Instruments of international order

Manchester University Press

KEY STUDIES IN DIPLOMACY

Series Editors: J. Simon Rofe and Giles Scott-Smith
Emeritus Editor: Lorna Lloyd

The volumes in this series seek to advance the study and understanding of diplomacy in its many forms. Diplomacy remains a vital component of global affairs, and it influences and is influenced by its environment and the context in which it is conducted. It is an activity of great relevance for International Studies, International History, and of course Diplomatic Studies. The series covers historical, conceptual, and practical studies of diplomacy.

To buy or to find out more about the books currently available in this series, please go to: https://manchesteruniversitypress.co.uk/series/key-studies-in-diplomacy/

Instruments of international order

Internationalism and diplomacy,
1900–50

Edited by
Th. W. Bottelier and Jan Stöckmann

MANCHESTER UNIVERSITY PRESS

Copyright © Manchester University Press 2024

While copyright in the volume as a whole is vested in Manchester University Press, copyright in individual chapters belongs to their respective authors, and no chapter may be reproduced wholly or in part without the express permission in writing of both author and publisher.

Published by Manchester University Press
Oxford Road, Manchester, M13 9PL

www.manchesteruniversitypress.co.uk

British Library Cataloguing-in-Publication Data
A catalogue record for this book is available from the British Library

ISBN 978 1 5261 7255 6 hardback

First published 2024

The publisher has no responsibility for the persistence or accuracy of URLs for any external or third-party internet websites referred to in this book, and does not guarantee that any content on such websites is, or will remain, accurate or appropriate.

Typeset
by Deanta Global Publishing Services, Chennai, India

Contents

List of figures		*page* vi
List of contributors		vii
Preface		ix
Introduction – Th. W. Bottelier and Jan Stöckmann		1
1	Becoming national: self-determination as a tool in international politics – Georgios Giannakopoulos	17
2	The League of Nations and the new uses of sovereignty – Lukas Schemper	35
3	Ascertaining the truth in Albania: inquiry as a League of Nations instrument of international order – Quincy R. Cloet	55
4	The chemical weapons discourse as an instrument of international order: the Second Italo-Ethiopian War – Anneleen van der Meer	81
5	'Weapons misused by barbarous races': disarmament, imperialism and race in the interwar period – Daniel Stahl	104
6	Colonial policy and international control: the American Philippines and multilateral drug treaties, 1909–31 – Eva Ward	127
7	In the eyes of the world: media oversight and diplomatic practices at the League of Nations Assembly – Robert Laker	152
8	The League of Nations and the advisory opinion of the Permanent Court of International Justice as 'preventive adjudication'? – Gabriela A. Frei	177
9	With or without the metropole: deferred sovereignty as instrument of racial governance – Pablo de Orellana	198
Index		227

Figures

4.1	Cartoon by David Low, 3 April 1936. British Cartoon Archive, Kent, LSE2294. Copyright Evening Standard Ltd.	*page* 82
7.1	Photograph of the Seventh Assembly in the Salle de la Réformation, 1926. United Nations Archives at Geneva.	160
7.2	Photograph of a delegate speaking at the First Assembly in the Salle de la Réformation, 1920. United Nations Archives at Geneva.	161
7.3	Photograph of the Eighteenth Assembly in the Palais des Nations, 1937. United Nations Archives at Geneva.	162
9.1	Crest of the Union Française established by de Gaulle. Drawn by Tally de Orellana from 1945 archival document photos.	205
9.2	Map of colonial Indochina showing the five 'Associated States' that made up the Indochinese Federation. Bibliothèque Nationale de France, Wikimedia Commons.	207
9.3	Colonial power in practice: High Commissioner for Indochina Thierry d'Argenlieu at his desk sometime in 1945–46. Undated. Archive Sainteny. The Contemporary History Archives, Sciences Po, Paris.	210

Contributors

Th. W. Bottelier holds a PhD from King's College London, where he completed a thesis on Franco-British-US alliance relations and internationalism in the Second World War. He was most recently Marie Curie Fellow at Sciences Po Paris, working on the global and environmental history of the Lend-Lease Act of 1941.

Quincy R. Cloet holds a DPhil in International Politics from the University of Aberystwyth. His area of expertise is the history of international organisation, in particular the League of Nations and its use of inquiry commissions. He co-edited the volume *Breaking Empires, Making Nations? The First World War and the Reforging of Europe*.

Gabriela A. Frei has earned a DPhil in History from the University of Oxford, where she is currently an Associate Member of the Faculty of History. She held research and teaching positions at the Bundeswehr University in Munich, the University of Oxford, the University of Cambridge and the Université libre de Bruxelles. Her research focusses on the role of international law in the politics of the nineteenth and twentieth centuries.

Georgios Giannakopoulos is a lecturer in Modern History at City, University of London. He is the author of *The Interpreters: Internationalism and Empire in Southeastern Europe (1870–1930)*, forthcoming with Manchester University Press.

Robert Laker is an independent researcher with a particular interest in exploring the lived experience of internationalism and its broader cultural, political and diplomatic consequences. He holds an MA in Modern History from Swansea University and since graduating has worked in various research roles outside of academia.

Pablo de Orellana is a senior lecturer in International Relations at King's College London. His interdisciplinary research interests include diplomacy, nationalism, the history of ideas and the relationship between art and conflict. In happier times, instead of researching nationalism, he drives his Vespa and pursues poetic and archaeological passions.

Lukas Schemper is a historian with an interest in international organisations, humanitarianism and responses to disaster. He is a research associate in the project 'Archipelagic Imperatives. Shipwreck and Lifesaving in European Societies since 1800' at the Leibniz Center for Literary and Cultural Research (ZfL) in Berlin. He received his PhD from the Graduate Institute of International and Development Studies in Geneva with a thesis on the history of attempts to govern 'natural' disaster through international institutions.

Daniel Stahl is a senior researcher at the Friedrich-Alexander-Universität Erlangen-Nürnberg. His research focusses on international and transnational history, disarmament and human rights. He has published, among others, the award-winning book *Hunt for Nazis: South America's Dictatorships and the Prosecution of Nazi Crimes* (2013, English edition 2018).

Jan Stöckmann holds a DPhil from the University of Oxford. His book, *The Architects of International Relations: Building a Discipline, Designing the World, 1914–1940*, was published by Cambridge University Press in 2022.

Anneleen van der Meer holds a PhD in strategic studies from the University of St Andrews and is a lecturer in war studies at Leiden University. Her research focuses on norms and strategic norm transgressions in warfare.

Eva Ward graduated from Wake Forest University in 2015 with a BA in History and Spanish and was awarded a 2016 US–UK Student Fulbright Award in order to undertake an MPhil in Politics at the University of Strathclyde in Glasgow, Scotland, focussing on austerity and social policy in Scotland. As a PhD student at Strathclyde, Eva was part of the Wellcome Trust-funded project 'The Asian cocaine crisis: Pharmaceuticals, consumers and control in South and East Asia, 1900–1945'.

Preface

The idea for this volume emerged during the centenary of the end of the First World War and the birth of the League of Nations. At one of several conferences marking the occasion, in Lisbon, Portugal, in September 2019, we observed the remarkable overlap between present-day diplomacy and the topics on the programme. Research on the history of internationalism covered an entire panorama ranging from collective security to humanitarian aid. Many of those present in Lisbon that autumn dealt with the same actors and institutions, and drew on the same sources, to tell stories about the astonishing work of internationalists: men and women who sought to solve international problems at an international level. Yet (we remarked to each other) we lacked a clear oversight of everything these people were doing – a manual, as it were, of the toolbox of international politics they helped create.

When we took a step back from the centenary celebrations, we realised that the League was embedded in a longer and more complicated history of internationalist practices that shook up established diplomatic traditions. This was mirrored in research trends. There was a body of recent scholarship on internationalism challenging old-school diplomatic history. But there was little conversation between the two. By focussing on the mechanics of internationalism, we thought, it might be possible to show how the two camps interacted with each other and how, in the process, they shaped twentieth-century history well beyond the 1920s.

This volume is also the product of its own time, as it was largely written during the COVID-19 pandemic and was made possible by the vastly expanded access to videoconferencing software. The essays that it consists of were first presented at a conference organised on the virtual premises of Helmut-Schmidt-Universität/Universität der Bundeswehr Hamburg in March 2021, gathering a group of excellent scholars from three continents, including some who are not in this book but who shaped the project nonetheless – Aden Knaap, Lorena De Vita, Sakiko Kaiga, Ana Carina Azevedo and Waqar Zaidi. We also want to thank our panel chairs Michael Jonas,

Marcus Payk, Nicholas Mulder and Giles Scott-Smith. Special thanks are due to Peter Jackson for delivering the keynote address and to Joe Maiolo for leading the concluding roundtable discussion.

Following the conference, we spent a year workshopping the chapters, meeting up monthly and virtually on Friday afternoons. In that sense, the collection you have before you attests to the amazing possibilities of present-day communication, but also to its limitations, as (it may surprise you to learn) the authors never met in person while composing it. We leave it to the reader to decide whether the product of our virtual teamwork stands up to what might have been in person. As editors, in any event, we are hugely thankful to our authors for their thoughtful feedback, their willingness to re-visit their own work and above all their patience during the publication process. We are equally thankful to the staff at Manchester University Press, particularly Rob Byron and Deborah Smith, as well as to the anonymous referees for their helpful comments and support. For her support in composing the index, we would like to thank Julia Zenzen. Further and special thanks go out to Chris Capozzola for attending each of our workshops and for his thoughtful and extremely useful comments.

As this volume entered the peer-review process, Russia began its full-scale war on Ukraine, a move that many in the West have interpreted as undermining fundamental international principles. And yet the instruments of international politics are omnipresent in the war: sanctions, public diplomacy, international monitoring, self-determination, sovereignty, international tribunals and other political designs that entered the mainstream of international life in the first half of the twentieth century. Once again, the protagonists of internationalism are facing the bitter realities of geopolitics. The human consequences are already catastrophic, and the effects on international order are likely to be severe. It will be up to future historians to make sense of these disruptions, and to assess the long-term lessons that this book might hold.

Finally, a few personal words of gratitude. Jan would like to thank his friends and family, and especially Emilia, for their generosity, support and patience; as well as Thomas for his intellectual vision, conceptual clarity, and positive energy throughout the project. Thomas is thankful to Jan for his camaraderie, hard work, attention to detail, organisational talents and sharp comments as co-editor, not to mention for coming up with the idea in the first place; to Pablo de Orellana and Filippo Costa Buranelli for their advice, reading tips and conversation on the subjects of diplomacy and international practices; and to his wife for putting up with the occasional rants of frustration that inevitably accompany the composing of a book.

Th. W. Bottelier and Jan Stöckmann
Paris and Berlin, September 2023

Introduction

Th. W. Bottelier and Jan Stöckmann

In the summer of 1928, fifteen governments from across the globe signed the Kellogg-Briand Pact renouncing war 'as an instrument of national policy'.[1] The treaty did not, of course, abolish war altogether and, despite being eventually signed by virtually all independent states, it is often remembered for failing to prevent violent conflict. Yet as late as 1936, prominent jurists still hailed the Pact as a 'great international instrument'.[2] Others praised the League of Nations as the most important 'instrument of cooperation'.[3] Both the Pact and the League have since been re-invoked by academics and policymakers in other contexts, notably at the United Nations. Today's international order is built on these historical experiments that once seemed outlandish but have since become widely accepted norms and institutions.

This book explores how instruments such as the Kellogg-Briand Pact or the activities of the League of Nations reshaped the practice of diplomacy, broadly defined, in the half-century between the First Hague Convention (1899) and the aftermath of the Second World War. In this period, many ideas, institutions and actors that, in the nineteenth century, had been considered at best marginal or, at worst, radical, became core elements of international relations. Among the new developments were international organisations; (binding) legal norms and policies such as international inquiries, arbitration and arms control; economic governance; interest groups such as pacifists, feminists or anti-colonial nationalists; and all manner of experts, from historians to international jurists and social scientists.[4]

Historians have done much over the past two decades to recall the rise of such new forms of internationalism, centred in the League and its successor, the United Nations.[5] Yet while these studies of internationalism have moved the boundaries of international history well beyond the confines of 'what one clerk said to another',[6] the full implications for the field remain to be explored. It remains unclear, for instance, how these new forms of international and transnational cooperation altered older, nineteenth-century practices of diplomacy and their logics of *raison d'état* and the 'balance of power'. Likewise, what was the relationship between established diplomatic elites and internationalist newcomers? Why were many of the latter's ideas picked up by the former, and to what extent were new forms of cooperation inflected with national interests as a consequence?

These are the kinds of questions the nine essays in this volume seek to address. One of our central aims is to link the traditional study of diplomatic history and power politics to the new history of internationalism, two approaches that have yet to meaningfully engage each other. In doing so, we also intervene in debates in International Relations (IR) theory and new diplomatic studies. We seek to do so through the concept of *instruments of international order* – a coherent, though neither fixed nor complete, repertoire of international practices and principles used by governments and non-state actors to shape international relations between roughly 1900 and 1950. While the first half of the twentieth century was the most innovative period, the implications of the argument run throughout the entire century, and well into the twenty-first.[7]

The concept of 'international instruments' allows us to take a fresh look at how the practice of diplomacy was transformed, by picking up a term that contemporaries used themselves. For the language of 'instruments', 'tools' and 'means' was remarkably widespread between 1900 and 1950, both as descriptive terms and as a way to prescribe policy recommendations. For example, the arbitration of competing French and British colonial claims in the Entente Cordiale of 1904 was praised by the Austrian pacifist Alfred H. Fried as an 'unprecedented instrument'.[8] Advocating the democratic control of foreign policy during the First World War, the British politician Arthur Ponsonby insisted that a lasting peace would require 'living instruments of binding obligation', that is, treaties agreed to by parliamentary democracies, rather than secret pacts negotiated by a few statesmen.[9] In the 1930s, the members of the Women's International League for Peace and Freedom (WILPF) rejected military power as an 'instrument of foreign policy'.[10] Like WILPF and its members, the term 'instrument' circulated beyond the Anglophone world. Thus we find Ivan Maisky, the Soviet ambassador to the United Kingdom from 1932 to 1943, privately thinking of the League as an 'instrument of peace' (*instrument mira*), and references to an '*instrument de politique international*' in French or '*Instrument der internationalen Politik*' in German.[11]

While pursuing different political ends, these actors all believed that international affairs could be handled effectively by devising new diplomatic tools, or by repurposing existing ones. In a 1916 textbook on the study of international affairs, the British politician Arthur Greenwood referred to tariffs as an 'economic instrument […] in the sphere of international politics'.[12] The revision of treaties was labelled a 'diplomatic instrument' by the British League of Nations Union.[13] Facing the crises of the 1930s, the well-known journalist and politician Norman Angell reminded his colleagues at Chatham House of the 'instruments' available to impose military sanctions.[14] The Welsh industrialist David Davies went a step further and suggested using aeroplanes as 'instruments of coercion' to settle international disputes.[15]

In the eyes of these internationalists, then, international politics could be done differently, using both old and new forms of transnational connection and cooperation. More than a few of their proposals became mainstays of international politics, to such an extent that the very concept of 'internationalism' was disassociated from diplomacy. Instead, it came to connote radical, Marxist-inspired or pacifist politics rather than the seemingly conservative conduct of statecraft.[16] This book seeks to recover the latter's internationalist genealogy, and at the same time explain what role statesmen (they were all men) played in solidifying it.

Instruments in historical perspective

Instruments of International Order brings together original research on the formation and implementation, during the first half of the twentieth century, of practices of diplomacy that became standard parts of the diplomatic toolbox, such as international inquiries, disarmament regimes, drug control, self-determination, media oversight and more. By focussing on *instruments*, the volume emphasises the constructed and experimental character of international society in the twentieth century. The term *international order* – broadly defined as the bundle of bargains, rules, norms, institutions and materialities that structure interaction across borders[17] – meanwhile directs attention to the ends that these instruments served. Then as now, these goals were often considered technical, seeking to solve particular problems of transnational cooperation. But they were also and fundamentally political, answering questions about how to organise and order international relations, based on which (if any) common values, and who got to define these.[18] Historically speaking, instruments of international order reflected the new confidence of state and non-state actors in shaping the international system like mechanics or craftspeople, using the rapidly growing toolbox of international law, including administrative law and standardisation.[19] Studying these instruments, finally, also helps to explain the relationship between political ideas and historical realities. It shows how internationalism worked in practice, as actors modified ideas and institutions – not always consistently – to pursue partisan goals across the political spectrum.[20]

Unlike domestic policies, the instruments discussed in this volume were employed across borders, sometimes on a global scale. Crucially, they were internationa*list* in that their proponents assumed that certain problems required the concerted action of an international society, rather than, say, one government imposing sanctions on another. Instead, these instruments were used by a growing set of actors, both governments and private actors, in order to coordinate and leverage their goals within a complex world of empires and nations. That is not to say that their goals were necessarily peaceful or idealistic.[21] Nor were they blind to national self-interest or military power, as often asserted.[22] Indeed, one of this book's key points is that the practice of internationalism was not limited to any particular ideology or part of the traditional political spectrum.

The 'instrumentalisation' of international politics is also linked to the broader trend of rationalisation in the field of international affairs since the late nineteenth century.[23] Policymakers, advisors and scholars increasingly conceived of international affairs as a practice that could be studied and learned. Citizens questioned government decision-making rather than accepting the course of international relations as passive spectators.[24] The media became a close observer of international affairs and organisations.[25] International politics was no longer the product of an 'art' reserved for a handful of diplomats but subject to scrutiny by critical journalists and public opinion. As such, the instrumentalisation of international politics was related to demands for democratisation.

The idea that international affairs were changeable or 'plastic' inspired political thinkers and practitioners to design a range of new policy solutions – at times humble and well-meaning, such as humanitarian aid or the control of international broadcasting, in other cases less so, such as the internationalisation of colonial rule.[26] But the majority of the instruments pioneered during the first half of the twentieth century were neither 'bad' nor 'good' – they were used and reused by actors according to their respective political preferences. The concept of self-determination, for example, was used to justify demands for autonomy, secession or independence that served a whole range of political purposes from liberal to violently anti-liberal, and from irredentist and colonial to non-violent, anti-colonial and emancipatory.[27] Self-determination, in other words, was employed as an instrument by holding plebiscites or by launching campaigns for national independence to achieve specific political goals. In this sense, instruments can be understood as flexible constructions or tools that depend on specific actors within a certain time and space.

The material impact of these instruments is hard to overstate. By the mid-century, it was impossible to ignore the role of multilateral institutions and internationalist practices, even if they rarely lived up to expectations. What mattered was the normalisation of internationalism as the standard mode of diplomacy. The United Nations system continued to serve as a platform for international questions ranging from nuclear security to global health. Governments continued to test the limits of this order. And, perhaps most significantly, scholars and commentators continued to discuss and revise the instruments invented during the first half of the century. Questions of self-determination and sovereignty still spark international conflicts, arms control is as pertinent as ever and sanctions are widely used in response to the Russian invasion of Ukraine. This book is an attempt to historicise this international order.

Instruments in historiography and theory

The past thirty years have seen an explosion of interest in pre-1950 internationalism, which has taken us far beyond old canards about naïve 'idealism' that, having abetted aggression and failed to prevent war through pacifism and appeasement, was superseded by a hard-boiled 'realism' that saw the West through the Cold War. The new work has shown these labels to be inapplicable in such a general sense, leading to a gross caricature of what was in reality a diverse body of thought that was not pacifist, appeasing or naïve about power.[28] Parallel work on the League and other international organisations has, since the 1990s, transcended the narrow focus on its failure to stop war in the 1930s, replacing the old image of the League as a 'utopian' chimera with a new vision of a pioneering innovator of modern global governance.[29] Some authors have taken an alternative approach, exploring the League and the 'dark sides' of liberal internationalism, notably their entanglements with empire, white supremacy, eugenics and the use of force.[30] Another recent trend is to look beyond the League and the liberal internationalists that advocated and worked for it, to recover the histories of a diverse set of alternative, oppositional and even violently anti-liberal internationalisms, linked to women's, socialist, Black, workers', pan-Asian, religious, communist and even fascist movements.[31]

Taken together, this research suggests the image of a mosaic of internationalisms, pushing for change in many different directions and in the service of many different political ideals, often quite beyond the control or direction of states and their organisations, like the League. It also demonstrates that internationalism – which can be loosely defined as an approach to international relations that seeks to go beyond the limits of traditional, bilateral, state-to-state diplomacy (without jettisoning it altogether)[32] – was practised by people of wildly different political creeds, nationalities and social and cultural backgrounds. Far from a specifically liberal pursuit or the exclusive project of Western elites, internationalism emerged in the first half of the twentieth century as one of the major political paradigms of the century.[33]

But there are areas that remain underexposed by all the new light that historians have shone on international history before 1950. For example, the new history of the League has made it abundantly clear that international institutions came to be concerned with provinces previously considered quite beyond their jurisdiction, such as colonies, border changes and public health. It is less clear how this expansion of what counted as international affairs affected the practice of diplomacy in its traditional and conservative core, that is, the representation of political communities and the preservation of international security.[34] We lack, in other words, a cogent narrative to replace the familiar tale of 'old' versus 'new diplomacy'. Rather than straightforwardly resist the transformation of international affairs, states and their servants often co-opted internationalist initiatives, especially after the First World War began. The international politics that emerged in many ways resulted from contact between the old and the new diplomacy. Thinking about this process through the perspective of instruments of international order is a first attempt to account for this.

A further, and related, aim of the volume is to contribute to ongoing debates on the nature of international history and how it should relate to kindred fields, such as global and transnational history, IR or diplomatic studies. Specifically, we aim to demonstrate the added value of marrying an interest in the workings of interstate relations with an insistence on the importance of transnational movements, networks, culture and ideas in these. We thus push back against a recent trend, among partisans of both traditions, of divorcing diplomatic history from the history of internationalism.[35] We do not agree that 'the history of internationalism parted ways some time ago with "international history", which focused [*sic*] on diplomatic relations among nations', and that new insights will be achieved by concentrating exclusively on 'social and cultural histories of empires, post-colonial settings and global networks'.[36] Conversely, we are convinced that recentring high politics and rejecting cultural and transnational approaches because, supposedly, they 'cannot without difficulty relate the transnational sphere to the operations of the state system', as the diplomatic historian Thomas Otte proposes, would be throwing the baby out with the bathwater.[37] There is some truth to Otte's charge, if only because many historians of internationalism have not directly addressed the question of how their subject relates to traditional accounts, or indeed evinced much interest in it to begin with. Nonetheless, following Otte would render us blind to the profound changes in the constitution and day-to-day operation of the state system wrought by the rise of the new internationalisms – in short, to the transformation of international society in the first half of the twentieth century.[38] We need to consider both sides of the medallion, both the 'old diplomacy' of the state system and its logic of *raison d'état* and the 'new diplomacy' of international organisation, transnational movements and normative international law. We suggest that the concept of international instruments helps to overcome the divide.

In order to deepen this claim, the volume also draws on and engages with the so-called 'practice turn' in IR and diplomatic studies.[39] We define instruments of international order as the shared practices of a community, working to establish new norms and build new institutions in international society. In its most basic sense, a concern with practice(s) implies a focus on the *doing* and *doings* of actors.[40] Traditional analysis might ask why an institution was built or a norm is consented to and look to the competing interests, resources or ideas of individual actors for explanation. Practice theories, by contrast, refocus attention on how institutions, norms and other forms of social life emerge from routine activities that are invariably social, that is to say irreducible to individual actors, actions and beliefs. Routes and rhythms of walking and driving are examples of practices of urbanism; diplomatic language is an example of a diplomatic practice.[41] As patterns, practices can and must be studied across time. As forms of social behaviour, they are changeable, open to initiative and creativity, though often as not unintendedly. Practices are comparable to games like chess or football: goal-oriented activities that follow both tacit and explicit rules and repertoires of conduct. Following these competently offers entry into and status within the group performing the practice, but they also, in another sense, constitute that group (or, more specifically, the 'field' of their play) to begin with.[42]

We suggest that thinking of instruments of international order in terms of practice(s) both illuminates the changes in diplomacy and internationalism we observe and has the potential to further extend the practice turn itself. 'Practice' was first of all an influential actor's category in the first half of the twentieth century, as evidenced by Sir Ernest Satow's widely read *Guide to Diplomatic Practice* (1917), which itself can be read as a defence of diplomacy as a useful tool for the coming reconstruction of world order.[43] This points to how many older, even ancient international practices, such as those constituting diplomacy, were recycled and reworked for a new era of world politics, even as they were joined by new ones, such as those performed for the League by the world's first international civil servants. Though, as in these examples, there was certainly purposive intent involved – which is why we write of 'instruments' rather than 'practices' of international order – this is not enough to explain how the practice of diplomacy was transformed in the first half of the twentieth century. The topics discussed in this volume, like multilateral drug control or international law, are phenomena that transcend the interests and actions of individual agents and reflect more than a zero-sum game between utility-maximising actors. In several cases and in time, they were so successful that they came to appear as natural elements of international politics – even habits, like sanctions or global economic governance.[44]

Second, conceiving of international instruments in these terms opens new channels for a more sustained conversation between international historians and IR scholars. *Instruments of International Order* itself embodies that conversation, as its authors represent both fields. The historians among us are not the first to turn to practice(s) to shine new light on the diplomatic and internationalist past.[45] Conversely, our concern with how internationalism worked *in practice*, how it was adopted by official diplomats, as well as our more general interest in how diplomacy came to be 'done differently' as a result, are things we share with the practice turn in IR.[46] What the historical cases presented in this volume add to that research agenda is to historicise processes that are often treated as if they were recent developments that represent a sharp break with the past. Especially notable here is the expansion of what counts as diplomacy and who practices it far beyond the realm of official interstate relations. More generally, given that each of the authors gathered here grapples with the issues of international change and the role of instrumentality, interests and ideas in practice, this volume also promises to advance the debate on these key concerns among practice theorists.[47]

Instruments in this volume

The chapters that follow do not constitute an exhaustive anthology of all the instruments pioneered or coined during the first half of the twentieth century. But they cover a fairly wide scope of themes and places, ranging from fundamental principles such as sovereignty and self-determination to more specific interventions such as international inquiries and drug control. Many of them had reciprocal or reinforcing effects on one another. Each of the chapters offers some historical background and theoretical context, before discussing examples of how instruments were applied in practice. All the authors focus on the ways in which these instruments were used, and re-used, by various actors and for various political ends. In doing so, the book surveys the 'package' of actors and practices usually subsumed under the term 'new diplomacy' but rarely understood as complex political constructions in their own right.[48]

Despite the thematic scope, there are a number of common patterns across the instruments discussed. First, the chapters reveal how instruments were formed by drawing on a growing body of international law and academic scholarship, thus invoking rational justifications for political ends. Second, they show that instruments outlived political regimes and historical periods, indeed lasted beyond the timespan of this book. That longevity, in turn, sheds light on the political motivations that underpinned what is often underestimated as 'technical cooperation'. The chapters also invite us to think about the spatial scope of instruments unfolding across the globe, juxtaposed with the echo-chambers of international bureaucracy in Geneva and The Hague. They also reflect the changing speed of international affairs, facilitated by new media and (military) technology. Finally, the instruments presented in this volume received growing levels of public attention and, as a result, have left many traces in archives and contemporary publications which inform our research. By using original sources, the chapters offer raw and unfiltered insights into the fabrication of international order.

One of the recurring issues that shaped twentieth-century international politics was self-determination. Yet as Giorgios Giannakopoulos shows, self-determination was neither a consistent concept nor a reliable instrument to solve international disputes. By drawing on examples from the Anglophone discourse on the Habsburg and Ottoman empires, he demonstrates how self-determination was used by various nationalist groups to advance their cause for independent statehood, and how these campaigns shook up a world dominated by 'great powers'. Despite its conceptual ambiguities and doubtful effectiveness in practice, self-determination turned into a widely accepted instrument of international order.

Underlying this new international order was the old but equally ambiguous concept of sovereignty, which saw a major readjustment during the first half of the twentieth century, especially with the foundation of the League of Nations in 1920. But how exactly did the League challenge the nature of nineteenth-century state authority? Who benefitted and who suffered from renegotiations of sovereignty? Why was the nation-state so resistant to aspirations of world governance? By drawing on a wealth of recent historiography, Lukas Schemper shows that rather than curtailing the model of the nation-state, the League actually strengthened and expanded it. In doing so, the League became a vehicle and accelerator for political experiments that re-configured notions of sovereignty.

Inquiry missions had been a common way for governments to control local developments for some time, but the League of Nations raised this instrument to a new, international level. Inquiries were significant, as Quincy Cloet argues, because they expanded the thematic and geographical scope of Geneva diplomacy. Apart from territorial questions, inquiries also covered questions of human trafficking, drug trade and forced labour. The question was whether it was possible to gather and verify facts by officials accountable to the international system. More generally put, how did international institutions deal with problems of information?

Anneleen van der Meer examines the discourse about chemical weapons, especially its imperial and racial undertones, as an instrument in its own right. Unlike other instruments, this discourse was used both by European and colonial actors. Based on the 1925 Geneva Protocol prohibiting the use of chemical and biological weapons in war, the Ethiopian emperor Haile Selassie appealed to the international community when attacked by Italian forces in 1935, hoping to generate legal and moral momentum in his favour. While not initially successful, Selassie's campaign shaped the notion of 'civilisation' as a rhetorical device which, as Paul Betts has recently shown, continued to underpin Europe's missionary zeal after the Second World War.[49]

Similarly, Daniel Stahl shows how the debate on the arms trade was shaped by imperial and racial categories. Banning specific weapons in specific places was a convenient way for colonial powers, notably the British, to prevent revolutionary uprisings and, at the same time, to protect their armament industries, all under the guise of peaceful cooperation. Crucially, the advocates of disarmament succeeded in putting arms control on the international level by integrating an instrument of international law into their agenda and thus strengthening imperial rule on a much broader level.

International drug control was another example of how the League of Nations picked up pre-1919 concerns of colonial governance. As Eva Ward shows in her chapter, American efforts at banning opium from the Philippines resulted in a complex web of multilateral summits and agreements that eventually led to the 1925 International Opium Convention. Rooted in religious doctrine and economic interests, the anti-drug movement brought together governments and non-state actors to find unprecedented forms of international regulation. What started out as a niche concern of colonial policy ended up as a global regulative framework with wide-ranging consequences far beyond the smuggle of opium.

The League of Nations Assembly should have been the ultimate forum of accountability and an instrument of political control. But the relationship between delegates, journalists and officials was often more complicated, as Robert Laker shows in his chapter. By drawing on plenary proceedings as well as the private papers of the British delegate Winifred Coombe Tennant, he exposes how diplomacy was often performed, rather than negotiated by genuine exchange of arguments. This performance of diplomacy played an important role in legitimising the League as a whole and has continued to shape the public-facing side of international politics.

Turning to the judiciary, Gabriela Frei examines 'advisory opinion', a little-known instrument used by the Permanent Court of International Justice. Unlike formal decisions or judgments, the Court could issue non-binding opinions on matters arising in the Council of the League of Nations. This offered an opportunity to discuss controversial questions, such as the German minority in Poland or the Finnish-Soviet dispute over Karelia, without antagonising any of the conflict parties. Advisory jurisdiction became a popular instrument during the interwar period and has continued under the United Nations, although it declined when its procedure was rendered less workable.

What happens when colonial governments refuse to play by the rules established by the metropole is the question Pablo de Orellana asks in his chapter, which rounds off the volume in the middle of the twentieth century. Focussing on French colonial governance in Indochina during the 1940s, he examines how colonial administrators challenged existing notions of sovereignty by carrying out their own diplomatic efforts and even starting their own wars. 'Deferred sovereignty', as he calls this phenomenon, became an instrument of racial governance with wide-ranging implications for the metropole and post-1945 international relations.

Taken together, these chapters reflect the diversity of actors and practices that formed the twentieth-century international order. They do not, of course, cover all policy areas. Nor can they explain the outbreak of wars or the making of peace. But considering these instruments can help to better understand the constituent elements of international affairs during this important period. And they invite us to think further about the instruments that continue to shape our world.

Notes

1 Kellogg-Briand Pact, General Treaty for Renunciation of War as an Instrument of National Policy, https://avalon.law.yale.edu/20th_century/kbpact.asp (accessed 25 March 2022).
2 Alfred Zimmern, *The League of Nations and the Rule of Law* (London: Macmillan, 1936), pp. 282–3.
3 Arnold McNair, 'Collective Security', *British Yearbook of International Law* 17 (1936), 150–64 (here: 160).
4 See, for example, Carolyn N. Biltoft, *A Violent Peace: Media, Truth, and Power at the League of Nations* (Chicago, IL: University of Chicago Press, 2021).
5 See, for example, Susan Pedersen, 'Back to the League of Nations', *The American Historical Review* 112:4 (2007), 1091–1117; Mark Mazower, *Governing the World: The History of an Idea* (London: Penguin Books, 2012); Glenda Sluga, 'Remembering 1919: International Organizations and the Future of International Order', *International Affairs* 95:1 (2019).
6 G. M. Young, *Victorian England: Portrait of an Age* (London: Oxford University Press, 1936), p. 103.
7 Jessica Reinisch and David Brydan (eds), *Internationalists in European History: Rethinking the Twentieth Century* (London: Bloomsbury Academic, 2021); Richard H. Immerman and Jeffrey A. Engel (eds), *Fourteen Points for the Twenty-First Century: A Renewed Appeal for Cooperative Internationalism* (Lexington, KY: University Press of Kentucky, 2020).

8 Alfred H. Fried, 'Das englisch-französische Kolonial Abkommen', *Die Friedens-Warte* 6:4 (1904), 61.
9 Arthur Ponsonby, *Democracy and Diplomacy* (London: Methuen and Co., 1915), p. 114 (all emphases added).
10 Women's International League for Peace and Freedom, *Report of the Seventh Congress* (Geneva: International Headquarters, 1932), p. 12.
11 10 March 1936, Gabriel Gorodetsky (ed.), *The Maisky Diaries: Red Ambassador to the Court of St James's, 1932–1943*, abridged ed. (New Haven, CT: Yale University Press, 2015), p. 67; Alfred Zimmern, 'L'Avenir de la Société des Nations', *Esprit International* 10:3 (1936); Paul Guggenheim, 'Völkerbunddenken', *Die Friedens-Warte* 27:8–9 (1927), 239. The term also circulated in Japan: see Thomas W. Burkman, *Japan and the League of Nations: Empire and World Order, 1914–1938* (Honolulu, HI: University of Hawaii Press, 2008), p. 199.
12 Arthur Greenwood, 'International Economic Relations', in A. J. Grant et al. (eds), *An Introduction to the Study of International Relations* (London: Macmillan and Co., 1916), p. 80.
13 League of Nations Union, *Treaty Revision and the Covenant of the League of Nations* (London, 1933), p. 3.
14 Norman Angell, 'Germany and the Rhineland: II', *International Affairs* 15:6 (1936), 26.
15 David Davies, *The Problem of the Twentieth Century: A Study in International Relationships* (London: Ernest Benn, 1930), pp. 367–8.
16 Glenda Sluga and Patricia Clavin, 'Rethinking the History of Internationalism', in Glenda Sluga and Patricia Clavin (eds), *Internationalisms: A Twentieth-Century History* (Cambridge: Cambridge University Press, 2017), p. 3; Peter Brock, *Freedom from War: Nonsectarian Pacifism, 1814–1914* (Toronto, ON: University of Toronto Press, 1991), pp. vii–viii.
17 Hedley Bull defined it, alternatively and more narrowly, as 'a pattern of activity that sustains the elementary or primary goals of the society of states' in *The Anarchical Society: A Study of Order in World Politics*, 4th ed. (Basingstoke: Columbia University Press, 2012), p. 8.
18 See the insightful discussion in Andrew Hurrell, *On Global Order: Power, Values, and the Constitution of International Society* (Cambridge: Oxford University Press, 2007), pp. 1–6 and *passim*.
19 Martin H. Geyer and Johannes Paulmann (eds), *The Mechanics of Internationalism: Culture, Society, and Politics from the 1840s to the First World War* (Oxford: Oxford University Press, 2001); Martti Koskenniemi, *The Gentle Civilizer of Nations: The Rise and Fall of International Law 1870–1960* (Cambridge: Cambridge University Press, 2001); Marcus Payk and Kim Christian Priemel (eds), *Crafting the International Order: Practitioners and Practices of International Law since c.1800* (Oxford: Oxford University Press, 2021).
20 See, for example, David Brydan, *Franco's Internationalists: Social Experts and Spain's Search for Legitimacy* (Oxford: Oxford University Press, 2019); Patrizia Dogliani, 'The Fate of Socialist Internationalism', in Sluga and Clavin, *Internationalisms*.

21 For an overview, see Sluga and Clavin, 'Rethinking'.
22 Norman Ingram, *The Politics of Dissent: Pacifism in France 1919–1939* (Oxford: Clarendon Press, 1991); David Long and Peter Wilson (eds), *Thinkers of the Twenty Years' Crisis: Inter-War Idealism Reassessed* (Oxford: Oxford University Press, 1995); Cecelia Lynch, *Beyond Appeasement: Interpreting Interwar Peace Movements in World Politics* (Ithaca, NY: Cornell University Press, 1999); Lucian M. Ashworth, 'Did the Realist-Idealist Great Debate Really Happen? A Revisionist History of International Relations', *International Relations* 16:1 (4 January 2002), 33–51.
23 See, for example, Lucian M. Ashworth, *A History of International Thought* (New York: Routledge, 2014); Patricia Owens and Katharina Rietzler (eds), *Women's International Thought: A New History* (Cambridge: Cambridge University Press, 2021).
24 See, for example, David Allen, 'Every Citizen a Statesman: Building a Democracy for Foreign Policy in the American Century' (PhD thesis, Columbia University, 2019); Helen McCarthy, *The British People and the League of Nations: Democracy, Citizenship and Internationalism, c. 1918–1945* (Manchester: Manchester University Press, 2011).
25 Jonas Brendebach, Martin Herzer and Heidi J. S. Tworek (eds), *International Organizations and the Media in the Nineteenth and Twentieth Centuries: Exorbitant Expectations* (New York: Routledge, 2018).
26 Amalia Ribi Forclaz, *Humanitarian Imperialism: The Politics of Anti-Slavery Activism, 1880–1940* (Oxford: Oxford University Press, 2015); Simon Potter, *Wireless Internationalism and Distant Listening: Britain, Propaganda, and the Invention of Global Radio, 1920–1939* (Oxford: Oxford University Press, 2020); Susan Pedersen, *The Guardians: The League of Nations and the Crisis of Empire* (Oxford: Oxford University Press, 2015).
27 See, for example, Adom Getachew, *Worldmaking After Empire: The Rise and Fall of Self-Determination* (Princeton, NJ: Princeton University Press, 2019); Philippa Hetherington and Glenda Sluga, 'Liberal and Illiberal Internationalisms', *Journal of World History* 31:1 (2020), 1–9; Joseph Massad, 'Against Self-Determination', *Humanity* 9:2 (2018), 161–91; Erez Manela, *The Wilsonian Moment: Self Determination and the International Origins of Anticolonial Nationalism* (Oxford: Oxford University Press, 2007).
28 See David Long and Peter Wilson (eds), *Thinkers of the Twenty Years' Crisis: Inter-War Idealism Reassessed* (Oxford: Oxford University Press, 1995); Nicolas Guilhot, *The Invention of International Relations Theory: Realism, the Rockefeller Foundation, and the 1954 Conference on Theory* (New York: Columbia University Press, 2011); Or Rosenboim, *The Emergence of Globalism: Visions of World Order in Britain and the United States, 1939–1950* (Princeton, NJ: Princeton University Press, 2017); Sakiko Kaiga, *Britain and the Intellectual Origins of the League of Nations, 1914–1919* (Cambridge: Cambridge University Press, 2021).
29 Most succinctly argued in Pedersen, 'Back to the League'. See further Akira Iriye, *Cultural Internationalism and World Order* (Baltimore, MD: The Johns

Hopkins University Press, 1997); Patricia Clavin, 'Defining Transnationalism', *Contemporary European History* 14:4 (2005), 421–39; Patricia Clavin, *Securing the World Economy: The Reinvention of the League of Nations, 1920–1946* (Oxford: Oxford University Press, 2013); Daniel Laqua (ed.), *Internationalism Reconfigured: Transnational Ideas and Movements Between the World Wars* (London: I.B. Tauris, 2011); Pedersen, *The Guardians*; Glenda Sluga, *Internationalism in the Age of Nationalism* (Philadelphia, PA: University of Pennsylvania Press, 2013).

30 Mark Mazower, *No Enchanted Palace: The End of Empire and the Ideological Origins of the United Nations* (Princeton, NJ: Princeton University Press, 2009); Matthew Connelly, *Fatal Misconception: The Struggle to Control World Population* (Cambridge, MA: Harvard University Press, 2008); Robert Vitalis, *White World Order, Black Power Politics: The Birth of American International Relations* (Ithaca, NY: Cornell University Press, 2015); Forclaz, *Humanitarian Imperialism*; Zaidi, *Technological Internationalism*; Thomas Willem Bottelier, 'Associated Powers: Britain, France, the United States and the Defence of World Order, 1931–1943', PhD diss., King's College (London, 2019).

31 See, for example, Jake Hodder, Stephen Legg and Mike Heffernan (eds), 'Special Issue: Historical Geographies of Internationalism, 1900–1950', *Political Geography* 49 (2015), 1–96; Jessica Reinisch (ed.), 'Special Issue: Agents of Internationalism', *Contemporary European History* 25:2 (2016), 195–371; Madeleine Herren, 'Fascist Internationalism', in Sluga and Clavin, *Internationalisms*, pp. 191–212; Talbot Imlay, *The Practice of Socialist Internationalism: European Socialists and International Politics, 1914–1960* (Oxford: Oxford University Press, 2017); Brydan, *Franco's Internationalists*; Jeremy A. Yellen, *The Greater East Asia Co-Prosperity Sphere: When Total Empire Met Total War* (Ithaca, NY: Cornell University Press, 2019).

32 Fred Halliday defined it as the idea, both analytical and normative, 'that states *are* becoming more interrelated, that this *is* reflected in a greater potentiality for cooperation across frontiers, and that the trend *is* a desirable one', in 'Three Concepts of Internationalism', *International Affairs* 64:2 (1988), 191. (Emphases original.) As Jessica Reinisch points out, conceptually, internationalism is closely related to, and overlaps with, transnationalism and globalization: 'Introduction: Agents of Internationalism', *Central European History* 25:2 (2016), 199–201.

33 This is the central argument of Sluga and Clavin's *Internationalisms*, *pace* G. John Ikenberry, *A World Safe for Democracy: Liberal Internationalism and the Crises of World Order* (New Haven, CT: Yale University Press, 2020).

34 Adam Watson, *Diplomacy: The Dialogue Between States* (London: Routledge, 1982); Ole Jacob Sending, Vincent Pouliot and Iver B. Neumann, 'Introduction', in Ole Jacob Sending, Vincent Pouliot and Iver B. Neumann (eds), *Diplomacy and the Making of World Politics* (Cambridge: Cambridge University Press, 2015), pp. 1–28.

35 See, in addition to the other footnotes to this paragraph, Joseph Anthony Maiolo, 'Systems and Boundaries in International History', *The International*

History Review 40:3 (2018), 576–91; Daniel Bessner and Fredrik Logevall, 'Recentering the United States in the Historiography of American Foreign Relations', *Texas National Security Review* 3:2 (16 April 2020).
36 Ana Antic, Johanna Conterio and Dora Vargha, 'Conclusion: Beyond Liberal Internationalism', *Contemporary European History* 25:2 (2016), 359–71 (here: 359).
37 T. G. Otte, 'The Inner Circle: What Is Diplomatic History? (And Why We Should Study It): An Inaugural Lecture', *History* 105:364 (2020), 5–27 (here: 21).
38 Erez Manela, 'International Society as a Historical Subject', *Diplomatic History* 44:2 (2020), 184–209.
39 The term was popularised by Theodore R. Schatzki, Karin Knorr Cetina and Eike von Savigny (eds), *The Practice Turn in Contemporary Theory* (London: Routledge, 2001).
40 The attentive reader may note the indebtedness of the following sentences to Michel de Certeau, *L'invention du quotidien*, ed. Luce Giard and Pierre Mayol, vol. 1: *Arts de faire* (Paris: FOLIO ESSAIS, 1990 [1980]). N.B. our formulation is less specific than most in IR. For overviews, see Emanuel Adler and Vincent Pouliot, 'International Practices: Introduction and Framework', in Emanuel Adler and Vincent Pouliot (eds), *International Practices* (Cambridge: Cambridge University Press, 2011), pp. 3–35; Christian Bueger and Frank Gadinger, 'The Play of International Practice', *International Studies Quarterly* 59:3 (1 September 2015), 449–60. For critiques: Friedrich Kratochwil, 'Making Sense of "International Practices"' and Raymond D. Duvall and Arjun Chowdhury, 'Practices of Theory', both in Adler and Pouliot, *International Practices*; and Jorg Kustermans, 'Parsing the Practice Turn: Practice, Practical Knowledge, Practices', *Millennium* 44:2 (1 January 2016), 175–96.
41 Certeau, *Quotidien* 1: chap. 7; Constanze Villar, *Le discours diplomatique* (Paris: Editions L'Harmattan, 2006).
42 Cf. Pierre Bourdieu, *Outline of a Theory of Practice*, trans. Richard Nice (Cambridge: Cambridge University Press, 1977 [1972]) and *Le sens pratique* (Paris: Les Editions de Minuit, 1980); Peter Jackson, 'Pierre Bourdieu, the "Cultural Turn" and the Practice of International History', *Review of International Studies* 34:1 (January 2008), 155–81.
43 See esp. Lassa Oppenheim's preface to Ernest Satow, *A Guide to Diplomatic Practice*, 1st ed. reprint, vol. 1 (Cambridge: Cambridge University Press, 2011). Cf. T.G. Otte, 'Satow', in G.R. Berridge, Maurice Keens-Soper and T. G. Otte (eds), *Diplomatic Theory from Machiavelli to Kissinger* (Basingstoke: Palgrave Macmillan, 2001), chap. 7; Iver B. Neumann, *At Home with the Diplomats: Inside a European Foreign Ministry* (Ithaca, NY: Cornell University Press, 2012), p. 5.
44 Nicholas Mulder, *The Economic Weapon: The Rise of Sanctions as a Tool of Modern War* (New Haven, CT: Yale University Press, 2022); Jamie Martin, *The Meddlers: Sovereignty, Empire, and the Birth of Global Economic Governance* (Cambridge, MA: Harvard University Press, 2022). On the difference between

practice and habit, see Ted Hopf, 'The Logic of Habit in International Relations', *European Journal of International Relations* 16:4 (1 December 2010), 539–61.

45 See esp. the pioneering work of Peter Jackson: 'Bourdieu' and *Beyond the Balance of Power: France and the Politics of National Security in the Era of the First World War* (Cambridge: Cambridge University Press, 2013); and also Karen Gram-Skjoldager and Haakon A. Ikonomou, 'The Construction of the League of Nations Secretariat. Formative Practices of Autonomy and Legitimacy in International Organizations', *The International History Review* 41:2 (2019), 1–23. Cf. Marie-Christine Kessler, *Les ambassadeurs* (Paris: Les Presses de Sciences Po, 2012).

46 Esp. with Neumann, *With the Diplomats* and 'Returning Practice to the Linguistic Turn: The Case of Diplomacy', *Millennium* 31:3 (1 July 2002), 627–51; Sending, Pouliot and Neumann, *Diplomacy and the Making of World Politics*.

47 Cf., in addition to fns. 39–40, Ted Hopf, 'Change in International Practices', *European Journal of International Relations* 24:3 (1 September 2018), 687–711.

48 Andrew J. Williams, 'Ideas and the Creation of Successive World Orders', in Stephen Chan and Jarrod Wiener (eds), *Twentieth-Century International History: A Reader* (London: I.B. Tauris, 1999), p. 51.

49 Paul Betts, *Ruin and Renewal: Civilizing Europe after World War II* (New York: Profile Books, 2020).

1

Becoming national: self-determination as a tool in international politics

Georgios Giannakopoulos

Introduction

On 6 December 1921, Britain's leading experts on international affairs gathered in the hall of the newly founded Royal Institute of International Affairs to hear the classicist and prominent figure in the League of Nations movement, Gilbert Murray, discuss the problem of the 'self-determination of nationalities'. Murray's paper was subsequently published in the inaugural issue of the *Journal of the British Institute of International Affairs*.[1] Murray's lecture did not delve much into the Germanophone origins of the concept of 'self-determination' and its semantics. His intervention was mostly preoccupied with the limits and application of the 'liberal ideal' of 'self-determination'.

Far from an abstract principle and a universal doctrine, Murray understood self-determination as a way of regulating the re-ordering of some of the territories unsettled by the war.

Although Murray's lecture took place well after the formal end of the proceedings of the Paris Peace Conference, the flames of war raged on. This was a period that one international historian has termed as that of the 'wars that would not end'.[2] Nationalist violence and aggression, refugees, famine and civil wars spread across continents from Ireland to central and eastern Europe, and from Russia and Turkey to Syria and Egypt. Scholars have convincingly made references to a 'greater war' decade starting with the Balkan wars in 1912–13 and ending with the conclusion of the Greek–Turkish war in 1922–23.[3] This wider perspective offers a more nuanced understanding of the global imperial transformations in this period and, in particular, of the crisis of legitimacy under Western, particularly Anglo-French, imperial rule.

Murray defined self-determination as a principle – a 'political formula' applicable only 'to the areas whose destiny had to be determined by somebody'.[4] Such a framing explicitly excluded the unchecked application of the doctrine to the British colonial world. In the second and most important part of his lecture, Murray discussed the practical problems inherent in the application of self-determination: How do we delineate the territorial limits of the unit having a right to self-determination? In response to this question, Murray dismissed the idea that small homogeneous regions had a de facto righteous claim to self-determination. To illustrate this point Murray turned to the ongoing conflict in Ireland. Small and ethnically homogenous parts of Belfast or Derry/Londonderry seemed prima facie to have a legitimate claim to a self-determining future. But, Murray reasoned, 'the general convenience here has to override the desire of the small unit'.[5] In many instances, he argued, 'the strategic interest of a large nation clashed with the desire of a small homogeneous group'. In other cases, distinct national groups were inextricably mixed making the act of separation an impossible task.[6] For Murray the question of self-determination as a principle to be applied in international politics was not a normative problem. Rather, it was a practical question and its application depended on a variety of factors.

Despite the ambiguities, Murray was clear that the horizon to the application of self-determination consisted of two conflicting imperatives: on the one end, the preservation of Western imperial dominance in world politics and on the other end adherence to the new liberal principles of open diplomacy and internationalism associated with the League of Nations. The League of Nations, Murray concluded, could become the most effective vehicle for channelling claims to self-determination. As the League of Nations grew in power, Murray concluded, the problems presented by self-determination would become 'soluble'.[7]

Four years later, in 1925, the world seemed a more stable place from the vantage point of the West. Building on the same rationale, Murray's son-in-law and leading expert in the *Royal Institute of International Affairs*, Arnold J. Toynbee, returned to the topic. During the Great War and its immediate aftermath, Toynbee had a direct exposure to the violent politics of self-determination in the world of the Ottoman empire in Asia Minor and Palestine.[8] Like Murray, Toynbee also approached self-determination as a regulatory principle of international politics. Using the language of political theory, Toynbee pointed to an inherent antinomy in the concept and practice of self-determination between the natural right of peoples to determine their own lives and the divine right of states to uphold their sovereignty.[9] Toynbee attempted to 'solve' the conundrum by applying a utilitarian formula to the problem balancing the collective right to self-determination and the right of a state to sovereignty. Both rights were flexible; their relation depended on moral, utilitarian precepts:

> the right of a people to self-determination is in inverse ratio to the justice, efficiency, reasonableness, and liberality of the government concerned, and also to the amount of prejudice which that government must inevitably suffer by the satisfaction of that people's claim; and conversely, the right of a state to

sovereignty is in inverse ratio to the injustice, misgovernment, intransigence, and repression with which it is treating the people by whom the claims to self-determination is being made, and to the amount of prejudice which that people must inevitably continue to suffer if the sovereignty of that government undergoes no modification.[10]

How did this moral formula translate to practical politics? Toynbee approached this question from two angles. His first point was a critique of the politics of national homogeneity. Forms of federalised statehood had a better chance in guaranteeing claims to self-determination. To illustrate this point Toynbee pointed to two examples of state systems which, in his mind, had 'solved' the nationality problem: the new Soviet state and the British Commonwealth. But Toynbee did not rest his hopes only with the federal solution, however real or imagined this might be. The ultimate guarantee in his views lay beyond the state in the recognition of the League of Nations as a legitimate arbiter of inter-national disputes.

Approaching self-determination in pragmatic terms as a right contingent on a myriad of factors was a common feature in the Anglophone debate of the period. Toynbee and Murray's interventions are exemplary of a way of thinking about national questions as problems in search of solutions.[11] They are instances of a distinct liberal, and imperialist, concern with regulating the explosive potential of collective self-determination when used as a tool in international politics.[12]

Murray and Toynbee's diagnosis of the limitations of self-determination as a normative principle has survived over time. Writing in the 1990s against the backdrop of the Yugoslav Wars, the historian of legal thought Martti Koskenniemi urged international lawyers to instill some kind of 'meaningful legal sense' into self-determination as a normative principle.[13] Koskenniemi concluded that the right to self-determination could not be consistently and universally applied as an abstract principle. He noted a 'paradox' at the core of the concept. Self-determination, Koskenniemi argued, 'both supports and challenges statehood' and it is impossible to delineate 'a general preference between its patriotic and secessionist tendencies'.[14] In order to explain this paradox, Koskenniemi found recourse to social contract theories and the classic binary between a Hobbesian view of sovereign statehood and a romantic Rousseauian understanding of the political community that constitutes the state. Koskenniemi concluded that the general problem with liberal views of self-determination is the tension between individualism and nationalism, between the rights of individuals and the rights of groups of individuals belonging to ethnic groups that seek collective recognition. Political philosophers have ventured to resolve the problem of reconciling individual with collective rights by articulating liberal theories of minority rights.[15]

Others follow a communitarian approach and understand self-determination as a collective cultural process that morphs into individual rights.[16]

The history of the concept and practice of self-determination is closely linked to that of human rights.[17] A new so-called 'revisionist' wave in human rights scholarship has drawn attention to the importance of claims to self-determination and national emancipation during the era of decolonisation in the 1950s and 1960s.[18] But it should be noted that for the United Nations, the right to self-determination rested on a view of sovereignty as the sole attribute of states; stateless people, or secessionist movements within states, were not deemed as self-determining subjects.[19] During the 1960s and 1970s, in Koskenniemi's words, international lawyers attempted to 'contain its potentially explosive nature by applying it principally to the relationships between old empires and their overseas colonies'.[20]

The post-war incarnation of self-determination and its complicated entanglement with the language of human rights has clear lines of continuity with the uses of the concept as a tool and practice in international politics during the nineteenth and early part of the twentieth century.[21] Historians and legal and political theorists, as well as International Relations (IR) scholars, broadly converge on the importance of the Great War and its aftermath as a turning point in the evolution of self-determination as a concept and practice. This period marked the increasing 'nationalisation' of the collective claim to self-determination and the pursuit of national homogeneous spaces. This political language of national self-determination did not vanish after the Second World War as some IR scholars have argued.[22]

Having established the importance of the period of the Great War and its aftermath for the historical evolution of self-determination, this chapter discusses how during this period, self-determination became an instrument of international politics. The first part of the chapter discusses the framing of self-determination in British internationalist commentary on national questions during the war. The following section briefly discusses one of the dominant accounts of thinking about self-determination in the aftermath of the Great War – Erez Manela's *The Wilsonian Moment* – and reflects on the recent framing of self-determination as an instance of 'world-making'. Then I turn to the Greek–Turkish conflict of 1919–22 and introduce a case-study showcasing the paradoxes in thinking about self-determination as an instrument of international order.

Self-determination as a solution to national questions

The historian Eric Weitz has convincingly shown how, during the Great War, what emerged in eighteenth-century German political thought as an

Enlightened concept became a doctrine to be applied in international politics. Despite the different ideological dimensions of the doctrine (liberal or socialist), its core was national; it applied first and foremost to communities defined in national terms.[23] Although the apostles of this new language of national self-determination are firmly located in the nineteenth century, the Great War therefore became a moment for the articulation of different claims to self-determination. The concept was embedded in different liberal and socialist political visions of social, political and international order. The customary antithesis is between socialist and liberal conceptions of self-determination. This antithesis is known in the literature as the great divide between Wilsonian and Leninist visions of international order.[24]

The focus on the split between Lenin and Wilson simplifies a complex story of different, and in some cases interlocking, political languages of self-determination that drew from liberal and socialist ideals of freedom. A case in point is the contributions of the Habsburg social democrats, conventionally referred to as Austro-Marxists. Doing politics in a period of gradual democratisation and operating in a complex multinational landscape, they articulated theories of cultural and national autonomy.[25] Although the political programme of the Austro-Marxists was defeated, scholars have shown how their conceptions influenced the Bolshevik reworking of self-determination.[26] It should also be added that the Austro-Marxist elevation of national self-determination to a regulatory political principle also influenced liberal understandings of 'the principle of nationality' and guided attempts to create political frameworks that could accommodate national units within liberal imperial units.[27]

The Wilsonian version of self-determination drew from a nineteenth-century tradition of thinking about liberty as the attribute of rational and autonomous individuals, or self-sovereign citizens. The Wilsonian vision of international order, in the words of Leonard Smith, envisioned a 'transnational community of liberal citizens' sustained by covenants between states.[28] The community of citizens imagined by the Wilsonian ideal of self-determination operated within clearly defined racial and religious boundaries.[29] It should also be noted, as Larry Wolff has shown, that Wilson's own understanding of self-determination was influenced by a wider Anglo-Saxon frame and exposure to the British liberal and Gladstonian cultural-political language of the so-called 'principle of nationality' that structured the English debate on national questions from the mid-to-late nineteenth century.[30] In other words, the intellectual origins of 'Wilsonianism' lie in the liberal-imperial heritage of Victorian England. This makes it therefore imperative to turn to the British context and analyse how self-determination was discussed in the British political debate on international order during the Great War and its immediate aftermath. The lines of the debate revolved around the centrality of self-determination as an instrument to create a new world order.

The outbreak of the Great War brought to the foreground a deluge of national questions framed as problems seeking solutions.[31] London became one of the major sites of political activity for central and eastern European nationalist groups and exiles fighting for national independence. The debate on the place of nationality and national self-determination in the new post-war world order polarised British experts and policymakers. Two groups of scholars and experts stand out.[32] The first group coalesced around the Union of Democratic Control – an anti-militarist group, part of a wider progressive transnational network arguing for greater transparency and democratic accountability in the conduct of foreign policy.[33] The members of the group supported the principle of popular consent in transfers of territory but cautioned against the elevation of nationality to the ultimate war-aim. Here is how one of the group's members, the journalist Henry Brailsford, framed the 'principle of nationality' – a codeword for national self-determination – in the early days of the war:

> [T]he more one emphasises the principle of nationality, the more intolerable it is that those who profit by it should themselves defy it … it is pleasant to express a facile enthusiasm for small nationalities, but for my part I feel that emotion chilled when I reflect that some of these small nationalities are themselves behaving like the largest and oldest of empires.[34]

Other scholars of international relations loosely connected with this group, such as Arthur Greenwood, harkened back to Lord Acton and viewed the problem of nationality as a question of national autonomy within a multicultural imperial state.[35]

This was largely the perspective adopted by those internationalists, such as J. A. Hobson and Leonard Woolf, whose contributions focused on the foundations of post-war international government. In his *Towards International Government*, Hobson argued that the 'real solution' lay not with the 'complete break-up of composite empires or kingdoms' but rather with

> substituting as far as possible the word and the idea of autonomy, effective self-government for the more confused and intransigent idea of nationality which often craves for itself an absolutism of independence and of sovereignty that is antagonistic to the needs of an international society.[36]

Similarly, although nationality played a key role in Woolf's conception of international governance, he argued that a new system of international governance should also be based on non-national group interests linked to social questions.[37]

On the other side of the debate lay a group of scholars and experts linked with the *New Europe* magazine. Among its prime instigators were the historian Robert Seton-Watson and the Moravian philosopher and politician Thomas Masaryk, who resided in London in 1916.[38] Scholars have credited the magazine with managing a successful campaign for the dissolution of Austria-Hungary and, more widely, pursuing the cause of national self-determination in central and southeastern Europe.[39] *New Europe*'s associates understood self-determination as a regulatory principle of international politics. The magazine represented the principles associated with Wilsonianism *avant la lettre*.[40] In Harry Hanak's words, 'so vital did national questions seem that the *New Europe* spent the greater part of its space examining them'.[41] This feature prompted its critics to refer to the magazine as an 'ethnological museum'.[42]

The *New Europe* group's view of self-determination harkened back to the mid-Victorian age. The liberal historian Ramsay Muir, one of the magazine's key collaborators, emphasised the role of the 'principle of nationality' as one of the key political ideals that the war put to the test. Muir understood the modern history of Europe as a process of building an international order based on national states.[43] Thus understood, 'internationalism [...] must take the place of cosmopolitanism'.[44] This understanding of internationalism as an organic outgrowth of national units drove the magazine's campaign for the dissolution of Austria-Hungary and the creation of a new central and eastern Europe.

New Europe's mobilisation of the political language of national self-determination as a remedy for the national questions stirred by the war had a tangible political outcome: the redrawing of the map of central and eastern Europe according to ethnographic principles. But as we discussed previously, other British scholars and experts presented an alternative vision of self-determination as a principle compatible with imperial rule. The guiding principle was the idea of national autonomy within large states.[45] During the apex of the self-determination rhetoric in the fateful year 1917, Brailsford wondered, 'must the aims of the war be sought by map making or may they be attained by organic changes, national and international?' In the event of the collapse of Austria-Hungary, Brailsford continued, a number of 'Ulsters' 'as perplexing and insurgent as our own' would come into existence under the arbitrary will of the majority. The federal 'solution' offered the only true guarantee to the unperturbed realisation of national sentiment.[46]

The references to 'Ulster' and the Irish question multiplied in the later stages of the war from those who opposed the break-up of Austria-Hungary. *The Nation* argued that the German population of Bohemia constituted a bigger 'Ulster' than that of Ireland. More broadly, the argument ran, a reordering of the map of Austria-Hungary along national lines would contain 'several Ulsters' that 'would make intricate problems for any League of Nations'.[47] In a piece from 1918, *The Nation* reminded its readers that 'Britain [...] does her appearance at the Areopagus as the advocate of a Czech Bohemia (with the suppression of the Teutonic Ulster) and of a national settlement of other equally hard cases of "self-determination". But, it affords no home rule for Ireland.'[48] Around the same time on the other side of the political spectrum the conservative MP and cabinet secretary Leo Amery, who masterminded the political integration of the Dominions in the British imperial system, paralleled the Czech demands over Bohemia to the Irish claims over Ulster and added that 'there is no possible solution which can wholly satisfy [regional Habsburg] nationalism, any more than there is any possible solution which can satisfy Irish nationalism'.[49]

When zooming in to the British debate during the Great War on self-determination, we observe the prevalence of earlier nineteenth-century discourses on the principle of nationality, dominated by representations (and misrepresentations) of the writings of scholars such as John Stuart Mill and Lord Acton. A wide spectrum of British liberals and internationalists welcomed the new epoch of self-determination but disagreed on the extent to which movements for national self-determination and self-government merited their own independent existence. From this perspective, the world of the British dominions, such as Ireland, and the world of central and eastern Europe appeared to be facing similar challenges.

Paris, world-making and the pursuit of ethnic homogeneity

During the Paris Peace Conference, the *New Europe* magazine reached the apex of its influence, famously making its way to Paris through the diplomatic sack of the British delegation. But this was part of a much wider story. At the Peace Conference, as Eric Weitz has put it,

> the language of self-determination moved to centre stage, the prominence of the concept evident in the wide array of statesmen and activists who deployed the term. Anti-war socialists, leaders from various belligerent countries, pacifists, and even, before the end of the war, the German occupiers of Eastern Europe all bandied about 'self-determination'.[50]

The year 1919 symbolises a period of novel experimentation on the applicability of self-determination in international politics. Key aspects of this new reality were the consolidation of the territorial national state; the 'mixing' of lands and the 'unmixing' of populations in central and (south)eastern Europe; the readjustment of European colonial rule across the Near/Middle East and Africa under the aegis of the mandate system; and the invention of a legal mechanism to protect and attribute minority rights[51] – as well as, of course, the emergence of the League of Nations with its associated institutions as a key arbiter of claims to self-determination.

Building on the work of scholars such as Antony Anghie, historians of international relations have convincingly argued that the employment of self-determination as a tool to stabilise and expand international society at a moment of the rapid aggregation of statehood brought about new hierarchies in the international system.[52] One of the key scholarly contributions that has set the tone for the academic debate on self-determination is Erez Manela's *The Wilsonian Moment*.[53] Manela argues that in the early 1920s, different political actors across the globe employed variations of the political language of Wilsonian self-determination in contrasting political frameworks. Manela describes how anti-colonial nationalism adapted the language of Wilsonian self-determination in attempting to subvert the existing colonial order.

Viewing self-determination as a principle that emanates from a clearly defined centre and is then diffused around the globe could be misleading. A recent volume on self-determination argues that

> when Wilson internationalised the language of 'self-determination' people around the world listened to his messages and drew upon his statements in their appeals for freedom.[54]

There are at least two problems with this assertion. First, Wilson did not internationalise by his own volition the language of self-determination; as Weitz has argued, 'the differences between the socialist and the liberal positions were lost on the hundreds of thousands in Europe, Egypt, China and India and somewhat later in Africa who found great hope in the promise of self-determination'.[55] Second, the local and regional 'Wilsonianisms' that emerged across the world were more dynamic and complex than what a static and monodirectional narrative of diffusion implies. Moreover, the Wilsonian variety of self-determination did not constitute a failed promise. As Adom Getachew has shown, self-determination, in its Wilsonian variety, became a principle regulating the unequal integration of the non-European world into the international system.[56]

Weitz has convincingly used the term 'Paris system' to describe the advent of a new system in the history of international relations – a passage from the principles of dynastic legitimacy and respect of state sovereignty which characterised the Vienna system to 'an ideal of state sovereignty rooted in national homogeneity'.⁵⁷ The Treaty of Lausanne – the last treaty of the Great War, which regulated the partition of the Ottoman Empire, set the terms of peace between Greece and Turkey and formalised the forced displacement of millions of Greeks and Turks. As Eric Weitz has argued, the Lausanne 'moment' reaffirmed the logic of the so-called 'Paris system'.

The case of the afterlives of the Ottoman Empire here presents itself as an instructive case-study. The Ottoman Empire after all had been one of the empires that had a spectral presence in the European international system during the nineteenth century, and its collapse appeared from the vantage point of the European metropoles to be more imminent than that of Austria-Hungary. In contrast to the fall of the Habsburg state, Western observers regarded the collapse of the Ottoman Empire as the culmination of a long-awaited process of disintegration.

In the early 1920s, the conceptual repertoire of Orientalism prevailed in the public commentary about the Ottoman space. The key term was that of 'awakening', peppered with anxieties about the future of the white race. British observers expressed fears for the prospects of the 'white race' after the awakening of 'sleepy Asia' in the absence of the Ottoman Empire, 'the avant-garde of Asia in Europe'.⁵⁸ The veil of the region had fallen, and an imaginary 'West' was called upon to manage the extension of self-government and protect its ascendancy. The references to 'awakenings' multiplied following the consolidation of modern Turkey in the wake of the Greco-Turkish war in Anatolia. Writing in 1925, the Victorian maverick Valentine Chirol argued that the people of the Orient 'are being roused from a long, lethargic sleep. [...] they are borrowing new weapons, even from the Occident's own arsenal and invoking against it its vaunted principles of nationalism and self-determination'. Turkey had indeed 'reawakened', Chirol continued, but it remained to be seen whether her re-awakening had brought 'a peaceful readjustment of the relations between the Orient and the Occident'.⁵⁹

How did this 're-awakening' materialise? Towards the end of the Great War, Greece undertook the task of becoming a temporary mandatory power in the Ottoman Empire and governing in the name of self-determination a region in Asia Minor. This gave rise to a military conflict in Anatolia between Greek expeditionary forces and Turkish irregulars between 1919 and 1922. During the war, the Turkish irregular forces formed a formidable political movement and garnered international support by mobilising anti-Western sentiment and appealing to the language of self-determination. The defeat of the Greek army marked the emergence of the Republic of Turkey as an independent state against the backdrop of a sizeable refugee crisis following the destruction of the port-city of Smyrna.

A vital aspect of the settlement negotiated in Lausanne in 1922–23, with the involvement of British political actors and the League of Nations, included the involuntary population exchange between Orthodox and Muslim populations located in Greece and Turkey respectively. This subsequently gave rise to a process of *minoritisation* of populations that found themselves uprooted. This process served to further homogenise both states, although minorities continued to exist within each state's border. Crucially, it brought into the limelight the paradoxical practice of population transfers as a means to protect and offer security to minorities.[60]

Since the outbreak of the Balkan Wars, populations had been on the move in southeastern Europe and the Near East. But what was new in 1922–23 was the scale, the legitimation and the engraving of the practice in the shrine of the new post-war international and legal order.[61] Subsequently, the League of Nations formed a committee to manage the settlement of populations in agricultural areas of Greece.[62]

The Greco-Turkish population exchange in the 1920s and 1930s offered a template for the resolution of 'national questions'. British officials involved in the negotiations and in the refugee resettlement efforts found the scheme reprehensible but nonetheless necessary, as it offered a lasting solution to a difficult question.[63] As early as 1925, the annual *Survey of International Affairs*, edited by Arnold J. Toynbee, noted that although the transfer of populations was essentially inhumane, the mutual antipathy inflicted by nationalism in the region had made 'segregation' a 'more *tolerable* alternative' (my emphasis) – a humane solution.[64] A year later, the first post-war British monograph on modern Turkey referred to the consequences of the population exchange in Turkey as follows:

> Turkey was now transformed into a homogenous Turkish national state, containing fewer extraneous elements than almost any other country in Europe or Asia. The way was clear for national development without hindrance from within.[65]

In 1927 a Greek commentator put it that

> the provisions relating to minorities have been laid out by the treaties that followed the Great War, not only for humanitarian reasons, but also for the purpose of preventing future wars by creating a tolerable life for minorities.[66]

Though controversial because it went against the current of minority protection, international observers and political actors regarded the Greco-Turkish population exchange as an effective arrangement. The political rapprochement between Greece and Turkey in the early 1930s gave the scheme a positive reputation and constituted a precedent for the attempts of the European dictatorships to solve their minority problems by mass resettlements.[67]

The first conclusion to be drawn from this case study is how liberal commentators and policymakers regarded the implementation of ethnic cleansing practices as an effective, yet no doubt illiberal, measure to ensure regional stability and protect some populations living in a de facto ethnically heterogeneous political landscape. Consequently, as Matthew Frank has shown, the Greco-Turkish population exchange set a key precedent for Nazi claims to territorial revisions and plans for population transfers articulated in the 1930s.[68] Frank has also argued that the spectres of the Greco-Turkish population exchange also framed the post-war thinking of liberal forces fighting the Nazis. An example in this direction is plans articulated in the aftermath of the Second World War by the liberal politician and Czechoslovak premier Eduard Beneš to forcibly dislocate Sudeten Germans residing in Czechoslovakia. Finally, the Greco-Turkish 'success story' became a reference point for settler colonial projects, and loomed over debates on the partitions of Palestine and British India.[69]

But there is more to this story. A second key feature of the Greco-Turkish population exchange concerns the link between settlement and colonisation, and the role of this specific incident as an instructive case of settler colonialism for the benefit of non-European regions of the world, such as the British Mandate in Palestine. In the mid-1920s, the refugee relocation settlements in the Greek region of Macedonia, which were overseen by the League of Nations and the Greek 'settlers office' (*grafeio epikismou*), drew the attention of British Zionists. Zionists regarded the successful resettlement of Turkish-speaking Christian populations in Macedonia as a project that could be instructive for the creation of Jewish settlements in Palestine.[70] The British Zionist and senior judicial officer of the British administration of Palestine Norman Bentwich was particularly impressed with the agrarian dimension of the refugee resettlement projects in Greek Macedonia. He noted how 'side by side with the transfer of population, a great agrarian reform has been carried out in Greece, as in the other countries of Eastern Europe'.[71] With an eye to ongoing settlement projects in Palestine, Bentwitch extolled the work of the relief commission in educating the new farmers on cooperative principles. Bentwich exclaimed that

> Macedonia, which was formerly the most desperate welter of nationalities and the traditional breeding ground for feuds and wars, has now obtained an almost homogeneous Greek population. The productivity of the land has already been doubled and in some cases trebled, by the settlers.[72]

With the passage of time, Greek Macedonia indeed became an ethically 'homogeneous' region. Following years of hardship, the Asia Minor refugees were successfully assimilated, while its indigenous Jewish community was virtually wiped out during the Nazi occupation. And in the early 1990s, the region became embroiled in a new 'national question' – this time provoked by a neighbouring state's (North Macedonia) claim to national self-determination. This time, at stake were not territorial claims; the struggle revolved around symbolic claims to the region's past and concerned the use of the very name 'Macedonia'. For the majority of the Greek Macedonians in the early 1990s, the multi-ethnic and multi-religious heritage of the region constituted a distant and repressed memory.

Conclusion

Difficult as it is to offer an all-encompassing account of the transformations of self-determination from a concept to a practice and an instrument in international politics, this chapter ventured to discuss some aspects of this process. I began by discussing key aspects of the contemporary debate on (national) self-determination as an international problem. Anglophone scholars in the main approach self-determination not as a normative concept but, rather, as a principle to be applied in international politics and as a solution to topical national questions. Then I zoomed in on the period of the Great War and discussed how self-determination or, put differently, the 'principle of nationality' framed the thinking of British liberals and became a key tool in imagining the future of the post-Habsburg and Ottoman worlds.

In line with the work of scholars such as Eric Weitz, I argued that the 1920s constitute a turning point in the transformation of self-determination from a concept to a political dogma and an international practice. By analysing the debate on the dissolution of the Habsburg and Ottoman Empires and the case of the Greco-Turkish population exchange, I showed the porousness of the conceptual boundaries between arguing for the protection of populations and promoting the destruction of minorities in the name of their protection. This is a paradox that seems to lie at the heart of the idea of human and national rights.

Notes

1 Gilbert Murray, 'Self-Determination of Nationalities', *Journal of the British Institute of International Affairs* 1:1 (January 1922), 6–13.

2 William Mulligan, *The Great War for Peace* (New Haven, CT: Yale University Press, 2014), p. 302.
3 Robert Gerwarth and Erez Manela (eds), *Empires at War 1911–1923* (Oxford: Oxford University Press, 2014); Robert Gerwarth, *The Vanquished: Why the First World War Failed to End, 1917–23* (London: Farrar Straus & Giroux, 2016).
4 Murray, 'Self-Determination of Nationalities', 10.
5 Ibid., 11.
6 Ibid., 12.
7 Ibid., 13.
8 Georgios Giannakopoulos, '"A World Safe for Empires?" A. J. Toynbee and the Internationalization of Self-Determination in the East (1912–1922)', *Global Intellectual History* 6:4 (2021), 484–505.
9 Arnold J. Toynbee, 'Self-Determination', *The Quarterly Review* 244:483-4 (July and April 1925), 137–338, at 328.
10 Ibid., 331-2.
11 Holly Case, *The Age of Questions: Or, A First Attempt at an Aggregate History of the Eastern, Social, Woman, American, Jewish, Polish, Bullion, Tuberculosis, and Many Other Questions over the Nineteenth Century, and Beyond* (Princeton, NJ: Princeton University Press, 2018).
12 Jeanne Morefield, *Covenants without Swords: Idealist Liberalism and the Spirit of the Empire* (Princeton, NJ: Princeton University Press, 2005); *Empires without Imperialism: Anglo-American Decline and the Politics of Deflection* (Oxford: Oxford University Press, 2014).
13 Martti Koskenniemi, 'National Self-Determination Today: Problems of Legal Theory and Practice', *The International and Comparative Law Quarterly* 43:2 (April 1994), 241–69, at 249. See also Antonio Cassese, *Self-Determination of Peoples: A Legal Appraisal* (Cambridge: Cambridge University Press, 1999); Nathaniel Berman, 'The International Law of Nationalism: Group Identity and Legal History', in David Wipman (ed.), *International Law and Ethnic Conflict* (Ithaca, NY: Cornell University Press, 1998), pp. 25–58.
14 Koskenniemi, 'National Self-Determination Today', 241–69.
15 Will Kymlicka, *Multicultural Citizenship: A Liberal Theory of Minority Rights* (Oxford: Oxford University Press, 1997).
16 Yael Tamir, *Liberal-Nationalism* (Princeton, NJ: Princeton University Press, 1993), p. 72. For a different perspective, see Irish Marion Young, 'Two Concepts of Self-Determination', in Stephen May, Tariq Modood and Judith Squires (eds), *Ethnicity, Nationalism and Minority Rights* (Cambridge: Cambridge University Press, 2009), pp. 176–96.
17 Eric Weitz, *A World Divided: The Global Struggle for Human Rights in the Age of Nation-States* (Princeton, NJ: Princeton University Press, 2019).
18 For a recent succinct overview, see Ronald Burke, Marco Duranti and Dirk Moses, *Decolonization, Self-Determination and the Rise of Global Human Rights Politics* (Cambridge: Cambridge University Press, 2020), pp. 2–8; Brad Simpson, 'Self-Determination and Colonization', in Martin Thomas and

Andrew S. Thompson (eds), *The Oxford Handbook of the Ends of Empire* (Oxford: Oxford University Press, 2018), pp. 418–30.
19 Michael Freeman, 'The Right of Self-Determination in International Politics: Six Theories in Search of a Policy', *Review of International Studies* 25 (1999), 335–70; Samuel Moyn, *The Last Utopia: Human Rights in History* (Cambridge, MA: Harvard University Press, 2012).
20 Koskenniemi, 'National Self-Determination Today', 241.
21 Samuel Moyn, 'The Universal Declaration of Human Rights of 1948 in the History of Cosmopolitanism', *Critical Inquiry* 40:4 (2014), 365–84; 'Giuseppe Mazzini in the History of Human Rights', in Pamela Slotte and Miia Halme-Tuomisaari (eds), *Revisiting the Origins of Human Rights* (Cambridge: Cambridge University Press, 2015), pp. 119–40.
22 Christian Reus-Smit, *Individual Rights and the Making of the International System* (Cambridge: Cambridge University Press, 2013), pp. 9–10.
23 Eric Weitz, 'Self-Determination: How a German Enlightened Idea Became the Slogan of National Liberation and a Human Right', *American Historical Review* 120:2 (April 2015), 463–96.
24 For a recent iteration of this distinction, see Mark Mazower, *Governing the World: The History of an Idea* (London: Allen Lane, 2012), pp. 154–88. See also Rita Augestad Knudsen, *The Fight over Freedom in 20th and 21st-Century International Discourse: Moments of 'Self-Determination'* (New York: Palgrave Macmillan, 2020), p. 75.
25 Ephraim Nimni (ed.), *National Cultural Autonomy and Its Contemporary Critics* (London: Routledge, 2005).
26 Weitz, 'Self-Determination', 484.
27 Benno Gammerl, *Subjects, Citizens and Others: Administering Ethnic Heterogeneity in the British and Habsburg Empires, 1867–1918* (London: Berghahn Books, 2017).
28 Leonard Smith, *Sovereignty at the Paris Peace Conference of 1919* (Oxford: Oxford University Press, 2018).
29 Simpson, 'Self-Determination and Colonization', pp. 418–19.
30 Larry Wolff, *Woodrow Wilson and the Re-Imagining of Eastern Europe* (Stanford, CA: Stanford University Press, 2020).
31 For the logic of 'questions' in the international politics of the period, see Case, *The Age of Questions*.
32 For a different reading focussing on nationalism and the language of psychology, see Glenda Sluga, *The Nation, Psychology, and International Politics, 1870–1919* (London: Palgrave Macmillan, 2006).
33 Jan Stöckmann, *The Architects of International Relations: Building a Discipline, Designing the World 1914–1940* (Cambridge: Cambridge University Press, 2022), pp. 42–6. See also Sally Harris, *Out of Control: British Foreign Policy and the Union of Democratic Control 1914–1918* (Hull: Hull Academic Press, 1996).
34 H. N. Brailsford, 'The Empire of the East', *The New Republic*, 7 November 1914.

35 D. I. Hughes, A. J. Grant, A. Greenwood, P. H. Kerr and F. F. Urquhart, *An Introduction to the Study of International Relations* (London: Book on Demand, 1916), p. 185.
36 J. A. Hobson, *Towards International Government* (London: George Allen & Unwin, 2015), pp. 125–6.
37 Leonard Woolf, *International Government* (London: Legare Street Press, 1915), pp. 356–7. There is a striking difference in tone and content between Hobson's and Woolf's account of nationality. For Woolf, 'the great stumbling-block in the theory of international inter-State government is the theory and passion for independence'. Nationality was an 'instinct' and not a 'sentiment'. He warned against the 'deification of geography and the worship of fictitious national ideas' and, without challenging the centrality of the nation in international organisation, he could see no reason 'why an international organisation which is based upon the nation as a unit should not be combined with an organisation which provides for the representation of group interests which are not national'. Ibid., pp. 347–7. G. L. Garvin found the 'anti-national' tone of Woolf's book 'unnecessary and hurtful, because world-government and world-partnership must depend for their progress on consenting activities and not on any super-national domination'. G. L. Garvin, *The Economic Foundations of Peace* (London: BiblioBazaar, 1919), p. xvi.
38 R. W. Seton-Watson, *Masaryk in England* (Cambridge: Cambridge University Press, 1943).
39 Harry Hanak, *Great Britain and Austria-Hungary During the First World War: A Study in the Formation of Public Opinion* (Oxford: Oxford University Press, 1962); 'The New Europe 1916–1920', *The Slavonic and East European Review* 39 (1961), 93, 369–99; Kenneth J. Calder, *Britain and the Origins of the New Europe* (London: Cambridge University Press, 1976); Hugh and Christopher Seton-Watson, *The Making of a New Europe: R.W. Seton-Watson and the Last Years of Austria-Hungary* (Seattle, WA: University of Washington Press, 1981). Erik Goldstein, *Winning the Peace: British Diplomatic Strategy, Peace Planning and the Paris Peace Conference, 1916–1920* (Oxford: Clarendon Press, 1991); Elizabeth Fordham, 'Le combat pour La New Europe: Les radicaux britanniques et la Première Guerre mondiale', *Mil neuf cent. Revue d'histoire intellectuelle* 23 (2005), 138–41.
40 Larry Wolf, *Woodrow Wilson and the Reimagining of Eastern Europe* (Stanford, CA: Stanford University Press, 2020).
41 Hanak, 'The New Europe', 378.
42 Henry R. Winkler, *The League of Nations Movement in Great Britain* (New Brunswick, NJ: Rutgers Unviersity Press, 1952), p. 145.
43 Ramsay Muir, *National Self-Government* (London: Constable & Co, 1918), p. ix.
44 Ramsay Muir, *Nationalism and Internationalism: The Culmination of Modern History* (London: Palala Press, 1916), p. 132.
45 Ibid.

46 H. N. Brailsford, 'The New Spirit in Austria', *The Contemporary Review* 1917:112 (1917). See also Brailsford, *A League of Nations* (London: Headley Brothers, 1917), pp. 108–9.
47 'The Tchecho-Slovaks', *The Nation*, 27 January 1917.
48 'The Irish Plea for Self-Determination', *The Nation*, 1 February 1919.
49 Amery to Balfour, 22 October 1918, *The National Archives* (TNA), FO/371/3136/17223.
50 Weitz, 'Self-Determination', 485.
51 Carole Fink, *Defending the Rights of Others: The Great Powers, the Jews and International Minority Protection, 1878–1938* (Cambridge: Cambridge University Press, 2018); Laura Robson, 'Capitulations Redux: The Imperial Genealogy of the Post-World War I "Minority" Regimes', *The American History Review* 126:3 (September 2021), 978–1000. From a legal history perspective, see León Castellanos-Jankiewicz, 'Negotiating Equality: Minority Protection in the Versailles Settlement', in Michael Erpelding, Burkhard Hess and Hélène Ruiz Fabri (eds), *Peace through Law: The Versailles Peace Treaty and Dispute Settlement after World War I* (Baden Baden: Nomos Verlagsgesellschaft, 2019), pp. 123–59.
52 Maja Spanu, 'The Hierarchical Society: The Politics of Self-Determination and the Constitution of New States after 1919', *European Journal of International Relations* 62:2 (2020), 372–96.
53 Erez Manela, *The Wilsonian Moment: Self-Determination and the International Origins of Anti-Colonial Nationalism* (Oxford: Oxford University Press, 2007).
54 Knudsen, *The Fight over Freedom in 20th and 21st-Century International Discourse*.
55 Weitz, 'Self-Determination', 485–6.
56 Adom Getachew, *Worldmaking after Empire: The Rise and Fall of Self-Determination* (Princeton, NJ: Princeton University Press, 2019). See also Michael Collins, 'Imagining Worlds beyond the Nation-State', *Comparative Studies of South Asia, Africa and the Middle East* 40:3 (2020), 601–6.
57 Eric Weitz, 'From the Vienna to the Paris System: International Politics and the Entangled Histories of Human Rights, Forced Deportations, and Civilizing Missions', *American Historical Review* 113:5 (December 2008), 1313–43, at 1314.
58 Henry M. Hyndman, *The Awakening of Asia* (London: Legare Street Press, 1919), p. 280. See also H. Charles Woods, 'The Capitulations and Christian Privileges in Turkey', *The Contemporary Review* (1922), 697–706.
59 Valentine Chirol, *The Reaweakening of the Orient and Other Addresses* (New Haven, CT: Yale University Press, 1925), pp. 5–6.
60 Weitz, 'Self-Determination', 487. See also Mark Mazower, 'Minorities and the League of Nations in Interwar Europe', *Daedalus* 126:2 (1997).
61 Umut Öszu, *Formalizing Displacement: International Law and Population Transfers* (Oxford: Oxford University Press, 2004).
62 Two years after the event, writing from Greece, a British humanitarian argued: 'Greece is doing its best, but had it not been for the Settlement Commission,

the solution for the refugee problem in that country would be indefinitely postponed'. Percy Alden, 'The Refugee Problem', *The Contemporary Review* 127 (January 1925), 569–75.
63 Mathew Frank, *Making Minorities History* (Oxford: Oxford University Press, 2017), pp. 49–96.
64 Toynbee would carry the idea that population exchange could offer protection to the minority question through to the Second World War. In 1942 he would tell an American audience that 'People were apparently much impressed with the success of the Greco-Turkish exchanges after the last war, which have been followed by a close friendship between the two erstwhile enemies. It is felt that such an exchange could be carried out without undue hardship to the people concerned if considerable economic aid were given them at once, possibly by an international agency.' Cited in Frank, *Making Minorities History*, p. 247.
65 Arnold J. Toynbee and Kenneth P. Kirkwood, *Turkey* (London: Ernest Benn Limited, 1926).
66 A. Andreades, 'The Greek Minority in Constantinople', *The Contemporary Review* 131 (January 1927), 34–40, at 35.
67 Frank, *Making Minorities History*, p. 97.
68 Ibid.
69 Cf. Laura Robson and Arie Dubnov (eds), *Partitions: A Transnational History of Twentieth Century Separatism* (Stanford, CA: Stanford University Press, 2019).
70 For background on Macedonia, see Elisabeth Kontogiorgi, *Population Exchange in Greek Macedonia: The Rural Settlement of Refugees 1922–1930* (Oxford: Clarendon Press, 2006).
71 Norman Bentwich, 'The New Ionian Migration', *The Contemporary Review* 130 (July 1926), 322–5, at 323.
72 Ibid., 323. Commenting on this very article, Dirk Moses has recently noted that for this type of discourse 'the refugee becomes the settler colonialist: the bearer of modernity and its democratic social system'. See Dirk Moses, *The Problems of Genocide* (Cambridge: Cambridge University Press, 2021), p. 344. See also A. Dirk Moses, 'Cutting Out the Ulcer and Washing Away the Incubus of the Past: Genocide Prevention through Population Transfer', in Ronald Burke, Marco Duranti and Dirk Moses (eds), *Decolonization, Self-Determination and the Rise of Global Human Rights Politics* (Cambridge: Cambridge University Press, 2020), pp. 153–78.

2

The League of Nations and the new uses of sovereignty

Lukas Schemper

Introduction

The founding of the first international organisations in the nineteenth and early twentieth centuries introduced an important instrument into the international order. Their creation facilitated new forms of inter- and non-governmental cooperation and led to the emergence of international governance in a number of areas.[1] Already prior to the First World War, international organisations started to influence the foreign relations of states,[2] began early experiments in international administration,[3] facilitated the emergence of common regional and later international standards[4] and enabled the transnational circulation of ideas and expertise[5] that led to the internationalisation of policies in scientific, technical, political, social and humanitarian fields. Historians and legal scholars have shown how the emergence of international organisations, both intergovernmental and non-governmental, changed the scope of state authority since the late nineteenth century.[6] They emphasised the role of international organisations as vehicles for liberal ideas against central government authority,[7] for anti-communism and for nationalism.[8] They have also problematised how governments began to value 'interconnectedness' as 'an indispensable tool of power', yet were torn between profiting from that interconnectedness and retaining sovereignty, 'national authenticity, autarchy, and uniqueness' (Madeleine Herren), even expanding their domestic role into the domains of economic and social regulation.[9]

This tension between preserving sovereignty on the one side and benefiting from the advantage of international cooperation on the other intensified in an unprecedented fashion with the creation of the League of Nations (hereinafter, the League) in 1920. Over the course of the League's existence, national governments, international bureaucrats, experts and activists not only discussed international and transnational challenges, but also debated what role and authority international organisations would have in the post-war world and what would remain the sovereign preserve of the state. Consequently, as this chapter argues, the institution that claimed to be the first universal world organisation had a decisive and lasting impact on how state sovereignty was conceptualised and practised.

What does it mean to conceptualise and practise sovereignty in different ways? Sovereignty is an elusive concept and appears in many shades. In the aftermath of the First World War, political thinkers defined sovereignty in various ways: as the monopoly of the state to use legitimate violence (Max Weber), the ability to decide on the conditions of exceptions (Carl Schmitt) or the representation of the people (Woodrow Wilson).[10] The political idea of a supreme, unchecked authority was unachievable in reality, as it presupposed the complete autonomy of a sovereign state in the world. The interwar legal theorists Nikolaos Politis and Hans Kelsen clearly pointed out the impossibility of reaching such a goal.[11] Bearing these limitations in mind, the contemporary legal understanding of sovereignty is the 'totality of powers that states have under international law'.[12] Sovereign power embraces not only the organisation of domestic public authority, but also the control of cross-boundary movements, and the international level (e.g. the mutual recognition of states or other entities), or what political scientist Stephen Krasner has termed Westphalian sovereignty, the exclusion of external actors from intervening in domestic authority.[13] It is this last definition of non-interference, shaped by the views of eighteenth-century thinkers such as Emer de Vattel or Immanuel Kant, that continued to dominate diplomatic and international legal practice after the First World War.

These different types and levels of sovereignty show that the concept of sovereignty is inherently socially constructed.[14] However, this social construction may change with the historical or geographical context. For instance, to what extent does sovereignty reside in legal criteria for state recognition, the congruence of territory and people, supposed 'standards of civilisation' or the monopoly of state violence at a given historical moment and place? In the same vein, as this chapter will show, the history of the League is a perfect illustration of the potential malleability of the otherwise timeless concept of sovereignty, of how older notions of sovereignty and statehood were debated, contested, re-evaluated and either preserved or reinvented in the *fora* of the world organisation. Despite the global reach of the League, sovereignty remained a legal fiction to much of the world outside Europe, as it was infringed upon or openly denied to it. Nonetheless, as this chapter attempts to show, the League also was an instrument occasionally used by peripheral actors to elevate their status in the international system.

Given the ubiquity of the issue of sovereignty within the scope of the League's activities, an increasing number of scholars have turned to the world organisation in their studies of this issue. This text makes use of such research to demonstrate how the various conceptualisations and practices of sovereignty were *instrumental* in shaping the international order. There has been a plethora of new research on the world body since the topic's 'rediscovery' by Susan Pedersen and others about a decade ago, and the League's 100th anniversary in 2019–20 further spurred interest in its history.[15] While early scholarship was primarily concerned with its impact on the relationships between states, with a focus on traditional diplomacy and matters of war and peace, the current literature has emphasised the transnational dimensions of the League's work, focussing on previously understudied actors and their roles in fields as varied as minority protection and health. This approach has occasionally resulted in a relative neglect of topics such as international security and disarmament. As this text shows, the two strands of literature are complementary in the sense that both contribute to our historical understanding of sovereignty.

Numerous historians have highlighted the perceived globalisation and collective management of sovereignty within the League supported by the proliferation of various transnational entities, hubs and associated interconnected systems. This chapter underscores the enduring importance of the concept of sovereign states and the acknowledgement of contentiousness over sovereignty within the operations of interwar intergovernmental organisations. The different elements mustered in support of this argument and around which this chapter is organised are: (1) the implications of the League's legal basis (the Covenant) for dealing with sovereignty claims; (2) the ways in which the League aided the design of new interventionist and state-like instruments of international administration; (3) how the problems associated with the League's work in disarmament and security were related to issues of sovereignty; and (4) how the League's work in the social and humanitarian domain struggled with problems of sovereignty and called for a reinvention of statehood. These examples demonstrate how the League standardised, strengthened, expanded and globalised the model of the sovereign nation-state.

Redesigning state sovereignty through the League's Covenant

One way to analyse the issue of sovereignty is through the lens of the League's legal foundation, the Covenant, which created an international order that was full of contradictions about the relationship between sovereign states. They were supposed to be the only legitimate agents of this new order, albeit their 'Wilsonian sovereignty' would henceforth be based on peoples' self-determination.[16] All sovereign states could join the organisation – at least on paper – although the defeated states of the war were at first excluded from membership and the criteria for sovereignty of many peripheral states had yet to be established. The idea of the sovereign equality of all member states (*de jure*) was nevertheless a break from the nineteenth-century system wherein this was never presented as the obvious solution to the problems faced by states. The League set an important precedent in this regard, but this should not disguise the fact that it was also, in Pedersen's words, a 'League of Empires and would-be empires, unequal in size, competing as well as colluding, but all determined to defend their right'.[17] This was reconcilable with Wilsonian liberalism, because, following a civilisational line of thinking, Wilson believed that those people excluded by race would only become fully sovereign once they were 'ready'. Inclusion and equality were only available to those who were eligible for it. While arguments for civilisational standards still dominated much of the debate around the question of accession of new member states, the League's existence still signified a novelty in the history of self-determination. Not only were already recognised smaller states like Argentina, Colombia and Iran able to use the League to foster their position in the international system, some peripheral and semi-peripheral entities such as Ukraine and the Iroquois also used the League as a forum to seek recognition as sovereign states (albeit unsuccessfully).

The League's rules for accession represent a change from nineteenth-century civilisational standards to more concrete legal procedures. Rather than basing exclusion of territories or populations on racial, cultural or religious grounds, the recognition of state sovereignty was grounded on specific technical requirements such as settled frontiers, stable government or commitment to obligations of international law. While this enabled the successful accession of countries like China and Ethiopia as full sovereign members, the League's mechanism of collective security failed to protect these states' sovereignty in the 1930s against Japan and Italy, respectively. While other entities such as the Iroquois were not recognised as sovereign states, the fact that their appeal was even debated at the League through the support of other smaller countries can be seen as a trend towards more inclusive rules for state recognition.[18]

Gradually, the League created new criteria of inclusion and exclusion, of legitimisation and delegitimisation for admission of sovereign states and for those entities striving for statehood. However, the question still remained about what the existence of the League actually meant for the exercise of sovereignty by those states eligible to join. For them, the League was conceived by the Entente Powers as the sum total of those states that indeed did compose it, not a non-state actor with state-like functions as its own source of sovereignty. Yet one could still argue that the League had more autonomy than initially planned. Its council functioned like a 'sovereign court' (Leonard Smith) to which aggrieved state parties could bring their problems and whose decisions could potentially be enforced through sanctions, the use of military force, or other forms of coercion.[19] From a technical standpoint, the League secretariat itself had extraterritorial status similar to a national embassy.[20]

Lastly, on a practical level, the League did indeed devote a considerable amount of effort to the domestic space of states, and not the space between them. One could object that the Covenant did mandate the non-interference of the Council in purely domestic interstate disputes. However, the wording was so ambiguous in defining what constituted a domestic dispute that it worried isolationists and internationalists alike.[21] Eventually, the League Council was charged with important functions such as territorial and financial administration, which traditionally were the sovereign prerogatives of states.

New forms of international administration

Although the creation of the League had brought the promise of self-determination and equality among states, it seldom succeeded in fulfilling it.[22] On the one hand, for countries like India and the British dominions, accession to the League as founding members represented emancipation and a modicum of recognition of sovereignty at least.[23] On the other hand, the decision as to which of these 'proto-states' should receive the privilege of being promoted to League membership was selective and did not prioritise the promotion of fair representation for diverse groups within the new organisation.[24] The membership of some territories was straightforwardly denied, and they were incorporated into the structure of the League as non-self-governing territories. Following the above-mentioned principles of Wilsonian self-determination, the Allied Powers reluctantly agreed to govern the ex-Ottoman and German territories, which they had conquered during the war, under 'mandates' from the League until the people in these mandates would be deemed ready for sovereignty and statehood. The threshold for statehood was not well defined, however.[25] Nevertheless, as legal historian Antony Anghie has rightly argued, this new system for (allegedly) ensuring the protection of non-European peoples meant a turning away from nineteenth-century positivist international law that endorsed their conquest and exploitation.[26] Anghie expanded on the issue of exploitation that the creation of the mandates signified, describing it as a separation of sovereignty and (Foucauldian) government, the latter which was mostly based on the furthering of economic development and the control of the economy.[27] Pedersen concurred with her authoritative study, agreeing that the mandate system denied the conquered powers full sovereignty. Furthermore, the publicity that the bi-annual reports on the practices of imperial rule in the mandated territories received changed the parameters under which the mandated powers could govern. This does not change the fact that neither the Covenant that created the Mandates Commission nor the Hymans Report (1920) that established the framework of the League's oversight regimen specified where sovereignty lay. Neither the mandatory powers nor the League or the mandated territories officially exercised sovereignty, an ambiguity that the mandatory powers could use to their advantage. The system allowed for zones in which sovereignty was completely separate from administrative authority or was entirely excluded.[28]

More direct was the League's oversight of territories in Europe as part of its security and conflict resolution policies. The League came up with several innovations: in the Memel dispute, only its port was internationalised while the territory itself was governed under sovereign law by Lithuania. However, in the case of Danzig, a 'free city' was formed as a semi-sovereign state with a League-appointed external supervisor. While the city enjoyed an extensive level of self-government in internal affairs, its external affairs were controlled by Poland, an arrangement historically referred to as suzerainty.[29] There were also cases of direct administration, in which, by institutional agreement, the League had the last word (*de jure*) and assumed all functions previously handled by governmental authorities. Such an arrangement was put into practice only in the case of the Saar Basin (under the treaty of Versailles) and the district of Leticia, which resulted from a League Council decision to address the conflict between Peru and Colombia over the territory in 1932. Historians have emphasised the precursor nature of these agreements, which became precedents for future types of territorial administration by international organisations after 1945 and the dispatching of international peacekeeping forces to places like Trieste in 1947 and Kosovo in 1999.[30] Despite these successes, this international system of direct administration by the League had limits and imperfections. For example, the international force deployed to Leticia by the authority of an appointed international commission was composed *de facto* entirely of Colombian troops, which had the positive result of reassuring Colombia that its sovereignty over the territory would be respected, while guaranteeing Peru that its population would not be mistreated.[31] Other research has shown that France clearly intruded into the internal affairs of the Saar as a member of the international commission during which it exploited mining rights, maintained French troops on the ground and used the franc as the official currency.[32] The failure of direct international administration was particularly blatant in the aborted idea of creating an international peacekeeping force composed of a number of League members and non-members under the aegis of the international organisation. The plan was to allow for the organisation of a plebiscite in the Vilna region in the context of the

Polish–Lithuanian conflict of 1921 without violating the sovereignty of the conflict parties, but budgetary constraints and a lack of political will among the League members caused the project to fail.[33]

The work of the League's Economic and Financial Organization on the stabilisation of the financial crises in Austria, Hungary, Bulgaria and Greece was not inherently territorial, yet it was deeply interventionist in terms of economic sovereignty.[34] It stood for a new form of global governance as represented also by other interwar international organisations such as the Bank of International Settlements, which operated in formerly protected and isolated domains of national economic policymaking, including certain development policies, austerity objectives and restrictions on certain products and exports.[35] An often-discussed example is Austria, which received financial aid in return for compliance with a programme of economic reconstruction, budgetary retrenchment and austerity. The country's leaders feared that Austria would be relegated to a mere colony of the League and its creditors because its economic stabilisation was overseen by a Commissioner General of Austrian Finances of the League. A foreign advisor was installed at the Austrian Central Bank, reminiscent of the early colonial precedents of financial stabilisation in Egypt and the Ottoman Empire. In the case of Hungary, too, its government accepted a weakening of its sovereignty in the short term, through financial reconstruction in return for the prospect of a bolstered sovereignty in the long term.[36] In most cases, however, foreign demands for the control of economic policies on tariffs, taxation, public spending or the management of currencies met fierce opposition, as any state that permitted an external authority to have significant control over its economic matters was seen as surrendering too large a part of its sovereignty. The above comparison with financial stabilisation in nineteenth-century Egypt and the Ottoman Empire shows the general belief that only non-sovereign states in imperial contexts could be subject to such interventions. Jamie Martin has recently argued that it was precisely during the interwar period that organisations such as the League 'open[ed] the internal economic spaces of sovereign states', in and beyond Europe, to foreign intervention under the banner of international cooperation rather than direct coercion, to make it appear less like imperialism. The stated goal of international cooperation made the interests of competing empires or the profits of powerful capitalist enterprises more readily acceptable to domestic audiences.[37] A counterargument to that claim is found in Nathan Marcus's recent work on the international financial control of Austria.[38] Despite the instrument of conditionality, the League was more 'respectful of national sovereignty than nineteenth-century creditors' and held opportunistic abuse by other states in check by setting strict rules and conditions.

Disarmament and security

Similarly intrusive for states were questions of international security that related to the issue of national disarmament. Although, deliberately, only certain issues of international security and disarmament were organised through the League (notable exceptions were the Washington Naval Conference of 1921–22 or the Treaties of Locarno of 1925), the task of disarming was explicitly mentioned in the Covenant as one of the League's main purposes. This was where public expectations and support were the greatest, and it is also where the League failed most spectacularly; hence, historical research on the League pictures disarmament as both the organisation's 'greatest crusade and its greatest disappointment'.[39] State sovereignty continues to be cited as the main obstacle to general disarmament, as it touches on the core competence that states were unwilling to give up. This tendency can be identified in the relevant disarmament articles 8 and 9 of the Covenant, whose contractual obligations were deliberately ambiguous and vague, exacerbating fears across the political spectrum of a transfer of national sovereignty to the League through an international disarmament agreement.[40] Andrew Webster has described the distrust with which governments viewed the expert civilian members of the League's Temporary Mixed Commission on Armaments, a 'semi-state-actor' whose independent experts must be considered as 'trying to serve two masters, both the League's disarmament vision and their own national interests'.[41] Even the more technical work of compiling and disseminating data on national armaments through a yearbook as part of a strategy of creating trust and 'moral disarmament' had to face unwilling governments; the argument was that considerations of national security and sovereignty had to be respected in the process of collecting data, making comparison across states difficult.[42]

Despite the easily identifiable impediment of sovereignty, research has shown that the study of apparent failures can be just as rewarding, historically, as the study of successes. New investigations have accordingly focused on the weak bureaucracy and lack of autonomy of the League's Disarmament Section (which was at least partly to blame for the failure of general disarmament);[43] internationalist activism for disarmament around the League (strong enough to influence national debates, but ultimately unable to support the League in producing a general disarmament treaty);[44] the role of women in both material and moral disarmament;[45] attempts at creating disarmament agreements as a strategy of rival states to increase their own security;[46] and disarmament negotiations as the basis of new moral norms and practices of global governance.[47] These new approaches do not exclude, but actually require, a reappraisal of the role of sovereignty in different contexts.

The social and humanitarian domain

Alongside the related questions of territorial administration, international security and financial stabilisation, the League also developed extensive programmes in the social and humanitarian sphere. On a closer look, these interventions were related to the *raison d'être* of the League – to ensure peace – since humanitarian disaster could potentially lead to political unrest. Despite the fact that only one of the Covenant's twenty-six articles, article 23, dealt with social and humanitarian activities, the League and its Social Section, the Health Organisation and the affiliated International Labour Organisation (ILO) accomplished seminal work in the transnational fields of the prohibition of slavery, child protection, education, regulation of prostitution, drug control, public health and workers' rights, as well as refugee and minority protection. Despite this meritorious agenda, the League's humanitarian and social work was often infused with beliefs in Western superiority and racism, confidence in scientific methods for social betterment and an upper-class humanitarian sensibility.[51] Some of this work was spearheaded by the head of the Social and Humanitarian Section, Dame Rachel Crowdy (1884–1964), who crafted strategies that involved direct intervention in issues concerning state sovereignty, advocating 'pooled sovereignty' in humanitarian and social matters.[48]

Thus, it is not surprising that the League's policies and operations frequently foundered against the obstacle of state sovereignty; for them to be enacted would have ideally required a reinvention of statehood and territoriality. If life and its protection, according to a Foucauldian understanding, are central objects of modern political governance – either in the sense that traditional sovereignty is the right to take life or let live or that biopolitics is the exact opposite, namely the attempt to give life or allow to die – then any form of intervention touching on these states' rights must be seen as interference, undue or not, in a state's prerogatives.[49] For example, in the context of international health work in East Central Europe, concerns about jeopardising state sovereignty and compelling member states to allocate resources towards the welfare of citizens in other states imposed constraints on the League's scope of operation.[50] Whether this desire to care for the citizens of other states is proof of the emergence of an early transnational 'human rights' programme in the interwar period is heatedly debated among historians,[51] but it is safe to assert that the interwar rights discourse constituted a challenge to state sovereignty.

The inclination of governments to support social and humanitarian interventions by the League in the affairs of other states was greater where the capacity to manage humanitarian crises and to exert sovereignty was perceived as weak. It could be argued that many interventions, whether for relief, reconstruction (as development was then termed) or state building (*avant la lettre*), took place in what would be called, in modern parlance, semi-sovereign 'failed states' and had a strong security component to them.[52] An informative example of this phenomenon was the creation of an international sanitary zone along the Polish–Russian border to deal with the emergence of epidemics after the First World War. This was a surveillance zone formed by quarantine stations, hospitals and hygiene institutes put under mixed jurisdiction and international oversight. In cases where state sovereignty appeared fragile, Western humanitarian actors, including the League and other international organisations such as the American Relief Administration and the Rockefeller Foundation, readily intervened. However, as can be seen from the example of the League's Epidemic Commission in Poland, the perceptions of the interveners did not always match the situation on the ground. The directors of the international humanitarian mission in Poland anticipated working within a void of sovereignty; yet Poland lacked neither the expertise nor the ambition to assume the authority necessary for building up greater capacity with resources provided from outside. In fact, Central and Eastern European states such as Poland used internationalism and international cooperation to *strengthen* sovereignty rather than to allow its erosion.[53]

Two other examples from the social and humanitarian domain that are closely related to the sovereign prerogatives of security and border control were the protection of minorities and the management of stateless persons. After the First World War, several states had to accept treaties to protect the rights of their minority populations in order to be recognised. It fell to the League to guarantee and supervise these agreements. To that end, it established a minority petition procedure, which created a path for minority groups to lodge transnational claims to improve international relations (though only for the minorities of newly created states). The petitions allowed minority populations that felt they were being unfairly treated to appeal directly to the League for redress without having their government interfering. While these petitions rarely led to noteworthy interventions, the procedure did widen the scope of action for stateless individuals, giving them independent standing in international law and endowing their cause with the publicity that it would otherwise not have received.[54] The minority protection by the League represented a first example of supranational state supervision in the 'state's management of internal difference' and the emergence of a 'spectrum of sovereignties' (Jane Cowan).[55]

The originality of the interwar European minority protection system as a form of non-territorial national autonomy has recently been put into perspective by new research showing that the attempt to disentangle the state from the nation through non-territorial arrangements predates the

First World War. It was pioneered in the Habsburg monarchy and its use appears to have inspired interwar discussions by transnational minority protection activists around the League.[56] Earlier research had insisted on the *caesura* represented by the minority protection system for better or for worse. For political scientist Stephen Krasner, the system was 'more firmly institutionalized than any of the universal human rights regimes that have existed since the Second World War', and was indeed the ultimate proof that the 'Versailles regime [...] was informed by principles that were antithetical to the Westphalian model'. Notwithstanding this, he pointed out the 'organized hypocrisy' that this new sovereignty represented as it was only enforced when it suited the interest of certain Western states.[57] The minority protection system indeed created a new yardstick for sovereignty that these Western democracies henceforth applied to the 'immature' states of Central and Eastern Europe, similar to the exclusive standard of civilisation that European powers had previously applied to the 'uncivilized' world in nineteenth-century international law.[58]

The League dealt not only with minority groups within states, but also with groups of people who did not belong to any state, contributing to the creation of the legal category of stateless persons. To protect them, it issued a travel document, generally known as the Nansen passport, that provided a modicum of international recognition. This practice was controversial for all sides: the stateless feared becoming a mandate of the League and some states saw the creation of this new legal category as an unwarranted intervention. In the end, the League's practice also reconfirmed the principle of the state's ultimate authority over border management and it did not put into question the international order that the League set out to ensure, based on state sovereignty and a clear distinction between national and international spheres.[59]

The treatment of stateless persons was an example of the League's general tendency to assume a leading role in the control of migration. The creation of an international regulatory procedure went hand in hand with a strengthening of domestic immigration control, not counter to it. The fact that governments sought international cooperation in tightening control (a break from the nineteenth-century view of free migration as a self-regulating process) was simply a recognition of the fact that no state could control migratory movements single-handedly. This conclusion was also evidenced by the work of the ILO's International Emigration Commission, which was founded in 1921 and tasked by the League to develop blueprints of immigration laws for states to adopt. Its compilation of migration statistics and laws fostered nationalistic conceptions of migration. The same applied to interwar international conferences dealing with migration questions. The degree to which immigrant destinations such as the United States and Australia participated in them set the stage for the international migration rights that were being adopted. When they participated, they used international institutions 'as platforms to disseminate ideas of national autonomy and self-determination' rather than to open borders. The result was the creation of a hollow 'universal right of migration' that could be suspended by the governments for any reason.[60] Part of the discussion on international migration centred on strengthening the passport procedure, which evolved along the same lines. The League's Committee on Communications and Transit and several international conferences tried to return to the open borders of the pre-war world. However, even self-proclaimed liberal states such as Britain had come to appreciate the increased ability to control mobility which they had become accustomed to during the war. The League had no choice but to content itself with assisting in the creation of a standardised passport system.[61]

The League's work in general, but in particular its work on social and humanitarian issues described above, relied on collaborations with voluntary agencies (later called non-governmental organisations – NGOs) and their staff. They participated in League committee meetings as assessors and experts and worked with members on the ground. Collaborations with humanitarian organisations such as the Red Cross (a movement that was explicitly mentioned by the League Covenant), the Save the Children International Union, the Young Men's Christian Association and the American Relief Administration allowed for humanitarian operations such as the repatriation of prisoners, the delivery of humanitarian aid for Russian refugees and the provision of nutritious meals for children in Central and Eastern Europe and the Near East.[62] Following up on the proposal of the Italian humanitarian Giovanni Ciraolo, the League also collaborated with the ICRC and the League of Red Cross Societies in the creation of the International Relief Union, the first intergovernmental organisation tasked with responding to disasters in connection to natural hazards. My own research has uncovered how governmental rejections of this project were based on the assumption that such an international organisation would cut deeply into the sovereign prerogatives of states. Talk of a right to relief policy for people struck by disaster and an obligation (financial and material) for states to come to the aid of other countries out of mutual solidarity set off alarm bells in more than one foreign ministry at the time. Not seeing itself in a position to stop the project, but sensing the lack of wide governmental support for the scheme, the League Secretariat organised the meetings and the final international conference necessary to create an international governmental organisation separate from the League and then left its management largely to the non-governmental International Red Cross organisations.[63]

The above examples show that the League's claim to humanitarian and social work brought a large number of NGOs and their lobbyists and networks into its orbit. On an informal level, it thus invigorated non-state activism, supported the emergence of an international civil society and facilitated global interactions between grassroots protagonists and elites.[64] On a formal level, it also elevated these non-state actors to new categories and recognised objects of international law, which still are with us today. This recognition went beyond the category of voluntary agencies, also including the various other actors discussed in this text such as peoples or nations seeking self-determination, minority groups, internationalised or mandated territories, mandatory powers and 'the international community'.[65] Some of these entities, previously of domestic jurisdiction, became subjects of international law in the eyes of interwar jurists as a result of the League's legal innovations.[66]

Conclusions

In light of the League's expansive intervention into the affairs of states described in the preceding sections, can it be argued that the League assumed functions previously the domain of the central or local authorities of a state? The fact that the League had a health section as well as social and humanitarian sections should not disguise the fact that most of this work consisted in researching, advising and coordinating. As a political scientist and former staff member of various League Secretariat Sections, Egon Ranshofen-Wertheimer observed that operational and quasi-governmental activities, albeit limited, were more prominent in the earlier years of the League than they would be later, and then were increasingly restricted. He argued that amongst other reasons, this had primarily to do with the fact that the way in which the League was organised went directly against an extension of direct administration. The way in which the League was imagined in the Covenant, as a typical 'headquarters organization', did not provide the staff or budget for direct administrative tasks.[67] Adopting an entirely different approach, Heidi Tworek used the example of epidemic surveillance by the League's Health Organisation to argue that even where it did not carry out hands-on work on the ground, the world organisation (despite being a 'headquarters organization') managed to 'broker shared sovereignty' through its international information infrastructure. At times of deglobalisation, when the movement of goods and people was restricted, Tworek averred that the League remained a globalising force through the collection and dissemination of information, creating a world that had not at its centre the nation state, 'but port cities, colonial networks, the sea, and the air'.[68]

While the view of a globalised, shared sovereignty managed by the League in the interwar period is convincing given the large number of new transnational actors, nodes and networks that emerged around the League, the present analysis has emphasised the continuing importance of the concept of the sovereign state as well as the practice of recognising or disputing sovereignty in the workings of the intergovernmental organisation and its member states. The analysis of the League's design as outlined in its Covenant showed that the world organisation was theoretically centred on the idea of sovereign nation states. The League became an instrument through which some claims for sovereignty were declared legitimate while others were not, and some entities were recognised as sovereign and others not. This allowed for the accession of non-European states such as China and Ethiopia and the recognition of colonies such as India and the British Dominions as member states, elevating their status. Rather than curtailing the model of the nation-state, the League standardised and disseminated it.

In new forms of international administration that it spearheaded, the League experimented with new forms of rule that either separated administrative and sovereign powers altogether or created semi-sovereign entities. Nevertheless, some of these arrangements turned out to be back doors for conventional state interventions, whilst others were at least perceived as such. Some national governments that were on the receiving end of such interventions only accepted interference in the hope of bolstering their own sovereignty. In other cases, the League and its interventionist instruments led states to fend off attempts at intervention and in return expanded their own role. Even in instances where states rejected intervention, the League made governments aware of their responsibilities on certain subjects and therefore expanded and refined the responsibilities of the state. In other cases, the League did exercise influence by encouraging the harmonisation of laws and norms among states. The social and humanitarian work of the League as discussed in the last part of this chapter provided several examples of this dynamic. Regardless, the continuing importance of state sovereignty 'under' the world organisation is proof that the nation-state should not be neglected in the fields of international and global history, fields that have increasingly chosen international organisations and international society as objects of study.[69] While many of the studies referenced in this chapter concur that the worldwide spread of nation-states overlapped with and was connected to the establishment of international institutions, the dialectic relationship between these two phenomena is frequently hinted at rather than rigorously investigated.

Notes

The idea for this text goes back to long conversations with Elisabeth Röhrlich and Bernhard Bardach at the University of Vienna, who had the idea of looking more closely at possible transformations of sovereignty within the context of the League of Nations. This text would not exist without their contributions. I am also indebted to comments received from Anca Cretu and Gary Bentley, and the authors and editors of this volume, as well as the anonymous reviewer. Research for this article has been made possible by the project 'Archipelagic Imperatives: Shipwreck and Lifesaving in European Societies since 1800' (AISLES) that has received funding from the European Research Council (ERC) under the EU's Horizon 2020 research and innovation programme (Grant agreement no. 863393). All errors and omissions are solely mine.

1 Examples of this were early public international unions such as the International Telegraphic Union (1865) and the Universal Postal Union (1874). For non-governmental cooperation, see the creation of the Universal Esperanto Association (1908) or the International Council of Women (1888), Akira Iriye, *Global Community: The Role of International Organizations in the Making of the Contemporary World* (Berkeley, CA: University of California Press, 2004), p. 20.
2 As examples, one may cite the creation of the Institute of International Law in 1873, which, for states, became an important private source of expertise on arbitration; and the creation of the Permanent Court of Arbitration in 1899, which could investigate the facts of an interstate dispute and provide arbitrators that states could draw upon to settle disputes. Daniel Gorman, *International Cooperation in the Early Twentieth Century* (London: Bloomsbury Academic, 2019), pp. 78–9.
3 Poignant examples were the Caisse de la Dette (1876) and the Ottoman Public Debt Administration (1881), which administered the bankruptcies of Egypt and the Ottoman Empire, respectively; and the creation of the international state, Etat indépendant du Congo through the Association Internationale du Congo. Madeleine Herren-Oesch, *Internationale Organisationen seit 1865: Eine Globalgeschichte der Internationalen Ordnung* (Darmstadt: Wissenschaftliche Buchgesellschaft, 2009), pp. 20–1, 29–30.
4 For ways that nineteenth-century internationalism and international organisations have promoted certain standards of European civilisation, see Mark Mazower, *Governing the World: The History of an Idea* (London: Allen Lane, 2012), pp. 65–115 (law and science), and, for focussing on the exploitation of the environment, Joanne Yao, '"Conquest from Barbarism": The Danube Commission, International Order and the Control of Nature as a Standard of Civilization', *European Journal of International Relations* 25:2 (2019), 335–59.
5 An example of how private transnational networks predated the creation of an international governmental organisation is described in Sandrine Kott, 'From Transnational Reformist Network to International Organization: The International Association for Labour Legislation and the International Labour

Organization 1900–1930', in Davide Rodogno, Bernhard Struck and Jakob Vogel (eds), *Shaping the Transnational Sphere. Experts, Networks and Issues from the 1840s to the 1930s* (New York: Berghahn Books, 2015).

6 Antonio Cassese, 'States: Rise and Decline of the Primary Subjects of the International Community', in Bardo Fassbender and Anne Peters (eds), *The Oxford Handbook of the History of International Law* (Oxford: University Press, 2012), p. 65.

7 Irye, *Global Community*, p. 13.

8 Glenda Sluga, *Internationalism in the Age of Nationalism* (Philadelphia, PA: University of Pennsylvania Press, 2014), p. 5.

9 Madeleine Herren, 'International Organizations, 1865–1945', in Jacob Katz Cogan, Ian Hurd and Ian Johnstone (eds), *The Oxford Handbook of International Organizations* (Oxford: University Press, 2016), p. 96; Bob Reinalda, *Routledge History of International Organizations: From 1815 to the Present Day* (New York: Routledge, 2009), ch. 8.3.

10 An overview of these two approaches can be found in Leonard V. Smith, *Sovereignty at the Paris Peace Conference of 1919* (Oxford: University Press, 2018), p. 7; the initial references are Max Weber, 'Wissenschaft als Beruf, 1917/1919; Politik als Beruf, 1919', in Wolfgang J. Mommsen and Wolfgang Schluchter (eds), *Gesamtausgabe* (Tübingen: J.C.B. Mohr/Paul Siebeck, 1992), pp. 158–9; Carl Schmitt, *Politische Theologie. Vier Kapitel zur Lehre von der Souveränität*, 10th ed. (Berlin: Duncker & Humblot, 2015), p. 13; and Wilson's Fourteen Points.

11 For an overview of these debates, see David Mitrany, *The Progress of International Government* (New Haven, CT: Yale University Press, 1933), pp. 67–8.

12 James Crawford, *The Creation of States in International Law* (Oxford: Clarendon Press, 2011), pp. 32–3.

13 Stephen D. Krasner, *Sovereignty: Organized Hypocrisy* (Princeton, NJ: University Press, 1999), p. 9.

14 Thomas J. Biersteker and Cynthia Weber, 'The Social Construction of State Sovereignty', in Thomas J. Biersteker and Cynthia Weber (eds), *State Sovereignty as Social Construct* (Cambridge: University Press, 1996), p. 1.

15 Susan Pedersen, 'Back to the League of Nations', *The American Historical Review* 112:4 (2007), 1091–1117. A great number of League-related studies in recent years also received an impetus at the conference 'Towards a New History of the League of Nations' co-organised by Pedersen with Patricia Clavin, Corinne A. Pernet and Davide Rodogno at the Graduate Institute of International and Development Studies in Geneva in August 2011. This research gained further traction through a variety of academic conferences around the centenary of the League and the ILO, some of which can be found on this list combined by the Geneva-based History of International Organisations Network (HION) webpage: https://www.hion.ch/centenary-events (accessed 10 September 2021).

16 Smith, *Sovereignty*, p. 10.

17 Susan Pedersen, 'Empires, States and the League of Nations', in Glenda Sluga and Patricia Clavin (eds), *Internationalisms: A Twentieth-Century History* (Cambridge: University Press, 2017), p. 137.
18 Arnulf Becker Lorca, *Mestizo International Law: A Global Intellectual History 1842–1933* (Cambridge: University Press, 2014), pp. 263–87.
19 Smith, *Sovereignty*, pp. 13, 226, 232.
20 Herren-Oesch, *Internationale Organisationen seit 1865*, pp. 54–5.
21 Jamie Martin, *The Meddlers: Sovereignty, Empire, and the Birth of Global Economic Governance* (Cambridge, MA: Harvard University Press, 2022), p. 18.
22 Wilson, along with Korean, Indian and Egyptian nationalists, believed that the formation of the League would 'allow demands for self-determination to come before a tribunal of the world community, shifting the balance of power in colonial relationships away from the colonial powers'. Erez Manela, *The Wilsonian Moment: Self-Determination and the International Origins of Anticolonial Nationalism* (Oxford: University Press, 2007), pp. 183, 217–18.
23 Stephen Legg, 'An International Anomaly? Sovereignty, the League of Nations and India's Princely Geographies', *Journal of Historical Geography* 43 (2014), 96–110.
24 Nigel D. White, 'Article 1', in Robert Kolb (ed.), *Commentaire sur le Pacte de la Société des Nations* (Brussels: Bruylant, 2015), p. 97.
25 Susan Pedersen, 'Getting Out of Iraq – in 1932: The League of Nations and the Road to Normative Statehood', *The American Historical Review* 115:4 (2010), 975–1000.
26 Antony Anghie, *Imperialism, Sovereignty, and the Making of International Law* (Cambridge: University Press, 2005), p. 116.
27 Ibid., p. 179.
28 Susan Pedersen, *The Guardians: The League of Nations and the Crisis of Empire* (Oxford: University Press, 2015), pp. 204–32; Pedersen, *Empires*, 2017, p. 122.
29 Erin K. Jenne, *Nested Security: Lessons in Conflict Management from the League of Nations and the European Union* (Ithaca, NY: Cornell University Press, 2015), pp. 90–108.
30 Ivan Ingravallo, 'L'administration directe de territoires dans la pratique de la Société des Nations', in Kolb, *Commentaire*, pp. 1224–30; Pierre-Etienne Bourneuf, 'La Société des Nations et la force internationale à Vilna (1920–1921): un projet précurseur pour le maintien de la paix ?' *Relations Internationales* 166:2 (2016), 87–102; Pierre-Etienne Bourneuf, '"We Have Been Making History": The League of Nations and the Leticia Dispute (1932–1934)', *The International History Review* 39:4 (2017), 592–614, at 17.
31 Bourneuf, 'We Have Been Making History', 7.
32 Ingravallo, 'L'administration directe', pp. 1210–18.
33 Bourneuf, 'La Société des Nations', 101.
34 Patricia Clavin, *Securing the World Economy: The Reinvention of the League of Nations, 1920–1946* (Oxford: University Press, 2013).

35 Martin, *The Meddlers*, p. 3.
36 Nathan Marcus, *Austrian Reconstruction and the Collapse of Global Finance, 1921–1931* (Cambridge, MA: Harvard University Press, 2018), pp. 79–80; Zoltán Peterecz, 'Hungary and the League of Nations. A Forced Marriage', in Peter Becker and Natasha Wheatley (eds), *Remaking Central Europe: The League of Nations and the Former Habsburg Lands* (Oxford: University Press, 2020), p. 165.
37 Martin, *The Meddlers*, pp. 3–5.
38 Nathan Marcus, 'Austria, the League of Nations, and the Birth of Multilateral Financial Control', in Becker and Wheatley, *Remaking Central Europe*, p. 142.
39 Andrew Webster, 'The League of Nations, Disarmament and Internationalism', in Sluga and Clavin, *Internationalisms*, p. 140.
40 Carolyn Kitching, *Britain and the Problem of International Disarmament, 1919–1934* (New York: Routledge, 1999); Emmanuel Bourdoncle, 'Articles 8 et 9', in Kolb, *Commentaire*.
41 Andrew Webster, '"Absolutely Irresponsible Amateurs": The Temporary Mixed Commission on Armaments, 1921–1924', *Australian Journal of Politics & History* 54:3 (2008), 373–88, at 388.
42 David Lincove, 'Data for Peace: The League of Nations and Disarmament 1920–40', *Peace & Change* 43:4 (2018), 498–529, at 498.
43 Haakon A. Ikonomou, 'The Administrative Anatomy of Failure: The League of Nations Disarmament Section, 1919–1925', *Contemporary European History* 30:3 (2021), 321–34.
44 Webster, 'The League of Nations'.
45 For example, through the Disarmament Committee of Women's International Organizations of the Liaison Committee of Women's International Organizations and its lobbying work at the League. Jaci Eisenberg, 'American Women and International Geneva, 1919–1939' (PhD thesis, Graduate Institute of International and Development Studies, Geneva, 2014), 254–73.
46 Webster, 'Absolutely Irresponsible Amateurs'.
47 Ibid.; see also the older David R. Stone, 'Imperialism and Sovereignty: The League of Nations' Drive to Control the Global Arms Trade', *Journal of Contemporary History* 35:2 (2000), 213–30, at 214.
48 Daniel Gorman, *The Emergence of International Society in the 1920s* (Cambridge: University Press, 2012), p. 12.
49 For Foucault's understanding of sovereignty, see the overview Banu Bargu, 'Sovereignty', in John Nale and Leonard Lawlor (eds), *The Cambridge Foucault Lexicon* (Cambridge: University Press, 2014); one important reference in Foucault's work on this issue is Michel Foucault, *Il faut défendre la société: cours au Collège de France, 1975–1976* (Paris: Gallimard/Seuil, 1997).
50 Sara Silverstein, 'Reinventing International Health in East Central Europe. The League of Nations, State Sovereignty, and Universal Health', in Becker and Wheatley, *Remaking Central Europe*, p. 71.
51 The origins of human rights have been dated either to the Enlightenment period, the aftermath of the First World War, the 1940s or the 1970s. Lynn

Hunt, *Inventing Human Rights: A History* (New York: W.W. Norton & Co, 2007); Bruno Cabanes, *The Great War and the Origins of Humanitarianism, 1918–1924* (Cambridge: University Press, 2014); Mark Mazower, 'The Strange Triumph of Human Rights, 1933–1950', *The Historical Journal* 47:2 (2004), 379–98; Samuel Moyn, *The Last Utopia: Human Rights in History* (Cambridge, MA: The Belknap Press of Harvard University Press, 2010).

52 The connection between peace and security with the creation of better social and humanitarian conditions was emphasised by the League's staff itself. Rachel E. Crowdy, 'The Humanitarian Activities of the League of Nations', *Journal of the Royal Institute of International Affairs* 6:3 (1927), 153–69, at 154.

53 Patrick Zylberman, 'Civilizing the State: Borders, Weak States and International Health in Modern Europe', in Alison Bashford (ed.), *Medicine at the Border: Disease, Globalization and Security, 1850 to the Present* (New York: Palgrave Macmillan, 2006); Silverstein, 'Reinventing International Health', p. 75.

54 Mark Mazower, 'Minorities and the League of Nations in Interwar Europe', *Daedalus* 126:2 (1997), 47–63; Jane K. Cowan, 'Who's Afraid of Violent Language?: Honour, Sovereignty and Claims-Making in the League of Nations', *Anthropological Theory* 3:3 (2003), 271–91.

55 Jane K. Cowan, 'The Supervised State', *Identities* 14:5 (2007), 545–78.

56 Börries Kuzmany, 'Non-Territorial National Autonomy in Interwar European Minority Protection and Its Habsburg Legacies', in Becker and Wheatley, *Remaking Central Europe*, 315–42.

57 Krasner, *Sovereignty*, pp. 95, 125–6.

58 Stefan-Ludwig Hoffmann, 'Introduction: Genealogies of Human Rights', in Stefan-Ludwig Hoffmann (ed.), *Human Rights in the Twentieth Century* (Cambridge: University Press, 2011), p. 13.

59 Mira L. Siegelberg, *Statelessness: A Modern History* (Cambridge, MA: Harvard University Press, 2020), pp. 49–82.

60 Adam M. McKeown, *Melancholy Order: Asian Migration and the Globalization of Borders* (New York: Columbia University Press, 2008), pp. 335–44.

61 Peter Becker, 'Remaking Mobility. International Conferences and the Emergence of the Modern Passport System', in Becker and Wheatley, *Remaking Central Europe*.

62 For a succinct overview, see chapter 4 in Silvia Salvatici, *A History of Humanitarianism, 1755–1989: In the Name of Others* (Manchester: University Press, 2019).

63 Lukas Schemper, 'Humanity Unprepared – International Organization and the Management of Natural Disaster 1921–1991' (PhD thesis, Graduate Institute of International and Development Studies, Geneva, 2016).

64 Simon Jackson and Alanna O'Malley, 'Rocking on Its Hinges? The League of Nations, the United Nations and the New History of Internationalism in the Twentieth Century', in Simon Jackson and Alanna O'Malley (eds), *The Institution of International Order: From the League of Nations to the United Nations* (New York: Routledge, 2018), p. 4.

65 Nathaniel Berman, 'Drama Through Law: The Versailles Treaty and the Casting of the Modern International Stage', in Michel Erpelding, Burkhard Hess and Hélène Ruiz Fabri (eds), *Peace through Law: The Versailles Peace Treaty and Dispute Settlement after World War I* (Baden-Baden: Nomos, 2019).
66 Natasha Wheatley, 'New Subjects in International Law and Order', in Sluga and Clavin, *Internationalisms*.
67 Egon Ferdinand Ranshofen-Wertheimer, *The International Secretariat. A Great Experiment in International Administration* (Washington, DC: Carnegie Endowment for International Peace, 1945), p. 5.
68 Heidi J. S. Tworek, 'Communicable Disease: Information, Health, and Globalization in the Interwar Period', *The American Historical Review* 124:3 (2019), 813–42, at 816, 829.
69 See, for this ongoing debate of why the state is important for the study of even a subfield of international history such as the study of the history of international society, Erez Manela, 'International Society as a Historical Subject', *Diplomatic History* 44:2 (2020), 184–209; and the related discussion in the H-Diplo article review forum 975.

3

Ascertaining the truth in Albania: inquiry as a League of Nations instrument of international order

Quincy R. Cloet

Introduction

From the outset, international bodies and organisations faced the problem of decision-making without access to reliable and full information. In the early twentieth century, for instance, the League of Nations was in need of detailed knowledge about subject matters related to security, disarmament and conflicts over borders and territory, cross-border trafficking of people or narcotics or even the economic development of countries and their surrounding regions.[1] The League's decision-making bodies, the Council and the Assembly, had to consider decisions and interventions in sensitive local and national matters, possibly with wider repercussions, not having a direct channel to first-hand accounts at their disposal. Could facts be verified and evidence be gathered by officials accountable to the international community, rather than having to rely on domestic press outlets or national diplomatic channels?

For the League of Nations, one means to overcome the lack of information was to send a group of persons on an ad hoc basis tasked with gathering information and reporting back to the League's decision-making bodies. This should be seen as part of a greater aspiration for rationalism in the conduct of international politics in the interwar years. Inquiry as an instrument was used on the basis (and belief) that reliable information obtained by the League's own methods and its chosen people would improve decision-making and lead to a more peaceful international system. This idea has continued to have an impact on international organisations in the second half of the twentieth century and the first decades of twenty-first, with the United Nations relying on inquiries to establish human-rights violations across the world and non-governmental organisations conducting their own fact-finding missions in the same as well as other fields.[2]

The aim of this chapter is to focus on inquiry as instrument of international order and how the League of Nations used it when dealing with a wide range of international issues during its lifetime. Although the League was not the first actor at the international level to do so – the chapter will briefly consider a number of precedents originating in The Hague, the Americas and in domestic and colonial contexts – inquiry commissions organised by the League were significant because of their unprecedented number and size and the broad range of issues they addressed. These ranged from more traditional ones such as border and territorial disputes in Europe and Latin America to new ones such as forced labour in Liberia and opium production in Persia and East Asia. Although inquiry was a pre-existing instrument, it was adapted by the League (as the first intergovernmental organisation of its kind) to address challenges arising from a new, more internationalist context.

The substance of this chapter is provided by one case study of the earliest period in the League of Nations history, a border delimitation dispute that created tensions between Albania and neighbouring countries, especially Greece and Yugoslavia, in the early 1920s.[3] While the case provides a good understanding of the overall process and life cycle of a League inquiry commission, it is meant for illustrative and analytical purposes. The aim is to give a broader understanding of what inquiry entails 'on the spot', as opposed to a regular committee meeting in Geneva; how investigative bodies were set up by the Secretariat in dialogue with the League's decision-making bodies; and how they ran their investigation on the ground and produced outputs (mostly in the form of reports). The question, in short, is how inquiry was instrumentalised in practice and what it meant overall for the League of Nations and interwar international politics. The chapter will use the materials of the Albanian case study in juxtaposition with elements from later inquiries to reach a greater understanding about the purpose of inquiry and whether it was an instrument genuinely devoted to resolving international issues through knowledge or rather one used by diplomatic actors to further interests and protect hierarchies embedded in the international order.

The chapter will show how officials and politicians at the League of Nations often spoke about truth, impartiality and independence when it came to inquiry, but left it unspecified how these aims could be fulfilled when commissioners were sent out to collect information on the ground. Individuals were chosen for their professional experience rather than their expert knowledge. In the absence of a clear blueprint and procedures, inquiries often relied on informal practices such as interviews with high officials and locals – through the assistance of interpreters – but also information obtained by foreigners present in the country. As a consequence, inquiry reveals itself not so much as an instrument of impartial knowledge or truth, but rather as a performative tool of diplomacy. Investigations could, for instance, serve as safety valves against further escalation, stretching the amount of time needed to come to an international agreement or a lasting decision in case of a conflict. While this is best epitomised by the Lytton Commission that was sent to investigate the Manchurian crisis, this chapter will instead focus on how the major powers, represented in the League Council or in Allied bodies such as the Conference of Ambassadors, sought to sustain the international system in the context of earlier interwar disputes.

The next section will focus on inquiry as an instrument and how the League of Nations built up its use of inquiry commissions during the interwar years. These inquiries supported decision-making about what were predominantly cross-border issues but often had far-reaching implications for the countries in question, visited by the commissions. The chapter then moves onto the case study of the Albanian inquiry, to focus on the patterns and practices developed by the League in this case and how they would differ or repeat themselves in future inquiries. The conclusion will address in greater detail the main observations as well as the question of instrumentality and inquiry as an instrument.[4]

Inquiry as a (League) instrument

In this chapter, the word 'instrument' connotes an identifiable set of recurring actions and practices that are followed to achieve a particular aim. When applied to inquiry commissions, 'instrument' means there is a visible pattern and intended use to these investigative bodies that distinguish them from other commissions. Before tracing the origins of the League's inquiry commissions and elucidating their underlying purpose, consideration must be given to what is meant by a commission of inquiry in this context.[5]

The League of Nations tasked a great number of commissions and committees with discussions about issues ranging from disarmament to health and mandates. Unlike inquiries, however, the majority of these took place at the institution's premises in Geneva. Inquiries did not have such a limitation, and while this appears to be a simple distinction, it helps to approximate a working definition of inquiry commissions: League inquiry commissions were ad hoc investigative bodies that were established on the basis of 'terms of references' to study an issue of international importance or concern, meet 'on the ground' to gather information and formulate an analysis with an advice or recommendation in the form of one or multiple reports.[6] Because of the temporary nature of their investigation of the specific subject matter, people chosen to fulfil the task were generally not League officials, except for some of the supporting staff.

As such, inquiries showed a relative consistency and coherence in their life cycle: they were established by a Council or Assembly resolution to work on a matter limited in scope and time (laid down in the resolutions or in a separate terms of reference); a selection and appointment of people was then made (a process chiefly organised by the League Secretariat). The task involved travel and work for a longer period abroad, providing periodical updates or reports before the provisions of a (final) general report about the issue. The above approximation of a working definition and life cycle is based on a total of nine League inquiry commissions that can be formally identified in the institution's archival sources. These nine inquiries were organised between 1921 and 1935 (see Table 3.1), thereby covering most of the League's existence, and dealt with a range of subjects not always limited to cross-border or international issues.

The relative degree of coherence among these examples of League inquiries is contrary to the fact that the Covenant of the League of Nations, the institution's foundational document, offers few traces of inquiry as an instrument beyond the label. A concise document overall, the Covenant mentions inquiry only twice, in Articles 12 and 17, and exclusively in the context of a dispute that may arise between countries.[7] While this points to the use of inquiry in other contexts – notably in arbitration, as will be explained further on – the foundational document does not capture the broader scope of the League's investigative undertakings in subsequent years. The nine examples show that inquiry commissions dealt also with issues well beyond interstate or border disputes.

The ad hoc nature of inquiries means there is nowhere a blueprint to be found in the archives with general rules for their establishment or a formal procedure for their organisation. For instance, inquiries are mentioned in the instructions on the League of Nations' financial administration ('action taken, in foreign countries by Bodies acting on behalf of the League'). However, these instructions concern only the payment of salaries and other

Table 3.1 Inquiry commissions organised under the auspices of the League of Nations.

Issue	Location	Timeframe
Border incident/delimitation	Albania	1921–22
Territorial	Mosul	1924–25
Women trafficking	30 countries	1924–26
Opium	Persia	1925–26
Border incident	Greece-Bulgaria	1925–26
Opium	East Asia	1928–30
Forced labour	Liberia	1929–30
Territorial	Manchuria	1931–32
Territorial	Chaco Boreal	1934–35

Data compiled by author.

expenditures and do not explain the organisation of inquiry commissions any further.[8] This is arguably one reason why individual inquiries have received considerable interest in the context of a specific topic, but inquiry as a general technique or instrument was overlooked up until recently as a League instrument, not to mention as a noteworthy instrument of international order.[9] As a consequence, inquiry as an instrument and as a set of institutional and social practices have to be discerned through specific case studies and actions found in the League archives or in available personal papers.

One reason, and perhaps the most significant one, for the relative absence of any formalised and legalised practice of inquiry commissions is that at this point in time an inquiry was a widespread and commonly understood phenomenon for most politicians, diplomats and officials involved with the League. These would have been exposed to royal commissions, parliamentary inquiries and special investigative bodies in a domestic and imperial context.[10] Another reason is that the ad hoc nature of inquiries in a relatively new, internationalist setting was seen as requiring a degree of flexibility and improvisation in practical terms, depending on the specific circumstances. Such a process is difficult to capture with a detailed blueprint or a fixed set of procedures, especially in the League's first years.[11]

To understand League inquiries at a more profound level and how these investigations were adapted in an internationalist context, it helps to understand where the idea and model(s) of international inquiry commissions appear to originate. Even though inquiry as a scientific endeavour has a very long history, when it comes to specific models of inquiry in a political and societal context with cross-border and international implications, there are three origins that are briefly worth highlighting.

First, inquiry was part of the system set up at The Hague in the early twentieth century that allowed states to settle disputes through a Permanent Court of Arbitration (PCA, established in 1899). In addition to instruments such as mediation and arbitration, it was a means to resolve interstate disputes. An international inquiry commission was organised to have a 'disinterested third party' pursue an independent and impartial investigation of the issue.[12] While the number of inquiries organised through the PCA were few and far between, exclusively related to incidents that occurred at sea, the Hague model was international in scope and identified an impartial and independent nature to the instrument, creating a precedent and inspiration for the Geneva-based international organisations in the interwar years.

Second, there were the often-overlooked experiments undertaken in the Americas throughout the nineteenth and early twentieth centuries when it came to the arbitration of interstate disputes in the Western hemisphere. Inquiry was included and often considered as an option in bilateral arbitration agreements or as the objective for a mixed commission. In the early twentieth century, the Taft and Wilson presidencies of the United States endeavoured to build a permanent arbitration system for the Americas that would also expand the role of inquiry to cover all types of interstate disputes (whereas the Hague's PCA only addressed disputes that did not risk touching upon vital national interests). Even though the possibility of including inquiry as an instrument of last resort – to stop a dispute from escalating – was never put in practice because the draft treaties failed to pass the US Senate, the possibility of expanding the use of inquiry as an instrument possibly had an influence on Wilson's later thinking in the design of the League of Nations.[13]

Third, the largest and most tangible body of precedents were set by national inquiry commissions organised in a domestic or imperial context. A large number of European countries relied on public inquiries, whether parliamentary or royal, to investigate broad societal issues or that served as a response to a political scandal requiring an examination of the facts. Of direct significance were investigations carried out in colonial territories or imperial dominions because they established another form of international inquiry, where metropolitan investigators would visit the territorial possessions and investigate the causes of a particular crisis and recommend a set of reforms. As such, empires proved to be significant laboratories for international instruments discussed here and elsewhere in this volume. For instance, the British Empire organised inquiries concerning narcotics and public expenditure in India as well as the defence of bases across the empire, the French Third Republic with regard to the colonial governance of Algeria and Belgium as a consequence of reports of cruelty and abuse perpetrated during King Leopold II's rule over the Congo Free State.[14]

The League of Nations could draw upon these earlier models in domestic and international spheres. Yet though the drafters of the League's Covenant were aware of the existing connections between inquiry and arbitration at the international level, they opted for an idiosyncratic approach to inquiry as an investigative instrument – adapting this older instrument to a new, internationalist context – since inquiries would not be directly linked to any court or arbitration procedure nor strictly address interstate disputes in the traditional sense (as seen with the Hague and bilateral arbitration agreements).[15] While League documents and meetings generally associated inquiry with the language of impartiality and independence, echoing the more legalistic, 'third-party' approach pursued at the Hague, there was no precise definition of such terms, no link with any international court nor any expectation that a fact-finding mission would result in a (court) judgment.[16]

On the contrary, inquiry was considered as one available instrument at the disposal of the Council or Assembly in its decision-making process.

The instrument was allowed sufficient flexibility in scope and procedure to deal with unforeseen international issues that would undoubtedly emerge in subsequent years, such as the production and smuggling of narcotics, the trafficking of women and children and the economic development of independent countries and regions.[17]

The significance of inquiry as fact-finding becomes clearer when it is set against the backdrop of the League of Nations' wider aspiration of rationalising the conduct of international politics in the post-war years. For instance, the League collected statistical data that informed the thematic sections of its Secretariat as well as its member countries, published relevant indicators in public memoranda and monthly bulletins and summarised key statistics about territory, population, economic production, commerce and public finance for each country in statistical yearbooks. The institution actively collected and compiled information – including from other international organisations – and triangulated official and unofficial sources for the purpose of 'accuracy'; it provided information because its officials considered that the 'very considerable volume of statistics' would be of 'great interest to Governments and business-men', informing them in their political or economic decisions.[18]

In this sense, the League experiment was not simply one of introducing new forms of conducting international politics (by means of e.g. public opinion, international territorial administration, minority rights and petitions). It also entailed a different approach to knowledge that put a greater emphasis on scientific progress, the importance of facts and impartial research and the role and authority of qualified experts. As a consequence, scientific terminology was introduced in the League's activities, which were often described as 'technical work' in the contemporary sources, and therefore it is important to understand instruments of international order also in this context.[19]

The League's rationalist aspirations in the realm of international politics gave formal coherence and purpose to its inquiry commissions. This is most palpable from the manner in which politicians and officials spoke about inquiry and what terminology they associated with the instrument. For instance, Spanish representative Salvador de Madariaga said that the Manchurian inquiry commission 'provides guarantees of knowledge and impartiality', while French foreign minister Aristide Briand justified the use of an inquiry because of 'the importance to the League of obtaining information by its own methods, by methods for whose accuracy it can vouch'.[20] In both official minutes and correspondence there were frequent references to an 'impartial' commission or persons with an 'unbiased' judgment and the required 'expert knowledge' – which often was understood as qualification rather than knowledge about a particular country or issue – with the overall aim being to 'ascertain the truth'.[21] Such references were chiefly used for rhetorical purposes since, in practice, the meaning of these terms and means to ensure impartiality and truth-seeking were left undefined and allowed room for interpretation. As a consequence, they cannot be taken at face value without understanding the context in which the instrument and its related practices were employed, which generally was one of power politics, imperial or economic interests and an adherence to a civilisational standard in relation to progress, as well as the belief in a racial hierarchy.[22] To bring the instrumentalisation of inquiry further into focus, the next section explores a case study concerning a commission that was sent to Albania in the early 1920s to investigate an ongoing border dispute with its neighbouring countries Greece and Yugoslavia in the absence of a final delimitation of Albania's frontiers.

The borders of Albania: an endeavour to 'ascertain the truth'

Albania's membership of the League of Nations, after the country's admission on 17 December 1920, was beset with difficulties in the first years because of an unresolved dispute with its neighbours about the frontiers and territory of the country, particularly the Kingdom of Serbs, Croats and Slovenes (Yugoslavia) as well as Greece. In November 1912, Albanians declared their independence, following a protracted struggle to separate themselves from the Ottoman Empire; this proclamation was confirmed by the Conference of Ambassadors (representing the great European powers) in December 1912 but was only the beginning of the demarcation of frontiers of the newly created state. While an international commission was appointed by the conference to draw the boundaries, and conferences organised in London and Florence during 1913 attempted to settle the entire matter, the concluded treaties did not put an end to competing territorial claims. Ongoing hostilities in the region had prevented a demarcation commission from drawing exact lines on the ground and the armed occupation of Albanian territories by neighbouring countries during the Balkan Wars and the First World War complicated the execution of the internationally agreed demarcation (with an attempt to supersede the earlier agreements and create a smaller Albanian state) and led to misunderstandings and recurring border incidents in the post-war years.[23]

Among others, the Paris Peace Conference had to reckon with the collapse of the Ottoman Empire and the intricate political map of the Balkans, including complicated ethnic, linguistic and demographic realities, following a decade of insurrections and armed struggle in the region. Specifically on the matter of Albania's borders, the Council passed the issue of finalising

Albania's frontiers to the Conference of Ambassadors once again – a diplomatic gathering of the main European powers which had dealt with the issue before the First World War – especially for those parts of the border that had not been delineated on the ground. The demarcation of Albania's frontiers was complicated by the fact that as a result of the First World War, troops of Serbia and Greece continued to occupy territories that had been previously assigned to Albania in 1913. Following its admission, Albania perceived the League of Nations as a preferred means to preserve its independence, because of continued fears of an invasion and forced break-up of the country, and to resolve all outstanding frontier issues, and it perhaps desired a quicker and more advantageous outcome by means of a Council (or Assembly) decision. However, Yugoslavia and Greece were less willing to have the League directly involved and showed resistance to a quick withdrawal of their troops from Albanian territory.[24]

The question whether the League of Nations had a role to play in the dispute came to the forefront during a Council meeting of 25 June 1921. Representatives of Albania, Greece and Yugoslavia were given the platform to state their views on the matter. Whereas the Albanian representative considered 'that the Albanian question should be discussed and decided by the League of Nations' and an inquiry commission would be the best means to observe the situation the ground, following incidents with foreign troops on Albanian territory within the frontiers agreed in 1913, the Greek representative questioned the League's right to intervene. He noted that 'agreements could not be ignored by an appeal with [sic] another authority [the League], before the authority [the Conference of Ambassadors] already dealing with the question had given its final decision'.[25] The Council followed in its decision the Greek representative's reasoning, stating that it was 'inadvisable to take up the question simultaneously' with the Conference of Ambassadors; however, it urged the latter to avoid further delay and to speed up the process.[26] While the Council opted not to get involved, it did not exclude the possibility of organising an inquiry 'at a later stage' – if the situation Albania warranted this.[27]

Because the Greek and Yugoslav troop occupation on Albanian territory continued over the summer of 1921 and a rebellion in Albania's Mirdite region erupted with alleged foreign assistance, Albania appealed to the League again in September. In light of the overdue response from the Conference, the Council passed the frontier question onto the League's Assembly (in September and October 1921), following Albanian reports that an escalation of the dispute was imminent because of Yugoslav advances into Albanian territory. The Assembly discussions confirmed the view that the Allied Powers (i.e. the Conference of Ambassadors) were still the 'appropriate body to settle the frontiers', but in its resolution of

3 October, the Assembly requested the Council to act on the proposal of organising an inquiry by appointing three persons to 'report fully on the execution of the decision of the Principal Allied and Associated Powers, as soon as it is given, and on any disturbances which may occur on or near the frontier of Albania'.[28] Shortly thereafter, on 9 November, the Conference of Ambassadors informed the League that a final decision about Albania's frontiers had been taken, largely confirming the agreements of 1913 except for a number of minor changes. The Conference also planned to send out a new delimitation commission in the nearby future to fix these formally agreed frontiers on the ground, a measure together with the tardy decision that were possibly also meant to de-escalate the dispute.[29]

In a special meeting on 19 November, the Council adopted the Assembly's proposal to organise an inquiry commission with the aim of keeping the League informed about the withdrawal of troops following the Conference's eventual decision about Albania's frontiers and the creation of a temporary neutral zone (to be demarcated on the spot by the delimitation commission). The League inquiry was instructed to keep in touch with the Conference's delimitation commission, to assist local authorities with the implementation of the troop withdrawal and to 'examine and submit to the Council measures to end the present disturbances and to prevent their recurrence'.[30] According to more detailed instructions provided to the commissioners by the League's Secretary General, Eric Drummond, the inquiry commission was also asked to send 'periodical reports on its work and on any event of importance'.[31] Unlike later inquiries organised by the League, these Council resolutions and accompanying instructions were precise and rather narrow in scope; they also demanded regular reports rather than one general report at the end of the inquiry's assignment.[32]

The other step was the composition of the inquiry and the selection of 'three impartial persons' for the assignment.[33] Throughout the League's existence, the Council President or the larger members of the decision-making body would be more closely involved in the process of appointing commissioners or having a country representative as part of the inquiry. However, for the Albanian inquiry, the League Secretariat and Secretary General Drummond were given a sufficient amount of autonomy to proceed with a chiefly informal selection process (i.e. relying on personal contacts with officials or diplomatic representatives) and worked during early and mid-November in parallel to the Council to confirm the appointed members. The Secretariat's correspondence regarding the commissioners reveals a strong preference, expressed by Drummond in his communication with others for candidates, for small and neutral European countries, for instance 'chosen from Scandinavia and Finland' or 'Swiss if there is a Norwegian member of the Commission'.[34]

While consideration was given to the nationality of the appointees, there is no extensive evidence in the League Secretariat documents that indicates attention was paid to the commissioners' particular knowledge of the region or country to be visited and any personal biases they may have with regard to the subject.[35] Often, a personal recommendation by a reliable person would be sufficient to consider and choose the candidate instead of any extensive vetting of this person – which could be challenging given the limited time.[36] Candidates under consideration were only male and often with a long career in politics, academia or the military – a tendency also palpable in all other League inquiries. Since appointments to an inquiry were never permanent, requiring a temporary break from another position or occupation, it also left unclear to what extent they could successfully serve the League's aim and interests in addition to their personal or professional interests. On 10 November, more than a week before the Council confirmed the details of the assignment, the Secretariat had already concluded the selection process and informed the candidates about the duties of the commission: the chosen commissioners were Major Jens Christian Meinich (Norway), Colonel Charles Schaefer (Luxembourg) and Dr Rolf Thesleff (Finland), and serving as secretary was M. H. de Pourtalès (Switzerland).[37]

The appointment of an inquiry was rarely if ever a straightforward process because last-minute or unforeseen changes to the composition of the commission were frequent. By the time the commission was preparing to travel to Albania, Rolf Thesleff had resigned from the commission for health reasons. The Finnish Foreign Service recommended to have him replaced by Professor Jakob Johannes Sederholm, a Finnish geologist, who joined the commission shortly thereafter.[38] The commission was also confronted by the poor health of Colonel Charles Schaefer, followed by his sudden death in January 1922. While he was not replaced, his death led to an unanticipated but extensive discussion at the League Secretariat about the organisation's legal liability and the payment of indemnity to the commissioner's widow on moral grounds.[39] Additionally, the repeated extension of the commission's assignment confirmed by the Council in 1922 and early 1923 – unlike future inquiries – would result in the prolonged engagement of Professor Sederholm as the League's (only) commissioner in Albania, albeit accompanied for most of the inquiry's remaining period by a new secretary, Count Frederick Moltke (Denmark).[40]

The inquiry commission travelled from Geneva to Albania, first to Durrës (Durazzo) and then to Tirana, in the second half of November 1921 to commence its activities on the ground, among others to inform itself about the troop withdrawal from the neutral zone and to gain a better understanding of the present situation in the country. Once in Albania, the League inquiry primarily dedicated time to conversations with representatives of the executive branch of government and 'other influential persons' that could shed light on the country's political system and form of government.[41] Among others, the commissioners spoke with Catholic bishops in Northern Albania, who possessed 'great authority' and 'whose opinions it was therefore necessary to obtain if a general idea of the situation in this district was to be gained'.[42]

After a few weeks, the commission also began to travel to smaller villages across Albania and gather opinions from local representatives and inhabitants – chiefly with the help of interpreters – for instance to clarify the situation in the Mirdite region and to understand the underlying causes behind a rebellion against the central government.[43] Unable to speak the local languages and because of limited access and availability of local newspapers, it was 'difficult for the Commission to keep in touch with public opinion in all parts of the country';[44] therefore, the inquiry often relied in subsequent weeks and months on the help of foreign citizens in the country who 'witnessed' events, could act as an interpreter or were perceived as possessing 'a thorough knowledge of the country' and willing to serve as advisers or confidential informants.[45] In one well-documented situation, the inquiry had to draw upon second-hand knowledge to inform the League Secretariat, which turned out to be inaccurate.[46]

The Council adopted new sets of resolutions on two occasions in 1922, which were generally prepared by the Secretariat and reflected the information received from the inquiry.[47] In January, the Council instructed the commissioners to focus on the situation in the neutral zone on the frontier with Yugoslavia after reports of incidents in December 1921 and suggested that it keep itself available for the Delimitation Commission once it was set up, after the inquiry had worked already for several months and submitted periodical reports regarding the evacuation of troops, the political situation and resources of Albania and the occurrences in the Mirdite region. In this context, a suggestion made by the inquiry commission to extend the neutral zone around Korçë (Koritza), close to Greece, was accepted by the Council and passed on the Conference of Ambassadors – and eventually put into practice in April 1922.[48]

After relations between Albania and Yugoslavia gradually improved, diplomatic relations were formalised and there were no major incidents to be reported or investigated, the inquiry shifted its focus to the internal political situation in Albania; it visited the neutral zone and subsequently remained in the country until the opportunity arose to meet the delimitation commission before returning to Geneva. Meanwhile, another inquiry commission proposal to form an Albano-Serb Mixed Military Commission was not accepted by the Conference of Ambassadors.[49]

Ascertaining the truth in Albania 67

In May, while expressing gratitude for the 'valuable work' done hitherto, the Council adopted new resolutions that saw one commissioner (Professor Sederholm) and a secretary (Count Frederick Moltke) travel to Albania and remain in the country – upon the inquiry's recommendation and Albania's request – for an extended period to continue to follow events in the country and consult with the government while the League was preparing economic assistance and 'to send experts to Albania to make a report on the measures necessary to encourage investment of foreign capital'.[50] Sederholm remained in the country for most of 1922 together with his secretary Moltke and he continued the assignment alone in Albania in early 1923 until the completion of the final report in May 1923.

The reduced inquiry dealt with minor incidents in the summer of 1922, including one involving an Italian postal office in Durrës. But the majority of the commission's attention went to the situation on the disputed frontier with Greece, where the evacuation of Albanian and Greek troops from the neutral zone had not been finalised and tensions continued to simmer over the creation of an autocephalous Albanian Orthodox Church. Sederholm spent a longer period of time in Korçë to understand the make-up of the population and the views of the inhabitants, including the Greek-speaking ones, and their perceptions vis-à-vis Albania and Greece.[51]

The inquiry commission reported back to the League of Nations in the format of regular telegrams with updates about travels and events, periodical overviews and general reports before each Council meeting discussing the Albanian question. A large number of documents were produced during the activity period (see Table 3.2).

Reports are an important step in the instrumental practice of inquiry, and the use of periodical ones meant that the commissioners could shift focus between reports. Moreover, it provided the League Secretariat – at the centre of communication between the inquiry, the Council and the Conference of Ambassadors – a means to engage with new (but not always accurate or complete) information and spur the organisation's decision-making bodies into action and at the same time put pressure on the Allied Powers. However, the variety of periodical reports also reveals a different treatment of some of them: the earliest reports were not widely circulated or deliberately summarised in a memorandum prepared by the Secretary General, because, while it was felt that the reports were 'probably quite accurate', they could provoke controversy among some League members because 'accusations against both sides [...] may render the future work of the commission difficult'.[52] Arguably, the fact that the initial reports were signed by only one commissioner and did not reflect the view of the entire commission was an additional reason to restrict circulation. Nevertheless, later reports signed only by Sederholm were generally made available through the

Table 3.2 Reports by the Albanian inquiry commission.

Title	Publication	Signed Author(s)
Report No. 1 on the proceedings and situation in the country	25 November 1921 Circulated to Council members	Schaeffer
Report No. 2 on the Mirdite question	6 December 1921 Not circulated/published	Meinich
Report of the commission on its work from 19 November to 20 December 1921	29 December 1921 Circulated to League members	Schaeffer, Meinich, Sederholm
Report of the commission in Albania (regarding the frontier with Greece)	March 1922 Published in the official journal	Meinich, Sederholm
Report of the commission of inquiry in Albania (regarding the neutral zone and civilian complaints)	April 1922 Published in the official journal	Meinich, Sederholm
General report presented by the commission to the Council of the League	19 April 1922 Circulated to League members	Meinich, Sederholm, Pourtalès
Supplementary report of the commission submitted to the Council	9 May 1922 Circulated to League members	Meinich, Sederholm, Pourtalès
Report of the commission of inquiry in Albania on its work from June until 18 December 1922	January 1923 Published in the official journal	Sederholm
Report of the commission of inquiry in Albania on its activities from 19 December 1922 to 1 February 1923	May 1923 Published in the official journal	Sederholm
Report of the commission of inquiry in Albania on its work from 1 February to the beginning of April 1923	May 1923 Published in the official journal	Sederholm
Final report of the commission of inquiry	May 1923 Published in the official journal	Sederholm

Sources: LONOJ, LONA/LONTAD.

League's official channels. In any case, signatures are a reminder that reports of inquiry commissions were in most cases a composite document prepared by multiple authors or, in the case of the majority of the reports in the table, the outcome of a single commissioner's activities (supported by a secretary).

In general, the reports shed light on what information the inquiry gathered during its work, what type of sources it was dependent on ('it is interesting to note a report confidentially received by the Commission from a trustworthy source') but also how it came to its judgments of a particular situation and in what manner it phrased these ('There seems to be no doubt that ...' and 'in no case was the Commission able to ascertain the truth of the same') as well as its conclusions or recommendations drawn at the end ('Albanians possess all the moral and material elements which go to form the basis of an independent State').[53] It was a common feature of inquiries to use statements implying the certainty of facts and the trustworthiness of gathered information while putting an emphasis on the authority and knowledge of the commission – that is, the production and qualification of information rather than the deliverance of truth. Additionally, Sederholm was the only commissioner to be involved from nearly the beginning until the very end; therefore, he presents the clearest indication of how a personality, profession or any personal and other biases shine through in the written output of an investigation. From the periodical reports, there are three thematic dimensions where his role was preponderant.

First, close attention to Albania's economic resources and in particular its geological ones was evident from the general report prepared by the inquiry but received even more attention in the final report presented by Sederholm to the Council. This stated that the country had sufficient mineral resources and fertile soil to be an independent state, but these would require a 'mining industry' and 'modern agricultural methods' respectively.[54] Much of the economic as well as political questions were framed in terms of development and modernisation along civilisational lines, with reports noting that administrative reforms might lead to Albania becoming 'a modern Occidental country' and emphasising that 'Europe cannot allow any part of the continent to remain permanently in a state of excessive backwardness'.[55]

Second, there was a racial component present both in the general reports and the ones signed by Sederholm that was used to justify the existence of an Albanian nation ('the only truly native race of the Balkans [...] they have been able to maintain the purity of their blood, their customs and their languages'). Nevertheless, it was also applied in hierarchical terms to talk about the path of development the country would have to pursue to become a 'modern state' ('The race is a gifted one, but at present it lacks experience and knowledge').[56] However, Sederholm did not apply race as a category or frame at every occasion or in all sections, and he may have used it to denote primarily a people or a nation. He also stressed the importance of cultural and linguistic factors, for example when discussing the situation in Southern Albania where there were multiple religious denominations and Greek and Albanian languages of instruction in schools. With regard to language, Sederholm drew upon his own country's history and the development – how the Finns developed their 'necessary stock of cultural words' and reduced the role of Swedish in education – to demonstrate with 'an encouraging example to follow' how Albania could develop its national language of instruction, legislation and administration.[57]

Third, Sederholm appeared at times to be aware of his own biases and limitations when it came to understanding the situation in Albania. With regard to the composition of the population in Southern Albania, he noted that 'it seems impossible to draw any certain conclusions in the present state of our knowledge'.[58] In the same report, he addressed 'the bias of the observers' and suggested that for foreign visitors arriving in Albania, it was easy for large welcoming events and official receptions 'to deceive many observers as to the real feelings of the population, especially when they see the apparent enthusiasm of the crowds'. Sederholm stressed that he had tried to find 'trustworthy' sources and double-checked information from other sources; while he showed a degree of consciousness about his personal bias,[59] his reports and arguably his extended presence in the country also turned him into a strong advocate of Albania's independence and the importance of the League's support to the country.[60]

A final element in this Albanian case concerns the impact of the inquiry commission on the country and what role this fact-finding instrument had in the League's decision-making process. As previously mentioned, there were many instances where the inquiry provided reports to the Secretariat, acting as a central information hub, which allowed the Council to act upon the commission's suggestions. The effect on the Conference of Ambassadors appears to have been more limited because the Allied Powers largely kept to their own agenda and timetable. They opted to address the delimitation question over a longer period of time and only began to speed up the decision-making process after indications of possible escalation and repeated requests from the League's bodies. At most, the interaction between the League and the Conference remained limited. More impactful perhaps was the factual presence of the inquiry in Albania and the performative role it played as the direct representation on the League on the ground.[61] The inquiry's presence in the country was a factor in the de-escalation of tensions between countries, improving interstate communication (when Albania had no diplomatic relations with its neighbours) and allowing a relatively quick verification of claims on the basis of 'trustworthy information' provided by locals – as one case of forced enlistment of Albanians in the Greek army demonstrates.[62]

When it comes to the inquiry's direct impact on the League's decision-making process, it is noteworthy that the 'valuable work' and 'wealth of precise information and sound conclusions' provided by the commission were recognised, however, without any discussions about the substance and the subject matter at the public meetings of the Council.[63] As a consequence, it is unclear to what extent the inquiry genuinely shaped the

Council members' thinking about the events in Albania (especially since the Secretariat drafted the majority of the respective resolutions). It is perhaps a reason why the experiment of using periodical reports was generally not repeated with future commissions, when it became common practice to produce a report with a single narrative at the end of the assignment. While the Council acted upon the commission's suggestion to extend the neutral zone, its success was minimal regarding other proposals (a mixed military commission) and in comparison to Albania's own diplomacy in the Council – to obtain a financial adviser and to extend the inquiry until his arrival – which had more palpable effects.

The inquiry reports had a lot to say about the enthusiasm in Albania for the League and the 'very great moral authority and prestige' the organisation enjoyed in the country, embodied by the presence of the commission. The written documentation was more ambiguous on the question of whether this was complementary to the inquiry's desire to 'ascertain the truth'. If so, what was that truth and how was it to be ascertained?[64] Nevertheless, seeing inquiry purely in terms of its diplomatic and performative role as the League's 'eyes on the ground' risks also overlooking signs of (individual) agency. The commission's and Sederholm's defence of Albanian independence – not unlike the stances taken in future reports about Persia and Liberia – focused attention on actions by internal factions or neighbouring countries that led to escalation or instability in the country. Meanwhile, the strong emphasis on the importance of the League in supporting Albania was a key component of such advocacy efforts. In sum, inquiry often came down to the agency and views of one or a couple of commissioners assigned to the task.

Conclusions

This chapter has explored how the League of Nations used inquiry as an instrument to examine a wide range of international issues. The Albanian case in the early years of the League already shows a number of formal characteristics that inquiry commissions would retain on future occasions, such as a recognisable life cycle from an initial request or resolution in one of the decision-making bodies until the delivery of a final report that concluded the assignment. While there was little of a detailed legal or organisational blueprint to inquiry at the League, there is a sense of common practices that were embedded in the League's wider rationalist and developmental aspirations. These practices ranged from the selection of commissions for the temporary assignment – taking a candidate's nationality, extensive career and any personal recommendation into account – to a presence on the ground to gather information and conduct interviews with high-level country representatives as well as inhabitants on the ground.

The League's model of inquiry was not created out of a vacuum. It drew on a number of earlier models and precedents, from international dispute settlement to domestic inquiries, creating a new form that was an adaptation of what could be understood as both an older instrument and an accompanying set of practices. While the context changed to one of internationalist action and internationalism under the auspices of the League and a greater emphasis was put on impartiality and disinterested advise, in practice inquiry did not differ too greatly from earlier precedents, such as commissions organised in an imperial or colonial setting.[65]

The League relied almost exclusively on Europeans and Americans for its nine inquiries (chiefly focused on what was perceived as the non-Western world). A number of them had a colonial professional background and they often came from countries with a direct interest. Despite their individual agency, commissioners shared discourses about civilisational development, modernity and a racial hierarchy while advocating (Western) assistance to ensure the 'progress' of a country or region. Even though the League relied on the internationalist setting and expert bodies to achieve a more rational conduct of international politics, in practice it was shaped by a very similar set of ideas and beliefs and a context that was permeated by imperial idioms, modes and repertoires.[66]

The practices comprising inquiry also rarely if ever occurred in a vacuum, as the Albanian case and other League inquiries demonstrate. At different levels, from the individual to the international, there were signs of tension and agency creating new dynamics. At the microlevel, the selected commissioners and their role on the ground were a crucial factor, because the different personalities and the degree of cooperation or competition created a complex dynamic that shaped the inquiry's activities and perception of events. At the slightly higher, local level, there was the significance of operating on the ground in a country or region mostly unknown to the commissioners, where travel conditions were difficult and where there was a great deal of reliance on interpreters or foreigners to converse with people or gather information. At the intermediate, national level, most inquiries (including the Albanian one) revealed a playing field of different political factions and parties that had an impact on the overall stability of the political system and the perception of the situation. Finally, the international level was often characterised by contestation between (neighbouring) countries, over territory and interests, or between rivalling powers and even international organisations, over which one had the ultimate authority. Here, the League's entanglement as a relatively new player in a broader, already established, imperial and international setting also became a lens through which an inquiry could be perceived.

Taken together, these multiple levels and considerations created a context for the investigative process that made neutrality or impartiality difficult to achieve on the ground because each commission was greatly constrained in its set-up and methods due to the absence of an organisational blueprint and detailed code of conduct or set of rules. In practice, there was great reliance on informal practices and the personal authority of individuals to produce and qualify information, while questions of what constituted reliable knowledge and truth were often brushed aside. As such, there was also a contrast between the institution's formal adherence to fact-finding and impartiality, a liberal and rational aspiration and the markedly different reality on the ground.

If inquiry was not an instrument of truth, then what kind of essence can be distilled from inquiry as an instrument of international order in the first half of the twentieth century? The Albanian case has shown the significance of a flexible presence in the country and the performative impact of the League having its chosen representatives acting as the organisation's eyes on the ground, which brought about a degree of pacification and de-escalation of the situation between Albania and her neighbours. While the inquiry contributed in part to a preservation of the peace – in the sense that it gathered and sent out relevant information, bringing different points of view to light, and ensured communication between the different actors through the Secretariat – there is no straightforward case to be made for fact-finding or even truth-seeking. If the definitions of Madariaga and Briand are taken as a benchmark, then impartial knowledge was meant to be guaranteed by representatives from small, neutral European countries, but the views and biases of commissioners were not actively considered. The accuracy of the League's own methods was difficult to square with the inquiry's reliance on foreigners in Albania for information and the fragmented and highly singular (i.e. personal) nature in which events were reported in periodical reports.

League inquiry is better understood if it is not strictly considered at face value, as a fact-finding instrument but rather as an instrument of diplomacy and the interwar international order. Serving as a fail-safe or safety valve, inquiry gave the larger European countries and international authorities (i.e. the Allied Powers, as permanent Council members and represented at the Conference of Ambassadors) a greater degree of flexibility to respond to an escalating conflict or a sensitive cross-border issue. Moreover, inquiry set a softer face on Western interference (through expertise, facts and recommendations), not unlike imperial and colonial inquiries, and avoided any form of direct intervention. In the Albanian case, the inquiry was a means to defuse tensions between neighbouring countries while allowing the Conference and the Allied Powers to stretch the delimitation question over a longer period of time. The on-the-ground presence of the League's commission tried to ensure some degree of stability in the region, at least until the Corfu incident in 1923, while its recommendations emphasised Albania's duty as an independent state to 'partake in [Europe's] economic current' as a means of civilisational progress to 'catch up the time she has lost through no fault of her own'.[67]

Notes

1 For example, see: Emma Post, '"Fighting a Ghost": Collecting Data and Creating Knowledge on Sex Trafficking in the League of Nations between 1921 and 1939', *Tijdschrift voor Genderstudies* 24:3/4 (2021), 296–314; Quincy R. Cloet, '"A Fuller Knowledge of the Facts": The League of Nations' Endeavours to Produce International Expertise', in Haakon A. Ikonomou and Karen Gram-Skjoldager (eds), *The League of Nations: Perspectives from the Present* (Aarhus: Aarhus University Press, 2019), pp. 150–60; David Lincove, 'Data for Peace: The League of Nations and Disarmament 1920–40', *Peace & Change* 43:4 (2018), 498–529; Daniel Laqua, 'Intellectual Exchange and the New Information Order of the Interwar Years: The British Society for International Bibliography, 1927–1937', *Library Trends* 62:2 (2013), 465–77.
2 Catherine Harwood, *The Roles and Functions of Atrocity-Related United Nations Commissions of Inquiry in the International Legal Order: Navigating between Principle and Pragmatism* (Leiden: Brill, 2020); Hans Thoolen and Berth Verstappen, *Human Rights Missions A Study of the Fact-Finding Practice of Non-Governmental Organizations* (Boston, MA: Kluwer Academic Publishers, 1986).
3 While the Albanian inquiry has been mentioned in general histories of Albania and the region, the investigation has only been subject of one article that provides a descriptive overview of its work in relation to the League of Nations decision-making process regarding the situation in Albania: Deona Çali, 'The Role of the Enquiry Commission in the Decision-Making at the League of Nations Regarding the Albanian Issue', *Studia Politica; Romanian Political Science Review* 16:2 (2016), 243–55. In addition to the League, the Carnegie Endowment for International Peace also sent out an expedition in this period, detailed here: Nadine Akhund, 'The Two Carnegie Reports: From the Balkan Expedition of 1913 to the Albanian Trip of 1921: A Comparative Approach', *Balkanologie* 14:1–2 (2012).
4 With regard to the source materials consulted for this chapter: many of the materials were gathered at the United Nations Library in Geneva during an archival visit in 2017 and complemented with additional primary sources collected through the League of Nations Official Journal (hereafter LONOJ) and the Total Digital Access to the League of Nations Archives (LONTAD) Project.

For Albania, the materials are predominantly from Boxes R555, R556 and R597 in the League of Nations Archives (hereafter LONA).
5 League archival sources and secondary literature have used both *inquiry* and *enquiry* interchangeably. While the former is more predominant in the United States and the latter in the United Kingdom, there is a minor semantic distinction between an enquiry (a simple question or request) and an inquiry (a more formal investigation). Given the nature of the subject, this chapter has opted for a consistent use and adaptation of *inquiry* as the preferred word form.
6 Council resolutions would specifically identify an investigations on the ground or 'on the spot'. For example, the Council resolutions of 10 December 1931 regarding the Manchurian crisis: 'to appoint a Commission of five members to study *on the spot* and to report to the Council on any circumstance which, affecting international relations, threatens to disturb peace between China and Japan, or the good understanding between them upon which peace depends' (emphasis added). From: Discussion at the 65th Session of the League of Nations Council, Box R1865, LONA.
7 For the background to Articles 12 and 17 and the drafting process of the Covenant, see Mary Florence Wilson, *The Origins of the League Covenant: Documentary History of Its Drafting* (London: Hogarth Press, 1928).
8 Commission of Inquiry in Albania: Instructions of the Secretary General to the Members of the Commission, Dossier 1 1–1661 1–17335, Box R597, LONA.
9 In comparison, the International Labour Organisation (ILO) was more specific about what an inquiry was and how it could be used in practice (see Articles 411–420 of the ILO's original Constitution of 1919).
10 Inquiry was a ubiquitous phenomenon in a lot of European countries, and in the United Kingdom, for instance, each year of the twentieth century had at least some form of inquiry underway. For an overview: David Butler and Gareth Butler, *Twentieth-Century British Political Facts: 1900–2000* (Basingstoke: Palgrave Macmillan, 2005).
11 Charles Howard Ellis, *The Origin, Structure & Working of the League of Nations* (London: Lawbook Exchange Ltd, 1928), p. 99; Wilson, *The Origins of the League Covenant*, p. 178; Nicolas Politis, 'Les Commissions Internationales d'enquête', *Revue Générale de Droit International Public* 29 (1912), 96.
12 J. Merrills, *International Dispute Settlement* (Cambridge: Cambridge University Press, 2005), p. 45.
13 John E. Noyes, 'William Howard Taft and the Taft Arbitration Treaties', *Villanova Law Review* 56:3 (2011), 536; Jackson Harvey Ralston, *International Arbitration from Athens to Locarno* (Clark, NJ: The Lawbook Exchange, Ltd., 2004), chapters 19–22.
14 Berber Bevernage, 'The Making of the Congo Question: Truth-Telling, Denial and "Colonial Science" in King Leopold's Commission of Inquiry on the Rubber Atrocities in the Congo Free State (1904–1905)', *Rethinking History* 22:2 (2018), 203–38; Ronen Shamir and Daphna Hacker, 'Colonialism's Civilizing Mission: The Case of the Indian Hemp Drug Commission', *Law*

and Social Inquiry 26:2 (2001), 435–61; Charles-Robert Ageron, 'Jules Ferry et la question algérienne en 1892 (d'après quelques inédits)', *Revue d'histoire moderne et contemporaine* 10:2 (1963), 127–46.
15 Quincy R. Cloet, 'Truth Seekers or Power Brokers? The League of Nations and Its Commissions of Inquiry' (PhD thesis, Aberystwyth University, 2019), 37–42.
16 Regarding to the Manchurian inquiry, Council discussions frequently referred to the 'impartial spirit' and the work conducted 'on the basis of impartial information only' (Boxes R1865–1866 and R1870, LONA). The inquiry commission's president, Lord Lytton, wrote that 'we are all agreed that our object is not so much to arbitrate between China and Japan on the subject of Manchuria' and he suggested that they 'disclaim from the outset the character of a Court, and offer our services in the character of a friend'. From: Memorandum of 5 February on the Organisation and Work of the Commission, Box S49, LONA.
17 Inquiries into border disputes and other issues often went beyond the strict nature of the conflict or issue, and commissions were generally instructed to look for underlying causes and provide recommendations regarding the development and modernisation of the country or region involved.
18 League of Nations, *International Statistical Yearbook* (Geneva, 1926), p. 7; League of Nations, *International Statistical Yearbook* (Geneva, 1927), p. 7.
19 This argument is developed in more detail in Bentley Allan, a discursive configuration where the League's central aims were coated in the language of scientific spirit; he argues that there is a strong orientation for civilisational progress and evolutionary development in the League, exemplified by the trust put in qualified experts and enquiries/surveys to gather impartial/authoritative information. See Bentley Allan, *Scientific Cosmology and International Orders* (Cambridge: Cambridge University Press, 2018), pp. 183–7.
20 Discussion at the 65th Session of the League of Nations Council, R1865, LONA; Discussion at the 66th Session of the League of Nations Council, January-February 1932, Dossier 1A-31334–34613, Box R1870, LONA.
21 For instance, in case of the opium inquiry in Persia, the Secretariat sought for experts in transportation and agriculture, see Services of a transport expert, Dossier 12A-45255–47747, Box R801, LONA; Services of an agricultural expert, Dossier 12A-45255–46962, Box R801, LONA; 'A Commission such as we have in mind ought to find out the actual truth of the Persian situation.' From: Expenses of the Commission, Dossier 12A-45255–45256, Box R801, LONA.
22 Andrew Linklater, *The Idea of Civilization and the Making of the Global Order* (Bristol: Bristol University Press, 2021).
23 Barbara Jelavich, *History of the Balkans: Twentieth Century* (Cambridge: Cambridge University Press, 1983), pp. 84–8; C. H. G., 'Greek Claims in Southern Albania', *The World Today* 2:10 (1946), 488–9.
24 Jelavich, *History of the Balkans*, pp. 136, 141–2, 177; C. H. G., 'Greek Claims in Southern Albania', 491; George F. Kohn, 'The Organization and the Work of the League of Nations', *The Annals of the American Academy of Political and Social Science* 114 (1924), 21–2.

25 It was not uncommon for a small countries such as Albania to resort to internationalism and attempt to use the League for greater leverage at the international level. See Minutes of the 15th meeting of the Council – 25 June 1921, 'The Frontiers of Albania', LONOJ (September 1921), p. 723.
26 Minutes of the 16th meeting of the Council – 25 June 1921, LONOJ (September 1921), p. 725.
27 Ibid., p. 726.
28 Overlapping authorities were not uncommon in this period and sometimes this could lead to frictions (for example, between the Pan-American Union and the League of Nations as experienced by the Chaco Commission). In these early years, the League did not seek confrontation with the Conference of Ambassadors on this assignment; Citations from: Albania – Memorandum by the SG – 17 November 1921, Dossier C.446.M.328.1921., LONA, p. 9.
29 Kohn, 'The Organization and the Work of the League of Nations', 21; Ibid.
30 Albania – Memorandum by the SG – 29 December 1921, Dossier C.547.1921. VII., LONA, p. 3.
31 Ibid.
32 This meant less of a single narrative of events than a succession of updates and the expansion of information gained on the ground. This was generally not repeated in other inquiries, except for the League's Shanghai Committee, a group made up of European diplomatic representatives in China, to report on events in Shanghai during the Japanese attack on China following the Manchurian incident.
33 Albania – Memorandum by the SG – 17 November 1921, p. 9.
34 Citations: Telegram to Wellington Koo of the Chinese legation in London (22 October 1921), Commission of Inquiry in Albania: Services of Major Meinich as member of the Commission, Dossier 1 1–1661 1–16759, Box R597, LONA; Exceptionally, a Venezuelan diplomatic representative was also approached for the inquiry, but he had to decline the invitation because of a conflicting assignment, see Commission of Inquiry in Albania: Services of Mr Escalantes as a member of the Commission – declined, Dossier 1 1–1661 1–116612, Box R597, LONA; Commission of Inquiry in Albania: Services of Count Horace de Pourtalès, Dossier 1 1–1661 1–16614, Box R597, LONA.
35 Greater consideration would be given to the specialism of each potential commissioner for inquiries that were not directly concerned with an international conflict or cross-border dispute in future years, although the League's rationalist aspirations would in this matter remain formal rather than substantial when it pertained to knowledge of local or regional conditions.
36 Commission of Inquiry in Albania: Services of Count Frederick Moltke, Dossier 1 1–1661 1–20964, Box R597, LONA.
37 Commission of Inquiry in Albania: Instructions of the Secretary General to the Members of the Commission, Dossier 1 1–1661 1–17335, Box R597, LONA; Albania – General report presented by the Commission to the Council of the League – 19 April 1922, Dossier C.202(A).M.148.1922.VII., LONA.

38 Commission of Inquiry in Albania: Services of Mr Thesleff as member of the Commission (replaced by Mr Sederholm), Dossier 1 1–1661 1–16944, Box R597, LONA.
39 Commission of Inquiry in Albania: Services of Colonel Schaefer as a member of the Commission, Dossier 1 1–1661 1–16613, Box R597, LONA; Albania – Memorandum by the SG – 20 March 1922, Dossier C.140.M.80.1922., LONA.
40 Commission of Inquiry in Albania: Services of Count Frederick Moltke, LONA.
41 Report No. 1 on the Proceedings and Situation in the Country, Dossier C.501.1921.VII., LONA, p. 1.
42 Report of the Commission on its work from 19 November to 20 December 1921, Dossier C.542.M.387.1921.VII., LONA, p. 2.
43 Report No. 2 on the Mirdite Question, Dossier C.5.1022..VII, LONA, pp. 2–3.
44 Report of the Commission on its work from 19 November to 20 December 1921, LONA, p. 5.
45 This was also a common feature of other League inquiries; Citations: Report of the Commission in Albania – 18 January 1922, Dossier C.93.M.48.1922.VII., LONOJ (April 1922), p. 264; Albania – Report of the commission of enquiry in Albania – 15 February 1922, Dossier C.113.M.67.1922.VII., LONOJ (April 1922), p. 324; Albania – General report presented by the Commission to the Council of the League (19 April 1922), LONA, p. 2.
46 This concerned the expulsion of a Greek clergyman. The commission noted that 'A foreign witness, who was present at the time of his departure, stated that there were no demonstrations on this occasion, either in favour of or against the Metropolitan' (Ibid., p. 2). Because the commission was not present in the region at the time, Psomas contends that Sederholm perceived a British citizen named Morton Frederic Eden as an unbiased Foreign Office source, even though he misinformed the commissioner about the specifics of the expulsion. See Lampros Psomas, 'A Spy in Albania: Southern Albanian Oil and Morton Frederic Eden', *International Journal of Intelligence and CounterIntelligence* 28:3 (2015), 590–609.
47 The Secretariat generally suggested a draft resolution to the Council rapporteur, although this autonomy and flexibility was less palpable in bigger inquiries where the stakes were higher and when the Council operated in a more autonomous fashion. See Note from Abraham to the Secretary General – 12 April 1923, Dossier 1 1–124 0–27763, Box R557, LONA.
48 Albania – Memorandum by the SG – 20 March 1922, Dossier C.140.M.80.1922., LONA, p. 3; Frontiers of Albania – Letter from the President of the Conference of Ambassadors – 5 April 1922, Dossier C.221.M.115.1922.VII., LONOJ (June 1922), pp. 486–7.
49 Albania – Memorandum by the SG – 20 March 1922, LONA, p. 5.
50 League of Nations Council – May Session 1922 – Resolution, Dossier C.260.I.1922.VII, LONA, pp. 1–2; Albania – General report presented by the Commission to the Council of the League (19 April 1922), LONA, p. 9.

51 Report of the commission of inquiry in Albania on its work from June until 18 December 1922, Dossier C.5.M.3.1923.VII., LONOJ (January 1923); Report of the commission of inquiry in Albania on its activities from 19 December 1922 to 1 February 1923, LONOJ (May 1923).
52 Citations from instructions and discussions among the Secretary-General and Secretariat officials as part of a folder containing a report. See Report No. 2 on the Mirdite Question, LONA.
53 Citations from: Report No. 2 on the Mirdite Question, LONA, p. 2; Report No. 1 on the Proceedings and Situation in the Country, LONA, p. 1; Report of the commission of inquiry in Albania – 18 January 1922, LONOJ (March 1922), p. 267; Albania – General report presented by the Commission to the Council of the League (19 April 1922), LONA, p. 9.
54 Albania – Final Report of the Commission of Enquiry, LONOJ (May 1923), p. 509.
55 Report of the commission of inquiry in Albania on its work from June until 18 December 1922, LONOJ (January 1923), p. 116.
56 Albania – General report presented by the Commission to the Council of the League (19 April 1922), LONA, p. 4; Albania – Final Report of the Commission of Enquiry, LONOJ (May 1923), p. 510.
57 Albania – Report of the Commission of Enquiry in Albania on its Activities from 19 December 1922 to 1 February 1923, LONOJ (May 1923), pp. 495–6.
58 Ibid. p. 500. Citations in the next sentence from Ibid., p. 497.
59 Citation: 'I have done my best to eliminate all causes of error which I could detect and to be fair in my judgment, in the firm conviction that the truth will be of best service to all parties' (Ibid., p. 497).
60 Citations: 'If Albania receives in the future the aid of Europe, through the League of Nations, she will continue to be a faithful adherent of the ideas represented by the League' (Report of the commission of inquiry in Albania on its work from June until 18 December 1922, LONOJ (January 1923), p. 116); 'If I may express a wish, it is that those who have shown confidence in me in Albania will feel that it has not been misplaced and that they will recognise that the criticisms I have felt it my duty to express in my reports have had no other motive but my earnest desire to serve Albania' (Albania – Final Report of the Commission of Enquiry, LONOJ (May 1923), p. 505).
61 For the role of performance and expertise, see IR scholarship such as: Berit Bliesemann de Guevara, 'Intervention Theatre: Performance, Authenticity and Expert Knowledge in Politicians' Travel to Post-/Conflict Spaces', *Journal of Intervention and Statebuilding* 11:1 (2017), 1–23.
62 'Telegram from Professor Sederholm (8 January 1923)', Albania – Professor Sederholm, Commission of Inquiry in Albania, Koritza, states that the Greek Government, ignoring the Albanian citizenship of men from the provinces of Koritza and Argyrocastro, is enlisting them in Greek army to fight their own kindred, Dossier 1 1–124 0–25522, Box R556, LONA.
63 Citations: League of Nations Council – May Session 1922 – Resolution, Dossier C.260.I.1922.VII., LONA, p. 2; Albania – Council of the League of Nations

– Fourteenth Session of the Council, Geneva, April 1923 – Resolution proposed by the Swedish representative and adopted by the Council with regard to the Commission of Enquiry in Albania, Dossier 1 1–124 0–27862, Box R556, LONA.

64 Citations: *Report of the Commission on its work from 19 November to 20 December 1921*, LONA, p. 2; *Report of the Commission in Albania – 25 January 1922*, Dossier C.98.M.53.1922.VII., LONOJ (March 1922), p. 267.

65 For instance, Allen identifies continuities when it comes to Palestine under the British mandate all the way to UN human rights inquiries. See Lori Allen, *A History of False Hope: Investigative Commissions in Palestine* (Stanford, CA: Stanford University Press, 2021).

66 Miguel Bandeira Jerónimo, 'A League of Empires: Imperial Political Imagination and Interwar Internationalisms', in Miguel Bandeira Jerónimo and José Pedro Monteiro (eds), *Internationalism, Imperialism and the Formation of the Contemporary World* (Cham: Palgrave Macmillan, 2018), pp. 87–126; Cloet, *Truth Seekers or Power Brokers?*, p. 247.

67 Albania – Final Report of the Commission of Enquiry, LONOJ (May 1923), p. 510.

4

The chemical weapons discourse as an instrument of international order: the Second Italo-Ethiopian War

Anneleen van der Meer

Introduction

In October 1935, Italy invaded Ethiopia following almost a year of rising tensions. In December 1934, the Wal-Wal incident had renewed older animosities stemming from the first Italo-Ethiopian war of 1887–96. It represented new attempts by Italy to conquer Ethiopian territory and expand its overseas empire in the Horn of Africa.[1] Soon, allegations of chemical weapons were levelled against Italy, but it was not until December that reports of a more official character were made.[2]

The chemical of choice for the Italians was sulfur mustard, a blister agent that was first introduced during the First World War and was responsible for the majority of gas casualties during that war. It is a fairly persistent substance that causes the skin to blister, exposing the victim to potential infections not only of the skin, but also of the respiratory system, although precise lethality is difficult to determine. In 1935, Ethiopian troops lacked protective gear, typically wearing light garments and sandals, thus making the use of these chemicals particularly effective for the Italians.[3] Apart from sulfur mustard, the Italians also used tear gas, and possibly chlorine and phosgene, over a period of several months from December 1935 until April 1936. Chemical weapons were usually delivered by air, using grenades, bombs and aerial spray tanks, protecting Italian supply routes and significantly disrupting Ethiopian infrastructure and morale.[4] One report estimates 15,000 gas casualties among the armed forces.[5] The number of casualties among the civilian population remains unclear, but ambulance units were reported to be treating more than a hundred victims a day by March 1936.[6]

There was significant international outcry against the use of chemical weapons by the Italian forces. Challenging Italy's argumentation about Ethiopia's supposed savagery, cartoonist David Low published a cartoon in the Evening Standard of 3 April 1936 (Figure 4.1). The cartoon depicts

82   *Instruments of international order*

Figure 4.1 Cartoon by David Low, 'Pah! They were uncivilized savages, without ideals', 3 April 1936, British Cartoon Archive, Kent, LSE2294.

a bulky Italian commander carrying poison gas cannisters. The background shows aeroplanes in the sky. Squinting his eyes, the commander points over his shoulder at people clearly in agony and dead bodies on the ground. The heading reads: 'Pah! They were uncivilised savages, without ideals.' The image is clear about whom Low believed the real savages to be. In the same month, a British delegate to the League of Nations noted in a Council meeting: 'there is one element in this tragic war about which I cannot pass over in silence': the use of gas.[7]

While Italy was sanctioned for its invasion, no sanctions were imposed in response to the use of gas. Collective security for a League member failed, and only two months after Italian forces had occupied Addis Ababa, the sanctions against Italy were lifted. The use of gas in Ethiopia is not the only example of chemical warfare during the Interbellum. Gas was also used by Spain during the Rif War (1921–26), after the Spanish suffered defeat at the Battle of Annual in 1921. Italy also used sulfur mustard and phosgene in Libya in the same period.[8] Another example was the large-scale use of chemicals during the second Sino-Japanese war of 1937–45, and there is strong evidence that Turkish forces used gas when trying to subjugate the Dersim people from 1937 to 1938.[9] What makes the Ethiopian case stand out, however, is the fact that Ethiopia was a sovereign state, being a member state of the League of Nations and signatory to the Geneva Protocol prohibiting the use of gas in war. This made Italy's invasion a war of aggression rather than a colonial operation, and its use of chemical weapons was a breach of the Protocol. While the Protocol was discussed at length in the League of Nations, it was ultimately not acted upon. The question is why.

Addressing the League's inaction is the first purpose of this chapter. The second purpose is to demonstrate how Ethiopian delegates attempted to instrumentalise the international discourse condemning chemical weapons in an effort to claim full statehood and protection under the Geneva Protocol, using the League of Nations' own legal instruments and norms. In other words, the chemical weapons discourse was used as an instrument of international order. While not immediately successful, Ethiopia was recognised as an independent state soon after the end of the Second World War. Megan Donaldson recently commented on this, saying that 'Ethiopia's use of the League to condemn the League's own failure may have had resonance over the longer term, helping ensure Ethiopia's re-emergence as a state after World War II.'[10]

Historicising chemical weapons and their prohibition

Hague Declarations

The moral history of chemical weapons has been examined by Richard Price, who traces the origins of the norm against these weapons back to the earliest legal agreement explicitly referring to asphyxiating gases.[11] He explains how the 1899 Hague Declaration became a reference point and a baseline for later understandings of the permissibility of chemical weapons. Interestingly, the topic of gas warfare was on the agenda in The Hague not because chemical weapons had been developed and used and a debate about their use was deemed necessary to limit future use. While proposals about using chemicals in war had been made, no weaponised chemicals had been created yet. Also, the connection with an older prohibition on poison was not evident. Instead, Price's genealogical analysis shows that the two topics were not connected in the proceedings. The prohibition on poison was copied directly from an earlier agreement text – the 1874 Brussels Declaration, which never took effect – while the topic of new explosives emitting asphyxiating gases was proposed and discussed separately. The poison prohibition did not generate debate about relative humanity, while the new topic of gas did. While some delegates proposed a relation between poisoning water and spreading asphyxiating gases, Price's conclusion is that the poison taboo was not instrumental for the inclusion of a gas prohibition in the Hague Declarations of 1899 and 1907. Catherine Jefferson agrees with this assessment in her 2014 examination of the chemical weapons norm.[12]

Unlike other weapon technologies discussed at the conference, such as submarines, asphyxiating gasses were prohibited in an absolute sense. The Declaration did not stipulate circumstances under which the use of gas would be allowed. However, the Declaration, which forbade the Contracting Powers 'from [using] projectiles the sole object of which is the diffusion of asphyxiating or deleterious gases', was only binding in the context of war amongst those same contracting powers. It ceased to be binding in the event of a war with a non-contracting party, or when a contracting party would be joined by a non-contracting state. As a result, the ban – although absolute – was not universal. It also introduced an element of restraint, namely that the contracting powers would abstain from a means of warfare even though it was unclear if this new weapon could be effective or decisive. At this time, the condition of 'war' was commonly understood to be a conflict between sovereign states.[13] As a result, colonial warfare was outside the scope of the agreement. The normative project to alleviate the horrors of war for combatants and non-combatants, which gave rise to the international conferences shaping the laws of war from the nineteenth century onwards, was therefore largely limited to the established colonial powers. Colonial warfare, although often waged with reference to a civilising mission and loaded with humanitarian discourse, was another matter entirely.[14]

In his analysis, Price points out a further implication stemming from the codification of a chemical weapons ban before such weapons had been invented: it became a moral standard. Usually when new weapons are developed and used, moral objections are raised by unprepared victims of these weapons as they suffer the consequences. After more powers incorporate the new weapon into their arsenals, such concerns often diminish. In the case of chemical weapons, however, such moral indignation upon first use would rather be shared by a circle of states who had agreed not to use such weapons, as there had been an a priori prohibition rather than just a victim calling for a prohibition. Victims now had a reference point on the basis of which they could object, and these objections could not be chalked up to the usual objections of a losing victim.

First World War

Beyond the Hague Declaration, no further refinement of this new class of gas weapons was undertaken in the legal field until the end of the First World War. Of course, as the weapons had not yet been developed, it was unclear what technology the Hague Declaration actually referred to. Tear gas was used by French troops as early as August 1914, while the German use of chlorine gas canisters on 22 April 1915 during the Second Battle of

Flanders near Ypres is usually referred to as the starting point of the chemical arms race of the First World War.[15] The new moral standard set by the Hague Declarations was now tested in practice for the first time.

The codification of the laws of war both restricted and legitimised the use of violence, creating a normative sphere in which violence was an acceptable policy option. However, as explained, the prohibition on the use of asphyxiating gases was absolute, and no distinction had been made between legitimate and illegitimate purposes, payloads or projectile sizes. Still, the actual declaration agreed upon in The Hague was very concisely worded and left room for interpretation. Initially, German justifications for the use of chlorine gas were based upon the principle of retaliation, namely that it was justified as a response to the French use of tear gas. This implies an understanding that the use of gas would be illegal if it had not happened in retaliation.[16] The fact that cannisters are not technically projectiles was also raised. In general, however, legal responses to the use of gas during the First World War were few, and no lively debate occurred about it, while other elements of the war were discussed in detail. None of the belligerents objected officially to the use of gas during the war, although some politicians denounced the German use of gas publicly.[17] Only on 6 February 1918 did the International Committee of the Red Cross address the issue, writing with reference to the principle of preventing needless suffering that 'we do not hesitate to demand openly that this atrocious method of warfare be renounced'.[18] Interestingly, this communication relies on the poison prohibition and the prohibition to use arms causing unnecessary suffering, both codified in Article 23 of the Hague Convention of 1907, rather than the Hague Declaration, which specifically deals with asphyxiating gases. The justification in response to this complaint was made by the Allied governments with reference to their obligation to protect their armed forces and provide them with 'equal offensive instruments' as the Germans had introduced first.[19]

Only after the war had ended did the legal debate about the permissibility of gas weapons start in earnest. Rather than historical objectivity, these debates were characterised by nationalistic tendencies and polarisation.[20] While the French had been the first to use tear gas, the burden to justify the use of gas weapons seemed to fall primarily on German scholars, who denounced the applicability of the Hague Conventions and Declarations, claiming that gas weapons did not cause unnecessary suffering, that gas was not poison and that the projectiles used during the war did not have the 'sole purpose' of spreading asphyxiating gas. The briefness of the Hague Declaration indeed left much room for interpretation, and legal historian Miloš Vec notes a more nuanced debate about gas in the Allied countries with arguments supporting and objecting to the legality of gas under the

Hague treaties.[21] In any case, a concerted effort to further codify the gas prohibition did arise in the decade after the First World War.

Versailles

The Treaty of Versailles (1919) imposed by the Allies on Germany was the first international legal text that refined the gas prohibition, and simultaneously introduced a form of hierarchy to the matter. Article 171 prohibits the manufacture, importation, and use of 'asphyxiating, poisonous or other gases and all analogous liquids, materials or devices'. The same article also prohibits Germany from importing or manufacturing 'armoured cars, tanks and all similar constructions suitable for use in war'.[22] These latter technologies were certainly not deemed counter to international humanitarian law for other states, and it can therefore not be concluded that the Treaty introduced a general or universal gas prohibition either. However, the League of Nations did initiate research in various committees to address and prohibit the use of gas in war, although no new legal texts were agreed upon until 1925. In 1924, the Fifth Assembly of the League of Nations did pass a resolution denouncing gas weapons.[23]

Washington and Geneva

The text of the Treaty relating to the Use of Submarines and Noxious Gases in Warfare (Washington, 1922), which never came into effect, proposed to universalise the gas prohibition. Article 5 read:

> The use in war of asphyxiating, poisonous or other gases, and all analogous liquids, materials or devices, having been justly condemned by the general opinion of the civilised world and a prohibition of such use having been declared in Treaties to which a majority of the civilized Powers are parties, the Signatory Powers, to the end that this prohibition shall be universally accepted as a part of international law binding alike the conscience and practice of nations, declare their assent to such prohibition, agree to be bound thereby between themselves and invite all other civilized nations to adhere thereto.[24]

The reason this Treaty never entered into force is that France failed to ratify it, based on objections regarding the provisions about the use of submarines, commerce raiding being a pillar of French naval warfare.[25] As a result, this treaty never became legally binding. However, it should be noted that article 5 regarding gas warfare was not the point of contestation. In other words, there was some consensus among the signatories of this treaty that the gas prohibition should be universal, rather than limited to those states who 'lost' the First World War.

Of course, such consensus hardly existed among policymakers and military experts, yet the use of such language was justified in part by reference to a desire to create consensus. Price examines the debates in the US Senate about the draft Washington Treaty, where one Senator noted that chemical weapons might not be as inhumane as suggested, an argument also proposed by other military experts. In response, Senator Lodge declared that '[The Washington Treaty] is expected to do something toward crystallizing the public opinion of the world against [the use of poison gases]', rather than actually describing the inhumanity of chemical weapons.[26] In other words, the legal processes were meant to establish an emerging norm rather than affirm it.

The next major legal development was the conclusion of the well-known Geneva Protocol of 1925, a separate protocol which added to the Hague Conventions and refined the gas prohibition. Worded after the failed Washington Treaty, it read:

> Whereas the use in war of asphyxiating, poisonous or other gases, and of all analogous liquids materials or devices, has been justly condemned by the general opinion of the civilized world; and whereas the prohibition of such use has been declared in Treaties to which the majority of Powers of the world are Parties; and to the end that this prohibition shall be universally accepted as a part of International Law, binding alike the conscience and the practice of nations [...] The High Contracting Parties, so far as they are not already Parties to Treaties prohibiting such use, accept this prohibition, agree to extend this prohibition to the use of bacteriological methods of warfare and agree to be bound as between themselves according to the terms of this declaration.[27]

While the Protocol generated much debate, the major European powers signed and ratified it within five years. The United States was more hesitant, owing to the lack of specification and the fear that tear gas would be included in the ban as well, and only ratified the Protocol in 1972. Many states, including France and the United Kingdom, ratified with the reservations that the Protocol was only binding among the state parties and would cease to be binding in a conflict wherein another state party would resort to the use of gas. The Protocol did not include a verification or sanctioning regime. This can be explained in the light of the mixed attitudes towards chemical weapons in the 1920s: there was a general fear and abhorrence towards gas among the general public leading to the general prohibition, yet everyone believed the next war would be a chemical one, and no one wanted to be left defenceless.

Mixed attitudes towards chemical weapons

In the 1920s, the story of chemical weapons was not straightforward or unitary. American Army Chief of Staff General Peyton C. March, who had seen the effects of gas first hand, called for a prohibition, claiming that chemical weapons 'reduce civilisation to savagery'.[28] The *New York Herald* published an article saying that '[o]rdinary killing is bad enough, but that a man should treat his fellow as he treats a rat or cockroach is inherently repugnant to all men for whom decent instincts have not fled'.[29]

Around this time, Spanish forces used gas with tacit agreement from the French during the Rif War, and there is evidence that Italy used phosgene and mustard gas in Libya as well between 1923 and 1930.[30] Some suggest that the United Kingdom used gas during this time as well in Mandatory Iraq, but Raymond Douglas concluded in 2009 that uncertainty about the legality of gas amongst members of the Cabinet and logistical problems, most importantly, prevented this.[31] While attitudes about the colonial order were changing after the First World War, the League had trouble intervening in these conflicts. During the Rif War in particular, the League emphasised that it was unable to intervene given the status of the Rif region as protected by Spain and the United Kingdom, and that the Rif was not a state.[32] Mandatory Iraq became a state party to the Geneva Protocol in 1931, but as sub-state and colonial entities, Libya and the Rif could not. As the Protocol formally only applied to state parties, there was no strict legal reason for Spain and Italy to abstain from chemical weapons use in the 1920s.

While controversial, none of these instances led to sanctions for the use of chemical weapons. The Protocol prohibits the use of chemical weapons in *war* and during *warfare*, an activity that was understood as a violent conflict between sovereign states.[33] When the colonies were concerned, government-mandated violence was rather a case of *policing*. Particularly when it came to tear gas, this distinction was explicitly drawn. At the same time, attitudes about this distinction were shifting, as evidenced by the debate in the British cabinet about the legality of using any type of gas in India and Iraq under the Geneva Protocol. Similarly, the United States Senate worried about the potential application of the Geneva Protocol to policing as well, pointing out that the use of tear gas for such purposes should not be prohibited.[34]

We can therefore conclude that attitudes toward chemical warfare during the 1920s were mixed. Especially in military circles, the assumption existed that any future war between major powers would include the use of gas, and there was no international consensus on whether the use of gas in colonial contexts was mandated. For instance, in response to accusations of French gas use in Syria, the vice-president of the Permanent Mandates Commission, the Dutchman François Willem van Rees, clarified that he would consider gas use against civilians problematic, but that such use against an armed adversary would not be problematic in his opinion.[35] At the same time, the use of gas in the Rif was heavily protested against by civil society across the world, including in the European press.[36] Additionally, the fact that the topic of chemical warfare returned to the agenda of the states that convened in Geneva in 1925 shows the perceived need to codify this emergent norm after the first attempt at Washington had failed.

The dual-use nature of the chemicals of concern as well as the potential strategic effects of these weapons were brought forward to prohibit legislation that would impose a complete ban on production as well as use.[37] It is also evident from the reservations put forward by the Geneva Protocol signatories that no state wanted to be caught unprepared in the event of a chemical war. At the same time, the interwar years were also marked by increasing stigmatisation of chemical weapons by political representatives of – mostly major – European powers of the time, using morally loaded language. Andrew Webster cites a 1921 resolution of the Assembly's disarmament commission calling gas weapons 'fiendish devices', and Price notes how such loaded language was not used for other weapon technologies which were also under legal review, such as the submarine.[38] It also appears that fear played a role in framing the narrative, exemplified both by the danger emphasised in official League reports and by independent gas experts, as well as popular science-fiction and fictional war novels.[39] Examples include H. G. Wells's *The Shape of Things to Come* and *Brave New World* by Aldous Huxley. The combination of air power and chemical weapons was often put forward in these publications as being the future of warfare, which would cause particular concern for non-combatants: the civilians hiding in their cities would no longer be safe from the horrors of chemical war. In his 1971 SIPRI study of biological and chemical weapons, Julian Robinson refers to a debate in British parliament in 1927, where one speaker said: 'These things [chemical weapons] make us realise that it is not war in the ordinary sense that we are talking about. ... We are faced with the wiping out of civilisation.'[40]

Research and development of chemical weapons was by no means halted after the Great War, if mostly for defensive purposes to prepare for the next war. This next war, so most experts thought at the time, would be a technological one, relying on a number of new technologies including the bomber, tanks and chemical weapons. This conviction was further strengthened by the limited scope of international law on chemicals in war. In his 1937 extensive volume on chemical warfare, one of Augustin Prentiss's first assertions was that the chemical weapons discourse at international conferences is used to create empty international law. It's 'a popular subject of condemnation'; an easy topic to reach consensus about and so a simple way of establishing common ground.[41] Therefore, in Prentiss's view, the chemical weapons discourse held no realistic promise for actual change. Indeed, he believes chemicals are 'destined to play an even greater role in future warfare'.[42] As a lieutenant colonel with the Chemical Warfare Service in the US Army, Prentiss did have an institutional interest in maintaining the position that chemicals would be crucial weapons in the next war, but he was by no means the only one.[43]

Thus, when it comes to chemical weapons, the decade preceding the Italian invasion of Ethiopia was marked by contradictions in the nature of the norm. The Geneva Protocol and efforts by the International Committee of the Red Cross to get it widely ratified,[44] as well as British domestic concern about the legality of the use of gas in the colonies,[45] and regular associations of chemical war with 'barbarity', are all indications of an emergent norm with universal tendencies. At the same time, the use of gas in the Rif War and mixed responses to it, as well as continued chemical weapons production and training by industrial states, show ambiguity and challenge universality, particularly as distinctions were made between colonial war (policing) and the conduct of war between civilised states.

This was the legal situation on the eve of the Italian invasion of Ethiopia in 1935. All major industrial powers possessed chemical weapons, and such possession was not illegal. It was also explicitly stated by several important states that the Protocol only applied to conflicts among state parties, not beyond that, and that it was a non-first-use pledge. Italy had ratified the Protocol without reservations, but did use both arguments associated with these reservations in its defence when the accusations of chemical war against Ethiopia were voiced. However, Italy did modify the second one, voicing the opinion that it was entitled to chemical retaliation in response to other war crimes committed by Ethiopia, not just in retaliation to the first use of chemical weapons. Anders Boserup notes that this interpretation of the Geneva Protocol is unique.[46] Ethiopia acceded to the Protocol in October 1935, when reports of chemical attacks were few and unverified. The accession, however, is indeed an indication that the threat of chemical war was perceived to be real. The Protocol, in combination with the infrastructure provided by the League of Nations, propelled the chemical weapons discourse to be an instrument of diplomacy that was about to be tested in 1935.

After the organised war effort in Ethiopia had ended, the evaluation of the use of gas was often done with reference to the distinct 'spheres' of warfare. The effectiveness of gas against unprotected (civilian) populations in the colonies was contrasted with expectations that a modern European army would be much better able to withstand chemical attacks. In this sense, the events in Ethiopia cemented the general association of gas with colonial war. Analysing American attitudes on the eve of the Second World War, Frederic Brown argued in 1968 that after the Italo-Ethiopian war, the '[American] military denied that there were any lessons to be learned from the use of gas as a weapon of opportunity against a totally unprepared enemy in a colonial war'.[47] While such suggestions in military circles mainly spoke to the strict usefulness of gas against unprotected populations versus modern armies trained in chemical defence, this distinction perpetuated and conformed to the earlier distinction between colonial war and 'modern' interstate war. Gas usage in one sphere was understood to be more acceptable than in the other.[48]

Ethiopia in the international order

The Ethiopian Empire had previously successfully thwarted an Italian invasion in 1896 and had entered into treaties with various European powers to maintain territorial security in the East Africa colonies. Haile Selassie's government and its precursors were therefore regarded as a legitimate international partner in the decades preceding this particular conflict and a member of the international society, to the extent that it subscribed to the institutions of self-governance, sovereignty and territoriality. In fact, because the Italian invasion was a war of territorial conquest, Haile Selassie's efforts to reclaim legitimacy before the League of Nations were existential for the Ethiopian state. They were also recognised as such.[49] At the time of the invasion, it was recognised that a formal sovereign state invaded another sovereign state, which was to be 'perhaps the most acute "classical" example of the failures of collective security and international law'.[50] Economic sanctions were imposed on Italy; the first multilateral sanctions in history, they marked a recognition of the severity of the moment for international order, yet failed to paralyse Italy's war effort.

However, several authors are careful to point out that Ethiopia's sovereignty only existed de facto, but was not fully internalised by the European states constituting international society.[51] Megan Donaldson calls Ethiopia's admission into the League of Nations in 1923 a 'startling expansion'.[52] Particularly as a result of the practice of domestic slavery in Ethiopia, the country was considered 'less-than-civilised', and therefore quasi-sovereign.[53] In other words, it remained potentially subject to intervention, either through war or through the formal pathways of the League of Nations.[54] This demonstrates the practical and ideological differences between membership of the League of Nations (i.e. formally being a state) and full and equal membership of the international society (i.e. being recognised as equal in status and normativity). Rose Parfitt describes the hybrid nature of Ethiopia as a state, both in the Orientalist-Semitic perspective of Ethiopia as 'in between white and black, civilised and barbaric, imperial and African', and in the Aksumite paradigm between northern, civilised Christians and southern, uncivilised non-Christians.[55]

In the Interbellum, the nature of international society, which had been dominated by European powers, was changing. Non-European states started playing important roles in the ordering of international society and within the instruments of the League of Nations. Nicholas Mulder describes the Interbellum as a period of 'de-Europeanization', pointing to the rise of non-European states in the global economy.[56] Other examples include the participation of Brazil and China in drawing the new boundary between Germany and Poland after the Silesian referendum;[57] the election of Cuban judge Dr Antonio Sánchez de Bustamante and Brazilian judge Dr Ruy Barbosa to the Permanent Court of International Justice in 1921;[58] and the significant reshaping by local health experts from East Asia of the International Sanitary Convention and the League of Nations Health Organisation in 1926.[59] This had been unimaginable before 1914.

In this changing world, Ethiopia as a state thus enjoyed semi-sovereignty. One term which has been used increasingly in International Relations Theory to conceptualise such a situation is 'liminality', which is derived from anthropological studies and signifies a transitional identity, one in between set categories of understanding. Consequently, being between such set categories, liminal actors are confronted with uncertain expectations.[60] Ethiopia was not fully colonial, having entered into bilateral treaties with Britain and Italy, being a member state of the League and having ratified multilateral treaties. However, neither was it fully sovereign, seeing the colonial ambitions of Britain, France and Italy in the region evidenced by the Tripartite Treaty of 1906 and the Anglo-Italian agreement of 1925, both of which laid out European economic interests in the region without consent from Ethiopian leadership.[61] Ethiopia was on the 'limen', the threshold, of international society.

The uncertainty associated with liminal identities could be regarded as the cause of the permissive attitudes towards the use of chemical weapons; it left room for Ethiopia to be understood as colonial and therefore a site for the use of chemical weapons. However, in concrete terms, the liminal identity was clearly informed by racial hierarchies rather than strict understandings of colonialism.[62] In other words, the fact that Ethiopians were not white prevented sustained political action against the use of gas. In this sense, the case of the Sino-Japanese war of 1937 bears striking similarities: a non-white state, enjoying outward markings of sovereignty, was attacked with the use of gas by a more established member of international society – although one that was also non-white. As a result, this case was not regarded as part of the scope of political action through the League. While the emerging norm against gas was invoked, no sanctions were imposed. An important difference, however, remains that Japan, unlike Italy, had not ratified the Geneva Protocol, adding further cause to the League's inaction in that case.

Ethiopia's liminal identity and the uncertainties that came with it also permitted Ethiopian officials to engage in a type of diplomacy and the expression of public opinion that were not accessible to 'traditional' colonial states. Being a member state of the League of Nations and being able to invoke the Geneva Protocol, Ethiopian officials were able to act using the same discursive and normative structures that the major powers did, meeting them on the same level. This opportunity was available to Ethiopian officials in ways that were not available for the Rif rebels or the people of Italian Libya a decade earlier.[63] However, Ethiopian officials not only participated in international diplomacy on the same level as their Italian counterparts did, they also explicitly challenged the social hierarchies that Italy was explicitly using to justify the invasion. Indeed, they even attempted to reverse the hierarchy completely; the chemical weapons discourse permitted them to cast Italy as the 'uncivilised' one. We will now turn to a brief analysis of Ethiopian communications in the League of Nations to illustrate this.

The Italo-Ethiopian war in the League of Nations

Ethiopian communications about the Italian invasion often characterise the war as a chemical one when speaking about the League's obligation to protect one of its members. For instance, in September 1936, rather than speaking of the Italian invasion in general terms, the Ethiopian delegate Taezaz said that protection from the League could not be expected 'after the invaders had sprayed the country with mustard gas and the League's assistance … had been found insufficient'.[64] Of course, it would be Ethiopia's position that Italy's aggression should be responded to by the League in any case, but the fact that chemical weapons had been used seems to have been an important qualification. In January 1936, Haile Selassie wrote to the Secretary-General: 'After bombing the Adowa hospital [and other medical facilities] and using gas, Italy proceeds on her barbarous course with impunity and, according to her own professions, in the name of civilisation.'[65] Such language harked back to the language of civilisation used in the Geneva Protocol as well as the Covenant of the League of Nations itself.

Similarly, a telegram submitted to the office of the Secretary General from the Ethiopian authorities still in the country reads: 'Is a peaceful people which loves its independence and has placed its whole trust in the League of Nations to be abandoned to its aggressor and to be exterminated by poison gas and bombs?'[66] This is reflected in Haile Selassie's famous speech of June

1936 at the League's General Assembly, which starts off by highlighting the unique nature of the ongoing war:

> Also, there has never before been an example of any Government proceeding to the systematic extermination of a nation by barbarous means, in violation of the most solemn promises made by the nations of the earth that there should not be used against innocent human beings the terrible poison of harmful gases.[67]

In fact, when detailing the means used by Italy to conduct the invasion, the use of chemical weapons was the only specific characterisation that Selassie offered in the speech, even though gas was not the only transgression of humanitarian law that the Italians were guilty of.[68] Selassie mentioned this specifically at the end of the first section of the speech, calling the use of gas the 'chief method of warfare': 'In order to kill off systematically all living creatures, in order to more surely to poison waters and pastures, the Italian command made its aircraft pass over and over again. That was its chief method of warfare.'[69]

Chemical weapons thus emerged as the main characteristic of Italy's war effort, but the barbarity of Italy's endeavour is also emphasised by other means. Ethiopian communications essentially attempted to reverse the Italian narrative that Ethiopia was uncivilised, instead proposing that Italy was the uncivilised party to the conflict because of its use of chemical weapons. This strategy of reversing the narrative and casting Italy as lacking civilisation comes forward very explicitly in the response to an accusation that Italy had made concerning slavery in Ethiopia made by Wolde Mariam, Ethiopia's representative in Paris. He wrote:

> The Ethiopian Government denounces the leaders of the Italian armies, who claim to be fulfilling 'a sacred trust of civilisation' when they are actually engaged in murdering the civil population – old men, women and children. [...] The Ethiopian Government and people reject such a 'civilisation' with horror.[70]

This communication is dated 16 November, 1935, before accusations of chemical warfare had gained official character. The 'sacred trust of civilisation' was copied from the Covenant of the League of Nations Article 22, which provided for the Mandate system. In the Covenant, the 'trust of civilisation' referred to all sovereign member states of the League sharing the responsibility (trust) to administer affairs in former colonies and non-sovereign territories of former empires. By invoking this clause, Italy justified its invasion. By referring to it here, Wolde Mariam not only rejected the frame that Ethiopia is not sovereign, but simultaneously challenged the way in which major powers in general sought to reorder international society during the Interbellum.

Ethiopian communications repeatedly sought to universalise the war by referring to future dangers and warning small states in particular of future aggression. For instance, in January 1936, the Ethiopian Government submitted to the Secretary General that the ongoing conflict with Italy was 'at present threatening the whole of humanity with the terrible danger of universal war', and later that Italy wanted to 'let loose a universal war'. In the same communication, Wolde Mariam wrote that 'The people of Ethiopia is firmly resolved to fight to the death for its existence', and that they 'are also defending the cause of all the small peoples'.[71] This language was repeated in various sections throughout Haile Selassie's speech to the Assembly in June of that year:

> It is my duty to inform the Governments assembled in Geneva, responsible as they are for the lives of millions of men, women and children, of the deadly peril which threatens them, by describing to them the fate which has been suffered by Ethiopia. [...]
>
> I did not hesitate to declare that I did not wish for war, that it was imposed upon me, and I should struggle solely for the independence and integrity of my people, and that in that struggle I was the defender of the cause of all small States exposed to the greed of a powerful neighbour. [...]
>
> [What is at stake is] the value of promises made to small States that their integrity and their independence shall be respected and ensured. It is the principle of the equality of States on the one hand, or otherwise the obligation laid upon small Powers to accept the bonds of vassalship. In a word, it is international morality that is at stake.

In a discursive twist, Selassie blamed not only Italy for violating the principles of international society, but also the other major European powers as they fail to intervene. He called attention to the way Italy sought to reimpose the colonial hierarchies of the pre-1914 era, by reaffirming his commitment to the right of small states to exist while challenging the commitment of others. Reminding his audience, he said that: 'It is international morality which is at stake and not the Articles of the Covenant.'[72]

These citations also show that Ethiopia did not employ just one discursive strategy to reaffirm its commitment to the post-war international society. The push to truly universalise the chemical weapons prohibition, even with the challenges posed by the increasingly anachronistic colonial wars, speaks to the wider argument about collective security and the right of small states to exist, participate and be sovereign. Interestingly, Haile Selassie's warnings were prophetic: throughout the twentieth century, it had never been the weak or small state that resorted to gas as a means of last resort. Instead, since the First World War, it had always been the strong state in any conflict that resorted to chemicals first: Spain vis-à-vis the Rif rebels, Japan in China and, later, Egypt against insurgents in Yemen, the United States in Vietnam and Iraq against Iran.[73] Looking back, the civilisation discourse – when viewed through the lens of chemical weapons – can often be reversed, leaving the founders of the twentieth-century world order to prove their civilisation to the new states.

The civilisation narrative, so intimately connected to the chemical weapons discourse, served the purpose of re-affirming Ethiopia's membership of the international society and the League of Nations. At the same time, however, the discourse was used to reconstruct the institution of civilised international behaviour as one that denounced the use of chemical weapons against small, semi-sovereign states. Formally, these principles aligned with each other, evidenced by the fact that League members reaffirmed the validity of the Geneva Protocol in the context of the Italian invasion of Ethiopia. In practice, however, the League appeared less than willing to formally denounce Italy as a chemical weapons user or to impose sanctions that would affect its war effort in serious and immediate measure. In their declarations, Ethiopia claimed full membership in international society, while attempting to exclude Italy from it and challenge the commitment of the major powers to the international order they had created. As a small, non-white state on the threshold of international society, Ethiopia 'provokes a collective rethinking about who belongs to a particular group and what separates insiders and outsiders'.[74]

The significance of this instrumentalisation of the League's own principles by Ethiopia was felt across the globe, particularly among Black communities across the Atlantic Ocean. For instance, on the island of Trinidad, 'Ethiopianism' – or Black self-government – was instrumentalised among the Black community for their own liberation, when Trinidadians of African heritage boycotted Italian imports and protested before the Italian consulate in Port of Spain, some of them self-identifying as 'Ethiopian'.[75] Similar movements were active in Jamaica and the United States. In Robbie Shilliam's words, the Italian invasion 'enabled regional issues of self-governance and self-sufficiency to be politically apprehended as part of a global colonial war against African peoples at home and abroad'.[76] William Edward Burghardt Du Bois, an American sociologist and historian, also pointed to the racial hierarchies implicit in Italy's actions, sketching Italy's perspective on the invasion as follows: 'We are going to reduce black men to the status of landless serfs. And we are going to do this because we have the power to do it, and because no white nation dare stop us and no colored nation can.'[77] He then paralleled this colonial action with the economic exploitation and social repression of Black citizens in the United States. In this way, the events in Ethiopia and Ethiopia's instrumentalisation of the League's own principles resonated with Black audiences and inspired a pan-African movement.[78]

Ethiopian officials were not alone in protesting the use of chemical weapons by the Italians during the invasion. We have noted the indignation of the British delegate in the introduction to this chapter.[79] Immediately universalising the issue, he continued with reference to the 1925 Geneva Protocol:

> Is there one nation here, one nation anywhere on the earth's surface, which is not interested in its observance? This protocol concerns the inhabitants of every great city in the world. It is for them a charter against extermination. If a Convention such as this can be torn up, will not our peoples, whether living in the thronged cities of Western Europe or in less densely crowded areas elsewhere, ask, and ask with reason, what is the value of any international instrument to which our representatives put their name; how can we have confidence that our own folk, despite all solemnly signed protocols, will not be burned, blinded, done to death in agony hereafter?

In response, the Council adopted a resolution reminding both parties of their commitments under the Geneva Protocol, without noting Italy as the transgressor.[80] The relevance of the Protocol was also recalled at the start of the war. When compiling a list of arms subject to an embargo, the Sub-Committee of Military Experts had included chemical weapons and means of delivery. The political Committee of Eighteen, upon insistence by the Swedish representative, included a footnote to this clause confirming that the use of these weapons was prohibited under the Geneva Protocol of 1925.[81]

The fact that despite these references, the League of Nations did not go as far as to recognise Italy as having transgressed the Protocol and to sanction Italy for it, signals the inability of the Council to universalise the chemical weapons prohibition even to non-white states that had ratified it. The chemical weapons prohibition was indeed applicable according to the Council, but while all the fears of international society concerning the use of gas had come true in Ethiopia, the legal instrument fell short.

By laying this bare, Ethiopian officials challenged the interwar international order and the principles on which it was built. The rejection of wars of aggression was the most important one of these, and while unsuccessful, sanctions were imposed against Italy in accordance with this principle. The prohibition of chemical weapons was another. While not part of the League's own instruments, it was part of the civilisation of post-war international society to reject these weapons as barbaric amongst themselves.

Crucially, Ethiopia's liminality as a semi-sovereign state unable to receive protections under the Geneva Protocol showed that interwar international society remained liminal itself, on the threshold between Eurocentrism and universalism.

Conclusion

In the fluidity of Interbellum international order, both Italy and Ethiopia sought to create certainty about which states were full members and which were not. Italy's decision to invade Ethiopia affirmed an understanding of international order that subjected non-white states to the possibility of colonial conquest. In response, the League's sanctions regime signalled that wars of aggression were no longer an acceptable form of foreign policy. By using chemical weapons, Italy further upheld the distinction between colonial conquest and civilised interstate warfare and the prohibition of gas in the latter, but not in the former. As a member state of the Geneva Protocol, Ethiopia was able to challenge this understanding more effectively than colonised peoples had been able to before, and affirm its understanding of international order as rule-based, equal, and universal. Ethiopia also pointed Italy's civilisational narrative right back at it. The League's inability to confirm this understanding demonstrated its institutionalised inequality. However, the fact that the Council confirmed that the Geneva Protocol applied to the case also showed that the League operated in an international society that had changed. The chemical weapons discourse thus emerged as an interesting instrument with which to seek order, and a revealing lens through which we can assess the nature of the Interbellum international society.

Of course, the ultimate failure of the League to preserve Ethiopia's sovereignty discredited the international order and the principle of collective security most prominently. Hans Morgenthau called it '*the* debacle of collective security'.[82] However, in saying that 'the real death of the League was in December 1935, not in 1939 or 1945', historian A. J. P. Taylor pointed to the prominence of principles.[83] Crucially, he referred to the publication of the Hoare-Laval Pact, a secret British-French proposal to end the war in Ethiopia by dividing up the land between Ethiopia and Italy. This proposal was pragmatic and 'in line with the League's previous acts of conciliation'.[84] The indignation that followed the publication and led to its rejection, according to Taylor, was an indication of the changes international society had gone through: it had become principled, and these principles could not be combined with the practical policy of the League.

Similarly, although hardly a norm yet, the principle of the non-use of chemical weapons was irreconcilable with the pragmatism of the League of

Nations, particularly for non-white peoples. Yet international society had changed and Ethiopia was able to pick at the principles and understandings of international order in ways that challenged the League's pragmatism. It effectively reversed the narrative.

While Italy was recognised as sovereign in Ethiopia in 1938 by most states, this situation was short lived. With the outbreak of the Second World War, the United Kingdom withdrew its recognition. Significantly, the United States never had recognised Italy's occupation in the first place. Following Italian defeat with the help of British forces in 1941, Haile Selassie resumed governance of Ethiopia. First, this was done with the United Kingdom taking control of Ethiopia's foreign, security and financial policy. In 1944, with American assistance, Selassie's government re-negotiated the Anglo-Ethiopian Agreement to be more favourable, although the British retained control over some areas until 1955.[85] Having acted as a full member of international society before, there was little debate about Ethiopia's membership after the Second World War. However, the racial hierarchies in the chemical weapons norm also remained.[86] It would not be until 1993 that international law on the topic was strengthened by the Chemical Weapons Convention.

Notes

1 Lina Grip and John Hart, 'The Use of Chemical Weapons in the 1935–36 Italo-Ethiopian War', *SIPRI Arms Control and Non-Proliferation Programmme* (2009), 1–7.
2 Richard M. Price, *The Chemical Weapons Taboo* (Ithaca, NY: Cornell University Press, 1997), p. 101; Julian P. Robinson, *The Problem of Chemical and Biological Warfare, Vol. I: The Rise of CB Weapons* (Stockholm: SIPRI, 1971), p. 143.
3 Grip and Hart, 'The Use of Chemical Weapons'.
4 Ibid., 3.
5 Robinson, *The Problem of Chemical and Biological Warfare*, p. 142.
6 Robinson, *The Problem of Chemical and Biological Warfare*, p. 144.
7 League of Nations. Official Journal, April 1936, 91st Session of the Council, Tenth Meeting, pp. 378–9.
8 Giorgio Rochat, 'L'impiego dei gas nella guerra d'Etiopia. 1935–36', *Rivista di storia contemporanea* 17:1 (1988), 74–109.
9 Güneş Murat Tezcür, and Doreen Horschig, 'A Conditional Norm: Chemical Warfare from Colonialism to Contemporary Civil Wars', *Third World Quarterly* 42:2 (2020), 366–84, https://doi.org/10.1080/01436597.2020.1834840 .
10 Megan Donaldson, 'The League of Nations, Ethiopia, and the Making of States', *Humanity* 11:1 (2020), 8, https://doi.org/10.1353/hum.2020.0005 .
11 Price, *The Chemical Weapons Taboo*.

12 Catherine Jefferson, 'Origins of the Norm against Chemical Weapons', *International Affairs* 90:3 (2014), 647–61, DOI:https://doi.org/10.1111/1468-2346.12131.
13 Dieter Langewiesche, '"Savage War" as "People's War": Nineteenth-Century African Wars, European Perceptions, and the Future of Warfare', *The Journal of Modern History* 94:3 (2022), 537–63, https://doi.org/10.1086/720789 .
14 Erik Linstrum, 'Domesticating Chemical Weapons: Tear Gas and the Militarization of Policing in the British Imperial World, 1919–1981', *The Journal of Modern History* 91:3 (2019), 557–85, https://doi.org/10.1086/704383 .
15 Jürgen Renn, 'Introduction', in Bretislav Friedrich, Dieter Hoffmann, Jürgen Renn, Florian Schmaltz and Martin Wolf (eds), *100 Years of Chemical Warfare* (Cham: Springer, 2017). https://doi.org/10.1007/978-3-319-51664-6.
16 Miloš Vec, 'Challenging the Laws of War by Technology, Blazing Nationalism and Militarism: Debating Chemical Warfare Before and After Ypres, 1899–1925', in Friedrich et al. (eds), *100 Years of Chemical Warfare*, p. 114.
17 Ibid., p. 116.
18 Foreign Relations of the United States (1933), 1918, Supplement II: The World War. Washington: US Gov. Print. Off., Doc. No. 902, File No. 763.72116/533. www.history.state.gov/historicaldocuments/frus1918Supp02/d902 (accessed 31 October 2022).
19 Ibid., Doc. No. 906, File No. 763.72116/551. www.history.state.gov/historicaldocuments/frus1918Supp02/d906 (accessed 31 October 2022).
20 Vec, 'Challenging the Laws of War', p. 124.
21 Ibid., p. 125.
22 Treaty of Peace Between the Allied and Associated Powers and Germany. Versailles (signed 28 June 1919, entry into force 10 January 1920) UKTS (1919) No. 4, Cmd. 153.
23 Vec, 'Challenging the Laws of War', p. 127.
24 Cited by ibid., p. 127.
25 Price, *The Chemical Weapons Taboo*, p. 88.
26 As cited in ibid., p. 87.
27 Protocol for the Prohibition of the Use of Asphyxiating, Poisonous or Other Gases, and of Bacteriological Methods of Warfare. Geneva (signed 17 June 1925, entry into force 8 February 1928) 94 LNTS 67.
28 As cited by Tim Cook, '"Against God-Inspired Conscience": The Perception of Gas Warfare as a Weapon of Mass Destruction, 1915–1939', *War & Society* 18:1 (2000), 47–69, at 63, https://doi.org/10.1179/072924700791201379 .
29 'Not Poisonous Gas!', *New York Herald*, 7 January 1923.
30 Tezcür and Horschig, 'A Conditional Norm'; Nicola Labanca, 'Colonial Rule, Colonial Repression and War Crimes in the Italian Colonies', *Journal of Modern Italian Studies* 9:3 (2004), 300–13, https://doi.org/10.1080/1354571042000254737 .
31 Raymond M. Douglas, 'Did Britain Use Chemical Weapons in Mandatory Iraq?', *The Journal of Modern History* 81:4 (2009), 859–87, https://doi.org/10.1086/605488 .

32 Pablo La Porte, '"Rien à ajouter": The League of Nations and the Rif War (1921–1926)', *European History Quarterly* 41:1 (2011), 66–87, https://doi.org/10.1177/0265691410385780 .
33 Linstrum, 'Domesticating Chemical Weapons'.
34 Price, *The Chemical Weapons Taboo*, p. 97.
35 Ibid., p. 82.
36 Ibid., pp. 74–6.
37 Andrew Webster, 'Making Disarmament Work: The Implementation of the International Disarmament Provisions In the League of Nations Covenant, 1919–1925', *Diplomacy & Statecraft* 16:3 (2005), 561, https://doi.org/10.1080/09592290500208089 .
38 Ibid.; Price, *The Chemical Weapons Taboo*, p. 84.
39 Webster, 'Making Disarmament Work', 561; Cook, '"Against God-Inspired Conscience"', 62–3.
40 Robinson, *The Problem of Chemical and Biological Warfare*, p. 101.
41 Augustin M. Prentiss, *Chemicals in War: A Treatise on Chemical Warfare* (New York: McGraw-Hill Book Company, 1937), p. vii.
42 Ibid.
43 Cook, '"Against God-Inspired Conscience"'.
44 Rainer Baudendistel, 'Force versus Law: The International Committee of the Red Cross and Chemical Warfare in the Italo-Ethiopian War 1935–1936', *International Review of the Red Cross* 322 (1998), 81–104.
45 Douglas, 'Did Britain Use Chemical Weapons in Mandatory Iraq?'; Linstrum, 'Domesticating Chemical Weapons'.
46 Anders Boserup, *The Problem of Chemical and Biological Warfare, Vol. III: CBW and the Law of War* (Stockholm: SIPRI, 1973), p. 103, note 6.
47 Frederic Brown, *Chemical Warfare: A Study in Restraints* (New York: Routledge, 1968), p. 145.
48 Price, *The Chemical Weapons Taboo*, p. 107.
49 Robbie Shilliam, 'Intervention and Colonial-Modernity: Decolonising the Italy/Ethiopia Conflict through Psalms 68:31', *Review of International Studies* 39:5 (2013), 113–47, DOI: 10.1017/S026021051300020X .
50 Ibid., 1132.
51 Rose Parfitt, 'Empire des Nègres Blancs: The Hybridity of International Personality and the Abyssinia Crisis of 1935–36', *Leiden Journal of International Law* 24:4 (2011), 850, https://doi.org/10.1017/S0922156511000409 ; Shilliam, 'Intervention and Colonial-Modernity'.
52 Megan Donaldson, 'The League of Nations, Ethiopia, and the Making of States', *Humanity* 11:1 (2020), 6, https://doi.org/10.1353/hum.2020.0005 .
53 Shilliam, 'Intervention and Colonial-Modernity', 1136.
54 Shilliam further argues that modernity is colonial in essence ('colonial-modernity'), and that as a result, modern interventions are conceptually no different from imperial conquest.
55 Parfitt, 'Empire des Nègres Blancs', 856. The Aksumite paradigm refers to the Ethiopian understanding of its history with its noble, Christian class descending from the Biblical King Solomon and settling in Aksum (approximating

northern Ethiopia), and various non-Christian groups from the south of the region being incorporated into the polity.

56 Nicholas Mulder, *The Economic Weapon: The Rise of Sanctions as a Tool of Modern War* (New Haven, CT: Yale University Press, 2022), p. 205.

57 Jean A. Laponce, 'National Self-Determination and Referendums: The Case for Territorial Revisionism', *Nationalism and Ethnic Politics* 7:2 (2001), 33–56, https://doi.org/10.1080/13537110108428627 .

58 Percy Alvin Martin, 'Latin America and the League of Nations', *American Political Science Review* 20:1 (1926), 14–30.

59 Tomoko Akami, 'A Quest to be Global: The League of Nations Health Organization and Inter-Colonial Regional Governing Agendas of the Far Eastern Association of Tropical Medicine 1910–25', *The International History Review* 38:1 (2016), 1–23, https://doi.org/10.1080/07075332.2015.1018302 .

60 Maria Mälksoo, 'The Challenge of Liminality for International Relations Theory', *Review of International Studies* 38:2 (2012), 481–94, https://doi.org/10.1017/S0260210511000829 ; Bahar Rumelili, 'Liminal Identities and Processes of Domestication and Subversion in International Relations', *Review of International Studies* 38:2 (2012), 495–508, https://doi.org/10.1017/S0260210511000830 ; Lerna K. Yanık, 'Constructing Turkish "Exceptionalism": Discourses of Liminality and Hybridity in Post-Cold War Turkish Foreign Policy', *Political Geography* 30:2 (2011), 80–9, https://doi.org/10.1016/j.polgeo.2011.01.003 .

61 Parfitt, 'Empire des Nègres Blancs'; Shilliam, 'Intervention and Colonial-Modernity'; Antoinette Iadarola, 'The Anglo-Ethiopian Agreement of 1925: Mussolini's "Carte Blanche" for War Against Ethiopia', *Northeast African Studies* 1:1 (1979), 45–56, www.jstor.org/stable/43660348; Edward C. Keefer, 'Great Britain, France, and the Ethiopian Tripartite Treaty of 1906', *Albion* 13:4 (1981), 364–80, www.jstor.org/stable/4048642.

62 Parfitt, 'Empire des Nègres Blancs'.

63 In International Relations Theory, such behaviour can be typified as a 'transgression of inclusion'. Such a transgression is not a violation of a moral rule (i.e. something that is 'wrong'), but rather a behaviour that runs counter to general expectations associated with an identity. As a non-white state that was still considered somewhat of an outsider by the major powers of the time, Ethiopia behaved as if it was one of them by engaging in the same diplomatic structures as they did. In this way, Ethiopia forced its audience to reconsider who 'belongs' and who does not. See Miles M. Evers, 'On Transgression', *International Studies Quarterly* 61:4 (2017), 786–94, https://doi.org/10.1093/isq/sqx065 .

64 League of Nations, Official Journal, December 1936, Situation in Ethiopia, C.414.M.256.1936.VII, pp. 1408–9.

65 League of Nations, Official Journal, February 1936, Document C.8.M.7.1936.VII, p. 242.

66 League of Nations, Official Journal, December 1936, Situation in Ethiopia, C.452.M.268.1936.VII, p. 1409.

67 Haile Selassie, *Appeal to the League of Nations*, 30 June 1936. shorturl.at/op qR8 (accessed 4 August 2022).
68 Sbacchi explains how Italy also regularly targeted non-combatants and Red Cross camps. See Alberto Sbacchi, 'Poison Gas and Atrocities in the Italo-Ethiopian War (1935–1936)', in Ruth Ben-Ghiat and Mia Fuller (eds), *Italian Colonialism* (New York: Palgrave Macmillan, 2005), pp. 47–56. https://doi.org/10.1007/978 -1-4039-8158-5
69 Ibid.
70 League of Nations, Official Journal, January 1936, Document C.457.M.239.1935.VII, p. 27.
71 League of Nations, Official Journal, February 1936, Document C.51.M.21.1936.VII, p. 256.
72 Haile Selassie, *Appeal to the League of Nations*, 30 June 1936.
73 Of course, in this latter instance, the Iraqi and Iranian forces were rather more balanced in terms of resources, but Iraq was organisationally superior and enjoyed most international support. It should also be noted that Japan and the United States had not ratified the Geneva Protocol, although both had signed it in 1925.
74 Evers, 'On Transgression'. Of course, Ethiopia was not a true outsider, but it could not enjoy the benefits of a full insider either.
75 Shilliam, 'Intervention and Colonial-Modernity', 1145.
76 Ibid., 1144.
77 W.E.B. Du Bois, 'Inter-Racial Implications of the Ethiopian Crisis: A Negro View', *Foreign Affairs* 14:1 (1935), 89, www.jstor.org/stable/20030704.
78 James Quirin, 'WEB Du Bois, Ethiopianism and Ethiopia, 1890–1955', *International Journal of Ethiopian Studies* 5:2 (2010), 1–26, www.jstor.org/stable/41757589; William R. Scott, 'Black Nationalism and the Italo-Ethiopian Conflict, 1934–1936', *The Journal of Negro History* 63:2 (1978), 118–34, www.jstor.org/stable/2717305.
79 League of Nations, Official Journal, April 1936, 91st Session of the Council, Tenth Meeting, pp. 378–9.
80 League of Nations, Official Journal, April 1936, 91st Session of the Council, Eleventh Meeting, pp. 392–3.
81 League of Nations, Official Journal, Special Supplement 145, Dispute between Ethiopia and Italy, Minutes of the First Session, 11–19 October 1935, pp. 63–4.
82 Hans Morgenthau, *Politics among Nations: The Struggle for Power and Peace* (New York: Alfred A. Knopf, 1948), p. 337.
83 A. J. P. Taylor, *The Origins of the Second World War* (New York: Simon & Schuster, 1961), p. 96.
84 Ibid.
85 Donaldson, 'The League of Nations'.
86 Tezcür and Horschig, 'A Conditional Norm'.

5

'Weapons misused by barbarous races': disarmament, imperialism and race in the interwar period

Daniel Stahl

Introduction

As a young man in his early twenties, Winston Churchill enrolled in the British Army and went to India. It was the end of the nineteenth century, and the British Empire was confronted with a series of violent conflicts in the North-West of India, one of its most turbulent frontiers. The Pashtuns, who inhabited the region that nowadays forms the border between Afghanistan and Pakistan, started to defend themselves against the steadily expanding British Empire and the regulations that colonial authorities tried to impose on them. In 1897, war broke out. Churchill was always looking for a chance to be deployed to war zones. He convinced his superiors to assign him as a journalist accompanying the imperial forces. Between August and October, he wrote as an embedded journalist for British newspapers about the campaign against the Pashtuns. The armaments of the enemy captured his attention:

> These struggles are not conducted with the weapons which usually belong to the races of such development. [...] The world is presented with that grim spectacle, 'the strength of civilisation without its mercy'. At a thousand yards the traveller falls wounded by the well-aimed bullet of a breech-loading rifle. His assailant, approaching, hacks him to death with the ferocity of a South-Sea Islander. The weapons of the nineteenth century are in the hands of the savages of the Stone Age.[1]

Breech-loading firearms with industrially produced rifled barrels were one of the important innovations of armament technology of the nineteenth century. The possibility of charging a gun within seconds increased the firepower of armies considerably, and the mass production of rifled barrels led to the global distribution of arms that provided projectiles with a spin, increasing their accuracy. Churchill was not the only one who considered the use of weapons with these technological features by colonised subjects as a threat to the security of the British empire and as opposed to the civilising process. Since the mid-1890s, British colonial authorities and the government in London had implemented gun control instruments at various levels of Britain's global empire. These instruments drew racialised lines between those whose access to guns should be restricted and those whose access should not. As one of the first, the arms market in India became strictly regulated.[2] However, British authorities soon concluded that it was not enough to control the flow of arms within their territories – they had to control the trade routes. This was only possible by signing international agreements. The Persian Gulf was an especially sensitive area. All important routes between Europe and India met here. Therefore, London forced the sheiks, who had no means to resist the forces of the empire and no powerful allies, to sign treaties that obliged them to introduce control measures defined by British authorities.[3] At the same time, the European colonial powers agreed to control the arms traffic in Africa.[4] However, the colonial gun market was a lucrative business for European armament companies and arms dealers, who often enjoyed the backing of their governments. Conflicts between colonial powers on gun control remained a constant issue during the years preceding the First World War.[5]

The readjustment of international relations at the Paris Peace Conference presented a new opportunity to create internationally recognised legal instruments to control the global arms market. This chapter explores how racialised instruments of arms control were adapted to the international system of the interwar period. The focus will be on to the question of how British authorities tried to categorise different kinds of weapons so that arms trade regulations could function as effective instruments of imperial control. First, I will show that the imperial powers used race as a determining factor to categorise arms by linking them to spatial concepts. By analysing imperial arms control as an instrument of international order, I will highlight the role of these instruments in maintaining racialised global hierarchies. Second, I will argue that it was not so much the governments of the colonial powers who pushed for the integration of these instruments into the League of Nations agenda, but primarily liberal internationalists whose goal was the creation of internationally binding disarmament instruments. In this way, this chapter contributes to the debate about the relationship between imperial and liberal internationalism – a debate that has increasingly come into the focus of research in recent years.[6]

So far, historians of international history have studied disarmament in the interwar period as an instrument for creating and maintaining peace between more or less equal powers, focussing on Western European states and on naval arms limitations.[7] More recently, scholarship has turned towards the role of experts within and outside the League of Nations.[8]

However, most of the research ignores the global dimension of these policies in general as well as efforts to regulate the arms trade in particular, which counted among the crucial measures of interwar disarmament policies.[9] By analysing attempts to regulate the arms trade through international law, this chapter shifts the focus of research on interwar disarmament policies to the unequal power relations between the imperial powers and the populations of their formal and informal empires. It argues that international arms trade regulations were both at the same time: instruments of disarmament and instruments of imperial control. The first part of the chapter looks at the peace conference in Paris. It analyses how the colonial powers drew on colonial laws and practices from the pre-war era and inscribed them into the new international order with the aim of creating not only a European peace but a global one – yet a peace that meant to create and to reinforce the hierarchies between imperial powers and their colonial subjects. The second part considers how these racialised instruments of disarmament became integrated into the League of Nation's agenda.

Racialised arms control instruments at the Peace Conference in 1919

Until the outbreak of the First World War, the colonial powers saw the 'uncivilized tribal warriors' of the imperial border regions as the primary addressees of imperial arms controls – as Winston Churchill's comments show. The global war, however, transformed societies and technologies, thereby creating new anxieties. It fuelled anti-colonial protests in different parts of the world. At the same time, political groups in Europe, Asia and Africa concluded that the time for massive changes in the international balance of power was ripe and that revolution was a promising road. While the British government concentrated its troops in Europe, the revolutionary Indian Ghadar movement saw an opportunity to organise a massive uprising. Germany was willing to provide them with weapons to destabilise the British empire. However, the colonial authorities uncovered the plan in February 1915 and killed or imprisoned many revolutionaries.[10] One year later, British authorities intercepted twenty thousand guns on their way from Germany to Ireland; the Easter Rising of April 1916 by Irish revolutionaries had to take place without these weapons.[11] Egypt was another trouble spot that worried the British authorities. When war broke out, London had declared the country a protectorate because of the importance of the Suez Canal. Egypt nationalists, however, were strong and deeply rooted in society. Thanks alone to the 82,000-strong occupation forces and harsh repressive measures, a revolt was unthinkable.[12]

Starting from the observation of these developments, Mark Sykes, a 35-year-old publicist, diplomat and protégé of Herbert Kitchener, Minister of War, formulated some basic ideas that would become key to British arms control policies. During 1915 and 1916, he travelled to India and the Near East. Most of the time he spent in Egypt. He helped to organise the Arab resistance against the Ottoman Empire and knew how important the transfer of arms was to destabilise an empire. At the same time, he held many talks with Arab intellectuals and became aware of the challenge that anti-colonialism posed to the British Empire.[13]

When he returned to London, he was invited to the Foreign Office to present his opinion on a series of meetings on the arms traffic of the Committee of Imperial Defence, an interministerial entity that worked on security and military issues. Sykes stated that in the past, 'tribesmen' had posed a considerable threat to the British Empire. It had not been easy to counter their sudden raids. But the further development of armaments technology during the First World War had increased the weapons technology superiority of Great Britain enormously:

> The sudden rush of the savage has almost become impossible owing to aeroplane reconnaissance [...] and can be met by machine gunfire on a scale hitherto unthought of. Instead of 600 men with two Maxims on wheels, we can, after this war, send 20 machine guns with every 100 men. [...] Therefore, assembled and organised rebellions of savages or irregulars will, after this war, be met by weapons beyond their ken or reach, and whether they have magazine rifles, single loaders, or musle loaders, their case will be bad.[14]

In addition, it would become easier to control the Persian Gulf and the Red Sea with the help of aeroplanes. Thereby, Sykes anticipated how important 'air policing' and 'air control' would become in securing imperial power in the interwar period. Concerns that had driven colonial authorities to stricter gun controls in the past would soon be outdated. Moreover, he prophesied, the increasing colonial penetration of space – civilisation, as he put it – with railroads and telegraphs would soon lead to the disappearance of the 'savage or semi-savage tribes'.[15]

However, technological progress was not only advantageous for the empire. There was a certain weapon that caused Sykes serious concern: the automatic pistol. 'These devilish inventions are cheap, accurate, small, and easy to smuggle.' Based on his observations during his stay in Asia and Egypt, he identified a new threat to the British Empire:

> This is the weapon of the intellectual, the anarchist, the town desperado and the secret revolutionary society. [...] I suggest that the disaffected intellectuals

of Cairo and the Indian towns, plus magazine pistols, will be a far greater danger than will tribes armed with modern rifles. Any fool can shoot a Viceroy or a police inspector; and an academic student of 15 years of age can easily knock out a police patrol of five men. 10 or 12 desperados can hold up a street for hours, and three or four hundred spread panic through a city.[16]

Sykes insisted that a new effort should be undertaken to negotiate an arms trade convention to suppress the traffic with guns in the colonies. The matter was urgent. It was very likely that the European powers would try to pay part of their war debts by selling surplus weapons. As threatening as that sounded, there was also good news. Magazine guns had disadvantages for colonised people. Unlike single-shot rifles, ammunition for magazine firearms could no longer be made in local factories or at home. The value of these weapons depended on the access to ammunition. Therefore, the control of the ammunition trade was even more important than the trade in guns.[17]

The Foreign Office started developing a draft convention on the arms trade based on treaties and practices from before 1914 and on the discussions during the series of meetings – Sykes's presentation and memorandum received special attention. The British draft started by defining 'arms of war'. It is worth noting that weapon systems produced for war. like tanks, warships, aeroplanes and armoured cars, were not included in this definition. According to the British draft, the term 'arms of war' only referred to small arms. The draft mentioned explicitly automatic pistols, breach-loading guns and ammunition – weapons that could be used for a variety of reasons.[18] This narrow definition shows clearly that the arms trade convention was not intended to regulate the trade between the Northern states. It targeted the colonised people.

As Sykes had warned, unrest increased in imperial spaces towards the end of the war, adding further urgency to the plan for an arms trade convention. The government in London drew heavily on the economic resources and populations of its empire for the purpose of war mobilisation. It bought up crops on a large scale and enforced low prices, causing the colonies' supply situation to deteriorate drastically. And it forcibly recruited men as soldiers or workers to expand the rail and telegraph networks, which they needed for the war.[19] This led to acts of sabotage, strikes and anti-colonial protests. Even the informal empire in the Persian Gulf was threatened by the upheavals of the war with the British order. This was particularly true of Persia. Broken trade routes cut off the country's imports and prevented exports, and the economic situation deteriorated drastically. Civil unrest increased; anger was also directed at British troops, who occupied the entire south of the country and openly flaunted British claims to power in the region.[20]

However, the British government did not interpret any of this as a reaction to war mobilisation, supply crises and repression, but suspected subversion emanating from the now Bolshevik-ruled Soviet Union.[21]

At the beginning of 1919, Britain's colonial rule and imperial supremacy was not under serious threat in India, the Persian Gulf or Egypt. But the British government felt compelled to act in the face of growing calls for self-determination, its own fears of communist infiltration in the colonies and the abundance of arms at the end of the war. The regulation of the arms trade was one instrument among many, like economic sanctions, unequal treaties or armies, that the British government intended to use to secure colonial rule in India and imperial supremacy in the Persian Gulf and Suez Canal in the face of these challenges. 'The matter is one of real urgency', the Foreign Office in London informed the delegation in Paris.[22] The topic was to be introduced into the Paris peace negotiations as an independent convention.[23]

It was not hard to convince the other colonial powers in Paris of the need for an arms trade convention. France was facing a similar situation. The recruitment of soldiers had led to a revolt in West Africa, which at its peak in 1916 included 20,000 insurgents.[24] In addition to using military means to suppress the resistance, the French colonial government also relied on stricter gun controls.[25]

At the end of June 1919, the Council of Four, made up of the heads of state of the victorious powers, set up a commission to draft a text of the convention. The commission included representatives from France, Japan, Portugal, Italy, Great Britain, the United States and Belgium. They managed to come up with a draft in just seven meetings that took place in July. On the one hand, this tempo can be explained by referring to the special Parisian context of 1919. Heads of state, foreign ministers and innumerable diplomats from the great powers gathered in one city and developed a certain routine in making far-reaching decisions in a short time. At the same time, however, the speed also indicates that there was a basic consensus on the matter. This consensus was imperial control. All European countries and Japan involved in the negotiations were colonial powers and after the war faced the challenge of reacting to social unrest and increasing calls for self-determination. There was general agreement that arms trade controls in the colonies could be an instrument of securing power in the volatile post-war situation.

The fact that the negotiating parties had a common basis of interest did not mean that there were not also conflicts. During the negotiations, the definition of weapon categories became one of the central issues of dispute. While from the British perspective the whole convention was about severe small-arms control, the Belgian delegation wanted to ensure lax controls for smaller weapons. The country's firearms industry played an important role in the military's mobilisation strategies and was also an important economic factor.[26] Nevertheless, Belgium was also not entirely uninterested in a convention, since it itself had a colony in Africa. Restricting trade in Africa was therefore a concern that the Belgian delegation also pursued.[27] For the Belgian delegation, it was therefore important that at least certain types of handguns were not mentioned in the definition of arms of war. In contrast to the British draft, they therefore proposed a definition that did not include pistols and revolvers – arms that were produced in Belgium. The British negotiator repeatedly tried to act against such a softening of the category, pointing out that it was precisely these weapons that were so dangerous in the hands of the 'anarchists'. But the Belgians insisted that pistols and revolvers were defensive weapons.[28]

Finally, a compromise was found by defining different rules for so-called prohibited zones that included only the colonised territories of Africa, as well as the Middle East. The Convention for the Control of the Trade in Arms and Ammunition, signed in September 1919, required states to subject all exports of arms of war to an inspection and to issue licences for legal exports. The licences should be subject to compulsory publicity. For the so-called prohibited zones, however, the convention laid down stricter conditions. It regulated the trade with all firearms and munitions and not just those that fell under the definition of arms of war. Furthermore, it defined very specific control instruments with which trade in these zones should be regulated in a binding manner under international law. It contained, for example, a right to control domestic ships under 500 tons and the obligatory establishment of warehouses for storing imported weapons – an instrument that the British had successfully implemented in the Gulf prior to the end of the nineteenth century.[29]

On September 8, 1919, the first international treaty was signed that regulated the arms trade internationally. The foundations for a global control regime were laid. This regime should not be seen as a byproduct of the peace negotiations; it was an integral part of a new international peace order. Even if the convention mainly created the international legal framework for instruments that had been used since the turn of the century, the colonial powers reacted with the treaty to a specific constellation created by the First World War. The war had not only increased social tensions in Europe and thus created the conditions for a revolution. By resorting to resources and people in the colonies in the course of war mobilisation, violence threatened to increase also outside Europe. After the colonial powers had successfully transferred part of the burden of war to the colonised societies, in 1919 the people in the colonies had to be prevented from acquiring the means to defend themselves. That was the reason why a racialised arms control regime was so important in the aftermath of the First World War.

But arms trade regulations were not only about denying certain groups the access to weapons, but also enabling others to have that access. There was one trade-off the British delegation had to make in Paris, as the staff of the Foreign Office noted:

> As first drafted by His Majesty's Government the definition of 'arms of war' covered only small arms, pistols and bombs, such weapons as could easily be procured and misused by barbarous races. However, due to the pressure of the US delegation, thedefinition was extended at Paris to include artillery and Machine guns, and thus restricted transactions in arms which could only be used by civilised Powers.[30]

Unlike the British and French government, the Americans were not concerned with preventing insurgent groups in the colonies from having access to small arms, but with being able to control arms exports to sovereign states in Central America, which also ordered larger weapons for their troops.[31] This had consequences for the definition of arms of war. From Washington's point of view, the inclusion of cannons was urgently needed.

The explicit mention of cannons started to cause serious problems for the British government during the early 1920s. The reason was Washington's refusal to sign the convention. In March 1920, Republican Warren Harding became the new US president. In contrast to Woodrow Wilson, whose government had worked out numerous international treaties in a rare feat in 1919, Harding's government was very sceptical about committing itself to international law. This also applied to the Arms Trade Convention, which had to be ratified by Congress. The Republicans, who had a majority in both chambers, had already made it clear during the 1919 presidential election how little they thought of Wilson's international law policy. Fresh in office, the new government informed the other contracting parties that, based on the existing legal situation, it could only ban arms exports in very few cases. Without new laws, however, it would not be possible to comply with the provisions of the convention.[32] The disinterest of one of the main arms-producing countries' government led to a standstill in the ratification process. The entry into force of the convention became increasingly unlikely.

The British government was in a bind because of the US refusal. On the one hand, it still had a vested interest in the convention and was eager to fully enforce its provisions in the Persian Gulf. Therefore, London insisted that the signatories had agreed in an additional protocol to adhere to the provisions of the convention until its coming into power.[33] In order to be able to give weight to this demand, British authorities were also obliged to comply with the provisions. On the other hand, Britain's defence industry was at risk of being disadvantaged by the United States' refusal to join or even comply with the convention. The colonial powers had included a provision that allowed the export of armaments only to other signatories. Any country that wanted to buy armaments in France, Belgium, Japan or the United Kingdom would have to adhere to the convention. This provision was intended to create pressure on other states to sign the treaty. After all, almost all states with an armament industry had participated in negotiating the convention.[34]

Washington's refusal, however, suddenly presented non-signatories with an attractive alternative. The British government feared that US arms companies could expand their business worldwide at the expense of the British. Suddenly, the treaty that was meant to consolidate imperial rule became a threat to the armament industry of the imperial powers. However, the ability to produce armaments was a key element to maintaining imperial control in the colonies. Britain needed a strong industry to construct the patrol boats, aeroplanes, machine guns and armoured cars that were needed to police their empires. Arms exports were important to maintain production capacities at times when the British government was buying fewer weapons. Out of this concern, Alfred Milner, Secretary of State for the colonies and fierce imperialist, proposed to limit the scope of the convention to small arms, as originally planned. 'Chief obstacles to legitimate trade with civilised countries would be thus removed while the most important feature of the Convention would be retained namely prohibition of export to prohibited zones of arms etc. likely to be used by turbulent tribes.'[35] In April 1920, the proposal was sent to the governments of Italy, France, Belgium and Japan.

While the Foreign Office awaited answers from the other colonial powers, the convention produced its first problems. Spain's government had started to build up its navy. Warships equipped with complex gun turrets and armour were Vickers' speciality, beside Armstrong, Britain's main armament company. Vickers was in a good position to land orders. Already before the war, it had signed a contract with Spain to arm warships with cannons. When Vickers tried to implement the contract, it was found that, according to the convention, guns could not be supplied as Spain had not signed the convention. The implications went even further. In the future, Vickers would not be able to deliver warships with armaments.[36]

Even though a solution could be found, Vickers' difficulties with exports to Spain made it clear to the British government that the dilemma posed by the convention was fundamental and needed a lasting solution. The Department of Overseas Trade lamented: 'This Department can only view the present position with the gravest apprehension for the future of a trade which has, in the past, been very profitable in times of peace and of the highest importance to the country in times of war.'[37] The British proposal, however, did not meet with the unanimous support of the other colonial powers. Eventually, all signatories except the United States agreed on a different solution: they would comply with the provisions of the convention regarding the prohibited zones, despite the lack of ratifications.[38] In view of this agreement, the signatory states considered ratification of the convention superfluous, and the treaty did not formally enter into force.

This does not mean the convention was a dead letter. From a British point of view, the agreement was quite convenient. It made it possible to ignore the unwelcome amendments that the treaty had undergone in the course of the negotiations and to concentrate on pacifying the empire. During the following years, British authorities demanded that the other colonial powers adhere to the provisions of the convention. Whenever they discovered arms entering their colonial possessions from a territory controlled by other powers, they complained about the breach of the agreement.[39] At the same time, the convention gained importance at a regional level, especially in the Persian Gulf. The region was important as India's frontier. From here, guns reached the Pashtuns living at the North-Western border of Britain's 'Jewel in the Crown'. Therefore, London pressured the Sheiks of the Gulf to implement arms regulations in accordance with the convention. Furthermore, the convention served as a legitimation to control and search so-called native vessels and, if weapons were found, to confiscate or destroy these vessels.[40] While the British arms trade with warships, aeroplanes and armoured cars started flourishing,[41] the agreement made it possible for British authorities to confiscate guns and pistols.

Liberal internationalism and imperial arms control

What role did the Arms Trade Convention play in Geneva, where disarmament policy became an important policy area in the interwar period? The treaty had been negotiated and signed before the League of Nations even began its work. However, the regulation of the arms trade was clearly identified in Article 23 of the League of Nations Act as a task for the newly founded international institution, and parts of Article 8 emerged from a debate on international business in the armaments industry. Therefore, it did not take long before the various League of Nations bodies began to define the implementation of the convention as their area of responsibility. The appropriation of an instrument of imperial control is not without a certain irony: the disarmament policy of the interwar period was seen as an expression of a 'new diplomacy', as a turning away from imperial power politics and towards a democratically legitimised foreign policy supported by 'public opinion'.[42] Historical research has shown that this dichotomisation does not do justice to the complexity of diplomatic action and that the policies sold under the new label were often not so new, but in many respects were linked to the great power politics of the pre-war period.[43]

With regard to the Arms Trade Convention, however, it is noteworthy that it was not just the governments of colonial powers such as Great Britain or France that lobbied in Geneva for its signing. Instead, the initiative to put the convention on the agendas of League of Nations bodies started with a group that pursued a liberal internationalist agenda. By *liberal internationalism* I refer to an ideology that places international law and international organisations at the centre of international relations. This group integrated the treaty negotiated by the colonial powers into its disarmament policy agenda – an agenda which it sometimes advanced in open confrontation with the great powers. It repeatedly appealed to public opinion and made use of the newly established instruments of international politics.

In May 1920, the League of Nations Council created the Permanent Armaments Commission (PAC) to implement the disarmament provisions of the Versailles Peace Treaty. Each Council member was allowed to appoint three representatives, one each for naval, land and air forces. The Armaments Commission was not bound to the League of Nations Assembly, but to the Council. In this way, it seemed as if two important points in the matter of disarmament had been set early on: firstly, it would be possible for the great powers to largely control the Geneva debates; second, the issue would be discussed primarily from a military point of view. Although the commission was responsible for implementing Article 8 of the League of Nations Act, in which all members committed themselves to disarmament measures, France managed to ensure that the commission initially concentrated almost exclusively on implementing the disarmament requirements of the loser powers.[44]

But the disarmament talks in Geneva soon developed a momentum of their own. Firstly, the less powerful states also knew how to use the newly created instruments of international politics. Second, the League of Nations was a projection screen for reform ideas, which were sometimes advocated by the delegates of the great powers, even if they conflicted with the interests of their governments. Before the League of Nations met for the first time in plenary in December 1920, the various thematic committees met in November. About 40 delegates attended the meeting of the Sixth Committee that was in charge of disarmament issues. The conditions for a lively debate were good. The high, mirrored room decorated with citrus plants provided sufficient oxygen; the large windows let in a lot of light. René Viviani, who was still French Prime Minister and foreign minister at the outbreak of the First World War, reported on the PAC's activities to date. It had been concluded, he explained, that without solid armament data, there could be no substantive discussions. After cursory statements on the topics of gas weapon bans and 'moral disarmament' (opinion-forming measures against militaristic tendencies), he already finished the first activity report of the PAC.[45]

Robert Cecil was deeply disappointed and launched into what was, for the diplomatique parquet, an unusually scathing criticism. He lamented that Viviani had only addressed a small part of the relevant topics. His presentation left many questions unanswered. This was proof that the PAC was not able to deal with the issue appropriately. He argued that the question of disarmament should not be reduced to a few technical details, but should be discussed on a much more fundamental level. If the League of Nations would not start immediately with a more determined approach to disarmament, it would create an unfavourable impression in the public. Cecil did not sit on the committee for Britain, but represented South Africa, which confused many fellow delegates who remembered him as a key figure in the British peace delegation in Paris. His former British negotiating partner, Jan Smuts, had meanwhile been elected prime minister of South Africa and had decided to entrust Cecil with representing his country at the League of Nations. This put him in a position to help shape the work of the newly founded organisation without being bound by the instructions of the British government, which he felt was not very interested in developments in Geneva.[46] Cecil, on the other hand, was still convinced of the importance of the League of Nations, whose core tasks, in his view, included general disarmament. In the years that followed, he was to invest a great deal of time and energy in this policy area.[47]

Cecil's speech set the tone for the upcoming meetings of the Disarmament Committee, which now set about defining the most urgent disarmament policy issues. The Scandinavian delegates played an important role in this. A year and a half earlier, at the peace conference, they had made it clear that general disarmament was very important to them. As small states with limited budgets, they had no way of keeping up with the military spending of the major powers around them. At the same time, they saw the great powers' arms race as a reason for wars, which in turn endangered their economies.[48] It was therefore not surprising that they sent armaments critics as delegates. The internationally well-connected Norwegian Christian Lange had been secretary of the committee awarding the Nobel Prize. As secretary general of the Nordic Inter-Parliamentary Union, he had played a crucial role during the war in promoting a peace agenda that contained the main points of liberal internationalism, such as free trade in colonies or spheres of influence, the institutionalisation of an international legal order, disarmament and democratisation of international relations. The Social Democrat

Hjalmar Branting, who had been prime minister of Sweden for just a month before leaving for Geneva, was a fierce anti-militarist. He represented a new approach to internationalism within the Scandinavian labour movement. Disillusioned by the failure of the international labour movement in 1914, Swedish and Danish Social Democrats placed the state and not the international proletariat at the centre of strategies to create a peaceful international order. Thereby, 'socialist and liberal versions of internationalism were made compatible and political consensus about peace politics broadened'.[49] This was especially true for disarmament policies – a field in which Lange and Branting would play an important role and cooperate closely during the years to come.[50]

Cecil, Lange and Branting, who had been elected chairman of the Disarmament Committee, set the pace in the meetings and carried out successful agenda setting. It was Cecil who made the Arms Trade Treaty the subject of debate – and not Viviani or H.A.L. Fisher, the two representatives of those great powers who had significantly advanced the negotiations. One of the critical questions that Cecil used to dissect Viviani's lecture was aimed precisely at this topic. What had been done about the Arms Trade Convention from 1919? He suggested that the Disarmament Committee of the League of Nations make it its task to press for the implementation of this convention. In doing so, Cecil did not fail to recognise that their primary aim was colonial control. On the contrary, from his point of view, this reflected the advantage of the League of Nations dealing with the convention: in the 'uncivilized countries', it had already helped to contain war and conflicts.[51]

In attempting to further push the debate, Cecil organised a presentation by his compatriot Cecil Hurst, who spoke about the 1919 Arms Trade Convention and emphasised its importance in securing peace: 'Arms of precision in the hands of individuals in the less civilized areas pose a great danger to the peace.' These remarks unquestionably echoed the words of Mark Sykes, who in 1917 had warned that small arms in the hands of resistance fighters were a threat to peace in the colonies. He related this threat to experiences that Europeans had had with revolutionary violence: 'Experience in all civilized countries during the last few decades has shown the use which persons of evil disposition, such as anarchists and criminals can make of high explosives, automatic pistols, and similar commodities.'[52] Statements like this reveal the racist and reactionary worldview of the European advocates of disarmament. They portrayed the population of the colonised territories as a threat to the international order they sought to establish through the League of Nations. The statement also makes it clear that they not only saw themselves as bringing peace to the European continent, but also understood their commitment as part of a civilising mission. At the same time, however, this racism also helped to make their concerns accessible to the delegates of the colonial powers. In any case, the Disarmament Committee soon agreed that the arms trade should be an important issue.

At the same time, however, Cecil and the Scandinavians went beyond the great power agenda and linked the issue of the arms trade to other concerns. They demanded to control the private manufacture of arms, to ensure that economic profit interests could not influence the global proliferation of arms and to establish an international office to control the arms trade. On these points the British Foreign Office had sent its delegate, Fisher, to Geneva with extremely vague instructions.[53] Although, as a British delegate, his voice carried great weight, he did not appear with his own substantive accents. Rather, he went in the slipstream of his diplomatically experienced countryman Cecil and followed the line he had set. An expert on education, Fisher neither had expertise in the field of armaments nor experience as a diplomat. It speaks to the Foreign Office's lack of ambition that it had earmarked him for the meetings of the Disarmament Committee, which was obviously not given much importance in Whitehall. Fisher, a committed liberal internationalist, found it easy to identify with Cecil's ideas and proposals.[54]

This created the conditions for the delegates in the Disarmament Committee to follow the suggestions of the Scandinavians and Cecil. In the resolutions they proposed and which the General Assembly passed, they emphasised the importance of the 1919 Arms Trade Convention in preventing the proliferation of arms in 'the troubled areas of the world':

> It is to be remembered that as the result of the war, there has been a great expansion in the machinery for the manufacture of arms and munitions, and in consequence a special danger that the demand for armaments may be stimulated by the enterprise of firms desirous of disposing of their surplus stock to the best advantage.

Therefore, they appealed to all signatory states to press ahead with ratification and to adhere to the protocol, which stipulated compliance with the provisions of the convention even before it entered into force. The Council of the League of Nations should also press ahead with ratification with renewed vigour.[55] The justification for the resolution makes it clear that the committee adopted the interpretation of the colonial powers and understood the convention as an instrument against social unrest in the colonies. On the other hand, it is noticeable that they avoided speaking explicitly of colonies and instead chose formulations that ascribed a global peace-building function to the convention. In addition, the members of the committee did not see the 'rebellious peoples' in the colonies as the core of the problem, but rather European companies.

Another resolution responded to Cecil's criticism expressed at the beginning of the proceedings. It recommended the setting up of a Temporary Commission as a further advisory body, composed of people with the 'necessary competence in political, social and economic matters'. Their task would be to develop proposals for the implementation of the disarmament article of the League of Nations statute. This resolution reflected the growing importance attached to experts in the environment of the nascent organisation. The design of the new diplomacy was based on the conviction that scientific methods of data collection, together with the specialist knowledge of experts, were important means of solving international problems. At the same time, calling on experts and their expertise has always been a means of bringing actors into position. The reference to the expertise that is necessary for the clarification of questions often conceals the fact that the problems they negotiated were essentially highly political.[56]

Based on this resolution, the Council established in February 1921 the so-called Temporary Mixed Commission (TMC), which was composed of 20 members. By appointing the members of the Council, the great powers, which were strongly represented there, secured a considerable influence on the composition of the Commission. But once appointed, the representatives of the new body were not bound by the instructions of any government. In practice, it was sometimes a bit more complicated. Both Viviani and H.A.L. Fisher, for example, were simultaneously delegates of their states to the League of Nations and independent members of the TMC. They were informed about their governments' interests in disarmament policy, and it would be foolish to believe that this knowledge did not also shape their positions in the commission. However, it also included people like Robert Cecil, who used the body to advance their own ideas about effective disarmament. In the years that followed, the TMC significantly shaped and promoted the debates on disarmament at the League of Nations. In 1923, it became apparent that the great powers could not prevent the members of the commission from pursuing an agenda that over time became increasingly at odds with the interests of the great powers [57]

At first, however, the Commission and the governments of the great powers were on the same page on this issue. At the League of Nations Assembly, for example, Fisher proudly presented his government's willingness to sign the Arms Trade Convention.[58] However, it is noticeable that the initiative to use the newly created structures of the League of Nations to strengthen the convention always came from the TMC. It was they – and not the PAC or the Council, where the influence of the great powers was far more direct – at whose urging the Secretariat of the Secretary-General took up the matter in 1921, sending letters to League of Nations members and the United

States urging the convention to finally be repealed to ratify.[59] The reason for this was obvious: the informal agreement reached between the colonial powers at the end of 1920 to apply the convention at least with regard to the prohibited zones largely fulfilled the expectations they had attached to the treaty. In their view, there was no urgency to formally put it into effect. Finally, in Whitehall in particular, people really appreciated that the informal character helped to circumvent the restrictions contained in the convention regarding states outside the prohibited zones. The efforts of the League of Nations for the convention ultimately failed. By the end of 1922, only ten Latin American and Asian countries and Finland had ratified the treaty. This fell far short of the number of ratifications that would have been necessary for entry into force. Those who mattered – the armaments-producing countries – feared export disadvantages for their own industry in the event of unilateral ratification.[60]

Conclusion

However, the League of Nations' involvement with the Arms Trade Convention of 1919 was not significant because the initiative was crowned with success, but for another reason: in Geneva, advocates of disarmament integrated an instrument of international law into their agenda that aimed at strengthening imperial rule. On the one hand, they pursued the goal of internationalising the convention and extending its reach to other regions of the world. Disarmament advocates such as Christian Lange and Hjalmar Branting pursued the strategy of strengthening the convention in order to promote the establishment of the international office to monitor the arms trade and thus pave the way for monitoring arms production. At the League of Nations Assembly in 1922, Cecil complained that from his point of view the convention would have been a suitable instrument, for example, to contain the violence in the Balkans, which continued there even after the end of the war. In addition, it could have prevented an armament of the Soviet Union, which in his view posed a considerable danger.[61]

At the same time, however, the advocates of disarmament inscribed measures of imperial control into the agenda of the League of Nations – not as an unintended by-catch, but specifically and as part of a peace policy programme with global aspirations. In 1922, the members of the Sixth Committee of the General Assembly stated that the Arms Trade Convention had one purpose above all:

> To prevent the importation of arms [...] to certain defined areas inhabited by backward peoples. [...] the task of preventing bloodshed in vast regions

of Africa and in the countries which border the Red Sea is rendered far more difficult if the inhabitants have access to unlimited quantities of arms and ammunition.[62]

Even if the Arms Trade Convention never came into force, the imperial control instruments laid down therein remained on the agenda in Geneva in the following years and played an important role in further attempts to regulate the international arms trade. Thus, it is an example of how instruments of international order of the pre-war order were adapted to the realities of the interwar period, in which the liberal conception of a 'new diplomacy' gained influence.

Notes

1 Winston Churchill, *The Story of the Malakand Field Force: An Episode of Frontier War* (London: Longmans, Green and Co., 1898), p. 23.
2 Emrys Chew, *Arming the Periphery: The Arms Trade in the Indian Ocean during the Age of Global Empire* (Basingstoke: Palgrave Macmillan, 2012); Lipokmar Dzüvichü, 'Guns in the Hills: Firearms Circulation along the North-East Frontier of British India, 1860s–1910s', *Journal of Modern European History* 19:4 (2021), 416–35.
3 Simon Ball, 'The Battle of Dubai: Firearms on Britain's Arabian Frontier, 1906–1915', in Karen Jones, Giacomo Macola and David Welch (eds), *A Cultural History of Firearms in the Age of Empire* (London: Routledge, 2013), pp. 165–90; Robert Crews, 'Trafficking in Evil? The Global Arms Trade and the Politics of Disorder', in James Gelvin and Nile Green (eds), *Global Islam in the Age of Steam and Print, 1850–1930* (Oakland, CA: University of California Press, 2014), pp. 121–42; Guillemette Crouzet, 'The Persian Gulf in Global Perspective: British Informal Empire and the Challenge of Arms Trafficking (c. 1870–1914)', *Journal of Levantine Studies* 10:1 (2020), 69–89.
4 Felix Brahm, 'Banning the Sale of Modern Firearms in Africa: On the Origins of the Brusells Conference Act of 1890', *Journal of Modern European History* 19:4 (2021), 436–47; Felix Brahm, *Merchandise of Power: Der Waffenhandel zwischen Europa und Ostafrika (1850–1919)* (Frankfurt am Main: Campus Verlag, 2022), pp. 201–27; R.W. Beachey, 'The Arms Trade in East Africa in the Late Nineteenth Century', *The Journal of African History* 3:3 (1962), 451–67; Jonathan Grant, *Rulers, Guns, and Money: The Global Arms Trade in the Age of Imperialism* (Cambridge, MA: Harvard University Press, 2007), pp. 47–64; Neil Cooper, 'Race, Sovereignty, and Free Trade: Arms Trade Regulations and Humanitarian Arms Control in the Age of Empire', *Journal of Global Security Studies* 3:4 (2018), 444–62.
5 Ball, 'The Battle of Dubai', p. 178; Chew, *Arming the Periphery*, p. 122; Brahm, 'Banning the Sale', 444.

6 Mark Mazower, *No Enchanted Palace: The End of Empire and the Ideological Origins of the United Nations* (Princeton, NJ: Princeton University Press, 2009); Jeanne Morefield, *Covenants without Swords: Idealist Liberalism and the Spirit of Empire* (Princeton, NJ: Princeton University Press, 2005); Jeanne Morefield, *Empires Without Imperialism: Anglo-American Decline and the Politics of Deflection* (Oxford: Oxford University Press, 2014); Susan Pedersen, 'Empires, States and the League of Nations', in Glenda Sluga and Patricia Clavin (eds), *Internationalisms: A Twentieth-Century History* (Cambridge: Cambridge University Press, 2016), pp. 113–38.

7 Maurice Vaïsse, *Sécurité d'abord. La politique française en matière de désarmement, 9 décembre 1930–17 avril 1934* (Paris: Pedone, 1981); Dick Richardson, *The Evolution of British Disarmament Policy in the 1920s* (London: Leicester University Press, 1989); R.G. Kaufman, *Arms Control during the Pre-Nuclear Era: The United States and Naval Limitation between the Two World Wars* (New York: Columbia University Press, 1990); B.J.C. McKercher (ed.), *Arms Limitation and Disarmament: Restraints on War, 1899–1939* (Westport, CT: Praeger, 1992); Rolf Ahmann, Adolf M. Birke and Michael Howard (eds), *The Quest for Stability: Problems of West European Security, 1918–1957* (Oxford: Oxford University Press, 1993); Thomas Richard Davies, *The Possibilities of Transnational Activism: The Campaign for Disarmament Between the Two World Wars* (Leiden: Brill, 2007); Richard Fanning, *Peace and Disarmament: Naval Rivalry & Arms Control 1922–1933* (Lexington, KY: University Press of Kentucky, 1995); Carolyn Kitching, *Britain and the Geneva Disarmament Conference: A Study in International History* (Basingstoke: Palgrave Macmillan, 2002); Richard Shuster, *German Disarmament After World War I: The Diplomacy of International Arms Inspection 1920–1931* (London: Routledge, 2006); David Stevenson, 'Britain, France and the Origins of German Disarmament, 1916–19', *Journal of Strategic Studies* 29:2 (2006), 195–224; Andrew Barros, 'Disarmament as a Weapon. Anglo-French Relations and the Problems of Enforcing German Disarmament, 1919–28', *Journal of Strategic Studies* 29:2 (2006), 301–21; Peter Jackson, 'France and the Problems of Security and International Disarmament after the First World War', *Journal of Strategic Studies* 29:2 (2006), 247–80; Andrew Webster, *Strange Allies. Britain, France and the Dilemmas of Disarmament and Security 1929–1933* (London: Routledge, 2019).

8 Andrew Webster, 'Making Disarmament Work: The Implementation of the International Disarmament Provisions in the League of Nations Covenant, 1919–1925', *Diplomacy and Statecraft* 16:3 (2005), 551–69; Andrew Webster, 'The Transnational Dream: Politicians, Diplomats and Soldiers in the League of Nations' Pursuit of International Disarmament, 1920–1938', *Contemporary European History* 14:4 (2005), 493–518; Andrew Webster, 'From Versailles to Geneva: The Many Forms of Interwar Disarmament', *Journal of Strategic Studies* 29:2 (2006), 225–46; Andrew Webster, '"Absolutely Irresponsible Amateurs": The Temporary Mixed Commission on Armaments, 1921–1924', *Australian Journal of Politics and History* 54:3 (2008), 373–88; David Lincove,

'Data for Peace. The League of Nations and Disarmament 1920–40', in *Peace & Change* 43:4 (2018), S. 498–529; Haakon A. Ikonomou, 'The Administrative Anatomy of Failure: The League of Nations Disarmament Section, 1919–1925', *Contemporary European History* 30:3 (2021), 321–34; Waqar H. Zaidi, *Technological Internationalism and World Order: Aviation, Atomic Energy and the Search for International Peace, 1920–1950* (Cambridge: Cambridge University Press, 2021).

9 For an exception, see David R. Stone, 'Imperialism and Sovereignty: The League of Nations' Drive to Control the Global Arms Trade', *Journal of Contemporary History* 35 (2000), 213–30; the special issue 'Arms Regimes Across the Empires', *Journal of Modern European History* 19:4 (2021); Daniel Stahl, 'The Decolonization of the Arms Trade: Britain and the Regulation of Exports to the Middle East', *History of Global Arms Transfer* 7:1 (2019), 3–19; Waqar H. Zaidi, '"Aviation Will Either Destroy or Save Our Civilization": Proposals for the International Control of Aviation, 1920–45', *Journal of Contemporary History* 46:1 (2011), 150–178; Waqar H. Zaidi, *Technological Internationalism*; Leon Julius Biela, 'Contesting Imperialism in Geneva. Interwar Arms-Traffic Conferences and the Anglo-Iranian Confrontation', in Leon Julius Biela and Anna Bundt (eds), *Interwar Crossroads: Entangled Histories of the Middle Eastern and North Atlantic World between the World Wars* (Würzburg: Transcript Verlag, 2023), pp. 121–52.

10 Thomas G. Fraser, 'Germany and Indian Revolution, 1914–18', *Journal of Contemporary History* 12:2 (1977), 255–72; Heather Streets-Salter, *World War One in Southeast Asia: Colonialism and Anticolonialism in an Era of Global Conflict* (Cambridge: Cambridge University Press, 2017); Judith M. Brown, *Modern India: The Origins of an Asian Democracy* (Oxford: Oxford University Press, 1994), pp. 194–207; Stephen Garton, 'The Dominions Ireland, and India', in Robert Gerwarth and Erez Manela (eds), *Empires at War, 1911–1923* (Oxford: Oxford University Press, 2014), pp. 152–78.

11 Niamh Gallagher, *Ireland and the Great War: A Social and Political History* (London: I.B. Tauris, 2019); Wilfried Pott, *Auf der Suche nach Unterstützung für Irland. Roger Casements Wirken in Deutschland und die deutsche Unterstützung des Osteraufstandes* (München: AVM, 2011).

12 Robert L. Tignor, 'Maintaining the Empire. General Sir John Maxwell and Egypt during World War I', *The Princeton University Library Chronicle* 53:2 (1992), 173–99.

13 Michael D. Berdine, *Redrawing the Middle East: Sir Mark Sykes, Imperialism and the Sykes–Picot Agreement* (London: I.B. Tauris, 2018), pp. 4–107.

14 The National Archives, London (hereafter TNA), CAB 29/1, Memorandum by Lieutenant-Colonel Sir Mark Sikes, Bart, M.P., 12 January 1917, p. 3.

15 Ibid., Committee of Imperial Defence, Sub-Committee on Arms Traffic, Third meeting, 20 January 1917, p 1. On the role of air policing and air control in the colonies, see Martin Böhm, *Die Royal Air Force und der Luftkrieg 1922–1945. Personelle, kognitive und konzeptionelle Kontinuitäten und Entwicklungen* (Paderborn: Verlag Ferdinand Schöningh GmbH, 2015); David E. Omissi, *Air

Power and Colonial Control: The Royal Air Force, 1919–1939 (Manchester: Manchester University Press, 1990); Priya Satia, 'The Defense of Inhumanity: Air Control and the British Idea of Arabia', *American Historical Review* 111:1 (2006), 16–51.

16 TNA, CAB 29/1, Memorandum by Lieutenant-Colonel Sir Mark Sykes, Bart, M.P., 12 January 1917, p. 3.
17 Ibid., pp. 1 f.
18 TNA, FO 608, 217/9–11, Draft Convention for the Control of the Arms Traffic, Art. 25, n.d.
19 Ellis Goldberg, 'Peasants in Revolt – Egypt 1919', *International Journal of Middle East Studies* 24:2 (1992), 261–80; Krishan G. Saini, 'The Economic Aspects of India's Participation in the First World War', in DeWitt C. Ellingwood and S. D. Pradhan (eds), *India and World War* (New Delhi: MANOHAR, 1978), pp. 141–76.
20 Abbas Amanat, *Iran: A Modern History* (New Haven, CT: Yale University Press, 2017), pp. 392–407; Chelsi Mueller, *The Origins of the Arab-Iranian Conflict: Nationalism and Sovereignty in the Gulf between the World Wars* (Cambridge: Cambridge University Press, 2020), pp. 78–81; Central Asia, Persia, and Afghanistan. Bolshevik and Pan-Islamic Movements and Connected Information, December 1919, in QDL/IOR/L/PS/18/A185; Situation in Middle East, Note by Major Bray, Political Intelligence Officer, attached to India Office, 18 November 1920, in ibid./B358.
21 Ibid.; Guilia Bentivoglio, 'The Empire Under Attack. Anglo-Soviet Relations and Bolshevik Infiltration in India in the Early 1920s', in Valentine Lomellini (ed.), *The Rise of Bolshevism and Its Impact on the Interwar International Order: Security, Conflict and Cooperation in the Contemporary World* (Cham: Palgrave Macmillan, 2020), pp. 93–111; Hugh Tinker: 'India and the First World War and After', *Journal of Contemporary History* 3:4 (1968), 89–107; Stephen White, 'Colonial Revolution and the Communist International, 1919–1924', *Science & Society* 40:2 (1976), 173–93; Martin Kitchen, 'The Empire, 1900–1939', in Chris Wrigley (ed.), *A Companion to Early Twentieth-Century Britain* (Malden, MA: Wiley-Blackwell, 2003), pp. 182–97, here pp. 186 f.; *Disorders Inquiry Committee 1919–1920: Report* (Calcutta: Superintendent Government Printing, 1920), pp. 154–6.
22 TNA, FO 608/217/9–11, Foreign Office to Peace Delegation, 1 February 1919, p. 2.
23 A printed version of the British draft can be found in Ray Stannard Baker, *Woodrow Wilson and World Settlement. Written from His Unpublished and Personal Material, Volume III* (New York: Doubleday, 1923), p. 131.
24 Marc Michel, *L'Appel à l'Afrique. Contributions et Réactions à l'Effort de guerre en A.O.F. (1914–1919)* (Paris: Publications de la Sorbonne, 1982); Patrick Royer, 'La guerre colonial du Bani-Volta, 1915–1916 (Burkina-Faso, Mali)', *Autrepart* 26 (2003), 35–51; Mahir Saul, Patrick Royer, *West African Challenge to Empire: Culture and History in the Volta-Bani Anticolonial War* (Athens, OH: James Currey, 2001).

25 Sokhna Sané, *Le contrôle des armes à feu en Afrique occidentale française (1834–1958)* (Paris: Karthala, 2008), pp. 110–46.
26 Lothar Hilbert, 'Waffenexport. Aspekte des internationalen Waffenhandels nach dem Ersten Weltkrieg', in Jürgen Heideking and Gerhard Schulz (eds), *Wege in die Zeitgeschichte. Festschrift zum 65. Geburtstag von Gerhard Schulz* (Berlin: De Gruyter, 1989), pp. 415–32; Chew, *Arming the Periphery*, pp. 80–96.
27 NARA, RG 256, Pub M820, Roll 180, Note de la Délégation Belge au sujet du projet de Convention relatif au contrôle du commerce des armes à feu et des munitions, n.d. in Commission pour la revision des actes généraux de Berlin et de Bruxelles, Procès-Verbaux et Rapport de la Commission, pp. 23 f., here p. 23.
28 Ibid., Procès-Verbal N° 1, Sénace du 8 Juillet 1919, pp. 5–10. Quote p. 6: 'les pistolets automatiques, très dangereux par exemple dans les mains des anarchistes', 'pistolet est une arme de défense'.
29 Convention for the Control of the Trade in Arms and Ammunition, and Protocol, Art. 6–21.
30 TNA, FO 371, 4419, Lindsay to Frank Polk, Acting Secretary of State, 9 March 1920.
31 Daniel Stahl, 'Confronting US Imperialism with International Law: Central America and the Arms Trade of the Interwar Period', *Journal of Modern European History* 19:4 (2021), 491–7.
32 TNA, F0 371, 4419, Exportation of arms to American countries, 18 March 1920.
33 Convention for the Control of the Trade in Arms and Ammunition, Protocol.
34 Ibid., Art. 1.
35 TNA, FO 371, 4419, Telegram Milner, Secretary of State for the Colonies, to the Officer Administering the Government of Canada and the Governors General of the Commonwealth of Australia, New Zealand and Union of South Africa and the Governor of Newfoundland, 9 April 1920.
36 Ibid., 4422, Rudkin (Vickers Ltd.) to Major R. Glyn (MP), 10 June 1920.
37 Ibid., 4419, Department of Overseas Trade: Memorandum to Foreign Office, 14 May 1920, quote p. 2.
38 Ibid., Seymour (Foreign Office) to the Under-Secretary of State, Colonial Office, 11 August 1920.
39 QDL/IOR/R/15/5/47, 95r, Telegram, Viceroy of India, to Secretary of State of India, 27 October 1921, as well as the attached statements in TNA, FO 371, 5530; ibid., India Office to the Secretary of State, 28 October 1921; procedures in ibid., 4421, 5527 and 7178.
40 Leon Biela, 'Disarming the Periphery. Inter-war Arms Control, British Imperialism and the Persian Gulf', *Journal of Modern European History* 19:4 (2021), 469–88.
41 David Edgerton, *Warfare State: Britain, 1920–1970* (Cambridge: Cambridge University Press, 2006), pp. 46 f.
42 See e.g. Alan Sharp, 'The New Diplomacy and the New Europe, 1916–1922', in Nicholas Doumanis (ed.), *Oxford Handbook of European History, 1914–1945* (Oxford: Oxford University Press, 2016), pp. 119–37.

43 Verena Steller, 'Zwischen Geheimnis und Öffentlichkeit. Die Pariser Friedensverhandlungen 1919 und die Krise der universalen Diplomatie', *Zeithistorische Forschungen/Studies in Contemporary History* 8:3 (2011), 350–72; Stephen Wertheim, 'Reading the International Mind: International Public Opinion in Early Twentieth Century Anglo-American Thought', in Nicolas Guilhot and Daniel Bessner (eds), *The Decisionist Imagination: Sovereignty, Social Science, and Democracy in the Twentieth Century* (New York: Berghahn Books, 2018), pp. 27–63, here pp. 36–47; Susan Pedersen, 'Back to the League of Nations. Review Essay', *The American Historical Review* 112:4 (2007), 1091–1117.

44 Andrew Webster, 'Making Disarmament Work: The Implementation of the International Disarmament Provisions in the League of Nations Covenant, 1919–1925', *Diplomacy and Statecraft* 16:3 (2005), 551–69, here p. 552 f.

45 Here and in the following: *Records of the First Assembly. Meetings of the Committees II* (Geneva: The League, 1920), pp. 247–50. A few short, silent video sequences exist from the first meeting of the sixth committee: https://www.criticalpast.com/video/65675029351_League-Committee-on-Disarmament_HAL-Fisher_Robert-Cecil_Viscount-Kikujiro.

46 George W. Egerton, 'The Lloyd George Government and the Creation of the League of Nations', *The American Historical Review* 79:2 (1974), 419–44.

47 Gaynor Johnson, *Lord Robert Cecil. Politician and Internationalist* (Cornwall: Routledge, 2013), pp. 185–200; Dick Richardson, *The Evolution of British Disarmament Policy in the 1920s* (London: Leicester University Press, 1989), esp. pp. 24–7; Carolyn J. Kitching, *Britain and the Geneva Disarmament Conference: A Study in International History* (Basingstoke: Palgrave Macmillan, 2003), esp. pp. 20–3.

48 David Hunter Miller, *The Drafting of the Covenant*, Vol. 2 (New York: G.P. Putnam's Sons, 1928), p. 357; Sami Sarè, *The League of Nations and the Debate on Disarmament, 1918–1919* (Rome: Edizioni Nuova Cultura, 2013), pp. 61–8.

49 Karen Gram-Skjoldager and Øyvind Tønnesson, 'Unity and Divergence: Scandinavian Internationalism, 1914–1921', *Contemporary European History* 17:3 (2008), 301–24, quote 312.

50 Webster, 'Making Disarmament Work', pp. 553 f.; 'The Transnational Dream: Politicians, Diplomats and Soldiers in the League of Nations' Pursuit of International Disarmament, 1920–1938', *Contemporary European History* 14:4 (2005), 493–518, here pp. 496 f.

51 *Records of the First Assembly. Meetings of the Committees II* (Geneva: The League, 1920), p. 250.

52 League of Nations, Armaments, Report of Committee No. 6 to the Assembly, 14 December 1920, in *Records of the First Assembly*, p. 344.

53 TNA, FO 371, 4426, Parliamentary Question Robert Richardson.

54 *Records of the First Assembly. Meetings of the Committees II* (Geneva: The League, 1920), pp. 250–74.

55 Ibid., pp. 504 ff.

56 On the role of experts in the League of Nations, see Patricia Clavin and Jens-Wilhelm Wessels, 'Transnationalism and the League of Nations: Understanding the Work of Its Economic and Financial Organisation', *Contemporary European History* 14:4 (2005), 465–92; Patricia Clavin, *Securing the World Economy. The Reinvention of the League of Nations, 1920–1946* (Oxford: Oxford University Press, 2015); Eckhardt Fuchs, 'Der Völkerbund und die Institutionalisierung transnationaler Beziehungen', *Zeitschrift für Geschichtswissenschaft* 54 (2006), 888–99.
57 On the TMC, see Webster, '"Absolutely Irresponsible Amateurs"'.
58 *Records of the Second Assembly. Meetings of the Committees I* (Geneva: The League, 1921), pp. 311 f.
59 *Records of the Third Assembly. Meetings of the Committees. Minutes of the Third Committee* (Geneva: The League, 1922), p. 80.
60 Ibid., p. 79.
61 *Records of the Third Assembly. Plenary Meetings and Committees* (Geneva: The League, 1922), pp. 244 f.
62 *Records of the Third Assembly: Plenary Meetings II. Annexes: Reports on the Work of the Council and Reports adopted by the Assembly* (Geneva: The League, 1922), p. 163.

6

Colonial policy and international control: the American Philippines and multilateral drug treaties, 1909–31

Eva Ward

Introduction

The 1905 *Act to amend the tariff laws of the Philippines, and for other purposes* was the first colonial ban on non-medicinal opium sale and use and thus an early victory of the transnational anti-opium movement. American colonial officials in the Philippines soon realised that enforcing the ban without international cooperation would be impossible. Anti-opium trade campaigners, particularly Episcopalian Missionary Bishop of the Philippines Charles Brent, subsequently pressured the American government to arrange multilateral summits for agreeing on international systems of drug control. The ongoing difficulty of enforcing prohibition in the Philippines led to the United States promoting an increasingly complicated international drugs regulatory regime, developed through the Hague Convention of 1912, the Geneva Conventions of 1924–25 and the Geneva and Bangkok Conventions of 1931. However, the United States frequently clashed with other colonial powers regarding the practicability of prohibition. Moreover, the international structures that the United States had a hand in creating also hindered its ability to act unilaterally against the illicit narcotics trade. By the last post-war multilateral summits in 1931, the United States had redirected its drugs diplomacy focus from the Asian colonial context of its origins to the domestic sphere, and refused to sign the Bangkok Convention. The colonial legacy lingered, however, with the newly independent Philippines adhering to post-war drug control agreements. This chapter examines American involvement in these early multilateral summits and resultant agreements as an instrument of international order, put in place in order to enforce colonial drug policies during the first three decades of the twentieth century, and it explores the eventual shift towards the metropole rather than the colonial world as a focus of American international drugs diplomacy.

From its initial formulation, the architects of American colonial drugs policy constructed it with an international audience in mind. The rejection in 1903 of a return to the legal opium monopoly system used by the Spanish resulted in an investigative committee, tasked with essentially a best practice review of drug regulations in southeastern Asia. The Philippines Opium Committee, led by Bishop Charles Brent, conducted this review via interviews with colonial officials, religious leaders, doctors and businessmen in various polities. Steffen Rimner's discussion of the 'overt transnationalism' of the Philippines Opium Committee in 1903–4 credits the Committee with later 'facilitating a breakthrough in international cooperation against the opium trade'.[1] The Philippine Opium Committee's recommendations were modelled on the Japanese system in Formosa and consisted of an end to the legal practice of opium smoking, albeit gradually. Over the next three years, legal opium sales through a government monopoly should be gradually reduced. Following the end of the three years in 1908, opium, as well as derivatives like morphine, would be entirely prohibited except for medicinal use. Anne Foster argues American prohibitory drugs policy was rooted in the goal of demonstrating their more civilised form of colonialism by limiting access to opium rather than profiting from the trade.[2] Americans' belief that they 'offered a new and better colonial vision which Europeans would do well to emulate' resulted in restricting opiates to medicinal and scientific use as one facet of the superior American method of colonial governance.[3] Foster claims that through prohibition in the Philippines, 'American colonial officials were demonstrating their benevolent intentions to improve the colony' in comparison with the purported exploitation of the legal opium sales of neighbouring colonies.[4] Alma Bamero concurs that 'the American colonial government managed to project the image' of 'self-sacrifice' in forgoing the profits of the trade.[5] Jessica Kuperavage argues that prior to the American occupation of the Philippines, Americans already viewed themselves as distinct from European nations in their vision of empire.[6] By the time of the Spanish–American War, American public opinion had already developed a strong opposition to opium sales financing imperial aims. In John Collins's words, 'Washington looked at the European monopolies not as a mechanism to control a complicated trade but as an attempt to provide legitimacy to a large source for potential diversion into illicit supplies.'[7]

David Musto, David Courtwright and others also attribute American colonial opium regulations to a larger foreign-policy strategy. However, they argue it was predominantly predicated on a desire to achieve greater access to the Chinese market and ensure the stabilisation of China for the purposes of uninterrupted trade, rather than present a purportedly morally superior form of colonialism. David Musto, David Courtwright, William McAllister and Arnold Taylor contextualise American opium policy in the Philippines within the desire to gain favour with the Qing government and further access to the Chinese market as well as ensure the stability of China in the interests of continued trade.[8] Tim Madge notes the multifaceted nature of foreign policy by reconciling both lines of inquiry as 'moral issues posed by the opium smokers of the Philippines would be combined with this desire to break into the Chinese market, creating a climate whereby Christian duty could happily sit with economic necessity'.[9] William McAllister concurs that following the conquest of the Philippines, 'America's East Asian interests ... were best served by maintaining Chinese territorial integrity ... to protect American trading, investment, and development opportunities ... an anti-opium policy complemented this general approach.'[10]

Once the ban on recreational opium sales and consumption came into effect in 1908, the international community took on new importance for colonial drug policy in the Philippines. Historians generally agree on the significance of the opium ban in the Philippines as an essential beginning to the international drugs regulatory regime and its largely prohibitionist nature. Carl Trocki describes the prohibition of opium in the Philippines as 'the first instance in which a major Western power had moved decisively to ban opium in any part of Asia ... the first step in the process of banning the opium trade on an international level'.[11] Ferdinand Victoria argues the 'current prohibitionist strategy in the global war against illegal drugs was an American legacy that was rooted in the Philippines' encounter with opium'.[12] However, the timing of the American push for drug control meant that it more broadly formed part of an era of colonial reform. Foster adds nuance to existing analyses in noting that 'the United States became a colonial power in Asia at the time when the other colonial powers were rethinking both the methods and the purpose of their colonial rule ... by 1900, officials everywhere were preoccupied with policing behavior as well as borders'.[13] The British, later believed by Americans to be their foremost opponent in suppressing the opium trade, had taken steps like the Anglo-Chinese Agreement in 1907 before the American opium ban in the Philippines had even taken effect.[14] The British were not the only producer state to have second thoughts about the wisdom of government involvement in the drug trade. John Collins states that 'imperial powers were at once conflicted and ambivalent about opium's role within the economic systems and societies they managed'.[15]

The existing work on the beginnings of the international drugs regulatory system addresses the early significance of the Philippines and issues of colonial reform. However, these authors do not discuss the later years of the American colonial era of the Philippines in the development of international drug regulations, nor the role of multilateral summits themselves for colonial drugs policy in the American Philippines. Furthermore, they do not address the policy shift by the early 1930s, where American involvement in international diplomacy was driven by a focus on drug control in the metropole rather than colonial concerns. This essay consequently seeks to elaborate on the existing analyses regarding the Philippines and the multilateral formulation of the international drugs regulatory regime.

Initial overtures, 1906–8

International diplomacy in support of prohibition began soon after the ban's passage in 1905. Having determined the future of colonial opium regulation, the United States promptly began lobbying other colonial powers in the region. In a letter dated 17 October 1906, Sir Edward Grey in the British Foreign Office wrote to Sir Mortimer Durand in the India Office on the subject of recent overtures by the US Ambassador. The American ambassador had told Sir Edward that 'his Government are much concerned with regard to the question of opium, which has been raised in connection with the Philippines'.[16] The ambassador had been directed to inquire regarding the British view of a Joint Commission or Joint Investigation of 'the Opium Trade and the Opium Habit in the Far East', to be carried out by the United States, the United Kingdom, France, the Netherlands, Germany, China and Japan.[17] The purpose of this exercise would be to 'come to a decision as to whether the consequences of the opium trade and opium habit were not such that civilized Powers should do what they could to put a stop to them'.[18] Grey refused to answer until consulting with the India Office on the subject, but was privately open to the possibility of considering the American proposal, subject to it being 'clearly proved that the result would be to diminish the opium habit'.[19] If, on the other hand, this undertaking resulted in the Chinese simply growing more opium themselves following a decrease in Indian opium production, the British sacrifice would be futile and financially damaging. This tension between the possibility of reducing the 'opium habit' and the financial risk it entailed, as expressed by Grey, would exhibit itself again in future British involvement in international diplomacy regarding the 'opium question'. As Collins notes, other powers such as Great Britain were 'reluctant to attempt grand experiments with social engineering such as prohibition'.[20]

The aftermath of the ban in the Philippines going into effect was particularly rampant smuggling, definitively demonstrating that international cooperation from regional opium producers and exporters was crucial for prohibition to be implemented successfully. Prohibition advocates framed the need for international cooperation as the continuance of the nobility of American policy towards opium in Asia. Historians have noted the role of religious figures, particularly Brent, in the beginnings of international cooperation on drug policy. Jerry Mandel notes that 'early on, missionary anti-drug crusaders saw the Philippines as an opening'.[21] David Musto states more specifically that 'the Philippine opium problem made Brent an international leader in the anti-opium movement'.[22] David Courtwright concurs, noting Brent's overtures to Roosevelt on the 1909 convention.[23] Paul Gootenberg asserts that out of frustration with smuggling following the ban, Brent realised prohibition could not be enforced 'in a vacuum' and prevailed upon the White House to call for international action.[24] Brent wrote to President Theodore Roosevelt that

> from the earliest days of our diplomatic relations with the East the course of the United States of America has been so manifestly high in relation to the traffic in opium that it seems to me almost our duty … to promote some movement that would gather in its embrace representatives from all countries where the traffic in and use of opium is a matter of moment.[25]

The overtures of American diplomats eventually bore fruit, as an international commission to be held in Shanghai from 1 February to 26 February 1909 was arranged. In addition to the United States, delegations from Austria-Hungary, China, France, Germany, Great Britain, Italy, Japan, the Netherlands, Persia, Portugal, Russia and Siam also attended. Brent was joined in Shanghai by Dr Hamilton Wright, an equally fervent proponent of suppressing the opium trade and eradicating the 'opium habit', and Charles Tenney, the Chinese Secretary to the American Legation in Peking (Beijing).

The International Opium Commission of Shanghai and The Hague Convention, 1909–12

Despite the primary topic of discussion during the Commission being the opium trade in the Chinese context, the Philippines also featured significantly in the deliberations in Shanghai. The US delegation noted in detail the difficulties the authorities had encountered in attempting to enforce prohibition in the Philippines. The primary obstacle was, of course, smuggling. The predominant smuggling routes were from Hong Kong, Singapore and British North Borneo to various ports throughout the islands. From the American point of view, 'the ease with which opium is smuggled makes it impossible to cut off the supply without international cooperation'.[26] Suppressing the opium trade was thus neatly framed as an international responsibility necessitating action on the part of foreign governments, rather than its actual legal status of a quixotic crusade undertaken by the American government in the Philippines.

The 1909 Shanghai Commission resulted in a series of resolutions calling for gradual suppression of the opium trade. This effectively represented a compromise between the financial interests of producer states like Great Britain, France, the Netherlands and their empires and the demands of the United States and China for prohibition to be put into effect as soon as possible. The most significant resolution, particularly for the purposes of the American government in the Philippines, was the agreement that the export of narcotics should be limited to countries that legally allowed their consumption. The Americans reasoned that if this could be enforced, then the shipments of narcotics from Hong Kong, the Straits Settlements in Malaya and Borneo that were subsequently smuggled into the Philippines would be depleted, lightening the burden of the customs officials. This resolution also demonstrated the beginning of the longstanding American ideological commitment to controlling supply as a means of suppressing the trade.

However, these resolutions were not legally binding, limiting their practical impact in preventing illicit trafficking. The prevalence of smuggling was soon reported in international media. The *Barrier Miner* in New South Wales, Australia, quoted a customs official in the southern Philippines, identified only as J. Evans, as stating:

> We have to cover the territory from Cebu to Borneo … Sandakan is the headquarters of the trade but Hong Kong sends out a great deal of contraband opium … In Cebu and Manila the work of the revenue officers is made up a great deal of breaking into Chinese establishments, of smashing down barricaded doors. We have had many fights. The natives baulk the work in every possible way, and it is far from pleasant.[27]

The ongoing difficulties with smuggling seemingly vindicated the US delegation to Shanghai's previous insistence that only assistance from other countries could effectively reduce the clandestine trade in opium. However, given the nature of the event as an International Commission rather than convention or conference, the agreement reached was not binding for the participants. Hamilton Wright's report on the proceedings of the Shanghai Commission was delivered to the US Senate Committee on Foreign Relations in February 1910. By this time, plans had already been drawn up for another session of international diplomacy regarding the opium trade. Wright stated that

> in consideration of its international relations and duties this Government is called upon to proceed with the work which it has initiated, and to support and pursue the project of a conference which shall effectuate as fully as possible by international agreement the recommendations of the Shanghai commission. The interests of the Government of the United States in and its obligations to the Philippine Islands and their inhabitants forcibly emphasize this duty.[28]

Moreover, 'as respects both the United States and the Philippine Islands it is most important to obtain, if possible, an international agreement preventing or restricting the shipment of opium from ports of export to countries prohibiting its importation'.[29]

Brent personally took an active role in lobbying for this agreement and used his connections in Great Britain to secure a meeting in July 1910 with Prime Minister Herbert Asquith and other officials. The *New York Times* described the British as 'not unwilling to go into another conference'.[30] However, 'the Indian Government for economic reasons is not prepared to go as far as the reformers desire in the matter of increasing the reduction of the production of opium'.[31] Despite the British reluctance to forgo a major source of colonial revenue, American efforts were successful enough that by January 1911, congressional hearings were held on the subject of allocating funding for US participation in the next round of international diplomacy.[32]

Finally, the *New York Times* reported in December of 1911 from The Hague that 'twelve nations will be represented at the International Opium Conference, which meets here tomorrow'.[33] The second round of international diplomacy on drug policy would take the form of a Convention, signifying a binding agreement for the signatories. Despite agreement from the other nations to participate, the timing of the Convention – over two years after invitations had been sent out to the countries that had participated in the first Commission in Shanghai – seemed to demonstrate to the US delegation the lack of enthusiasm on the part of many of the other nations in attendance, most notably Great Britain. Sir Edward Grey, in his capacity as the British Foreign Secretary, had despite Brent's best efforts 'advocated a preliminary commission of experts to inquire into the facts before delegates with full powers were appointed to an International Commission'.[34] The Americans viewed this as a delaying tactic by the British and believed subsequent British 'discussion on the necessity of a thorough consideration of the use of morphine and cocaine' during the Convention to be an attempt to divert attention from the trade in opium.[35] By the second decade of the twentieth century, neither of these substances were unknown in the Philippines, given the proximity to manufacturing sites in the Dutch East Indies.[36] Nonetheless, the US focus during the proceedings remained predominantly on opium.

Similarly to the 1909 Commission, the Philippines featured prominently in the US argument for the essential role of international cooperation in suppressing the opium trade. Brent once again presided, and submitted another report, nearly identical to that of 1909, on the state of the enforcement of the opiates ban in the Philippines. Manila, Cebu and the southern Philippines in particular continued to vex American opponents of the opium trade. Brent noted the lacklustre state of affairs regarding attempts within the Philippines to combat smuggling, stating that

> neither sufficient money nor men are provided for the vigorous enforcement of the law. The Filipino officials afford at best only passive aid. The customs officers and the internal revenue agents, who are Americans, are meeting the situation with moderate effectiveness and hopefulness.[37]

Consequently, Brent cited the previous commission's precedent, in that

> at Shanghai the difficulties of the Philippine government were urged upon the commission as a whole in favor of a resolution which called upon opium-producing countries to prevent at ports of departure the shipment of opium to countries which prohibit its entry.[38]

As a result, if narcotics smuggling were to be restrained, it 'should be conventionalized in the international conference that has been called by our Government to finally deal with the production and international traffic in opium and its products'.[39]

By the end of the deliberations in The Hague, the United States had managed to secure an agreement to this end. On 23 January 1912, the International Opium Convention was signed by delegates from China, France, Germany, Italy, Japan, the Netherlands, Persia, Portugal, Russia, Siam and Great Britain. The Convention not only restricted the exports of opium and other drugs to countries permitting their consumption, but also obligated the signatories to regulate domestic consumption within their territory and work towards restricting it to medicinal use. The Convention stated

> The contracting Powers shall use their best endeavours to control, or to cause to be controlled, all persons manufacturing, importing, selling, distributing, and exporting opium, morphine, cocaine, and their respective salts, as well as the buildings in which these persons carry on such an industry or trade.[40]

This agreement was the fruition of years of work by anti-opium activists. Despite being the first binding international agreement regarding drug control, the Hague Convention nonetheless ushered in a new era of international clashes over the nature and implementation of its provisions. As McAllister states, the agreement 'exemplified the emerging regime's possibilities and limitations'.[41]

Despite the ongoing issue of smuggling and the Hague Convention earlier that year, the extent to which the United States was willing to enter into international agreements on drug trafficking was still limited. In October 1912, acting Secretary of State Huntington Wilson was questioned about a rumoured Dutch–US treaty regarding drug control between their respective Asian colonies. Wilson replied, 'I never heard of it ... I think that matter should be referred to the Opium Commission, in common with many other pipe dreams.' [42] The *New York Times* reported that the geographical proximity of the American and Dutch colonies could reasonably form the basis of a bilateral anti-smuggling agreement but noted 'there is nothing to show, however, that the United States Government regards any agreement of this character as necessary for the Philippines'.[43]

The Hague and Harrison's administration, 1912–21

The Philippines were in close proximity to British as well as Dutch colonies, and American colonial officials expressed much greater concern over the significance of drug trafficking from the colony of British North Borneo to the southern Philippine provinces of Mindanao and Sulu, which accounted for a large part of the illicit opium traffic in the Islands. The report of the provincial governor of Mindanao and Sulu for 1916 noted that the 'largest number of violations of the opium law were recorded in Sulu on account of the proximity thereof to Sandakan and North Borneo points'.[44] Philippines Governor-General Francis Harrison claimed that, in regard to preventing illicit trafficking, that the American colonial state 'would be fairly successful in that endeavor were it not for the British North Borneo Government Opium Monopoly in Sandakan'.[45] This served a dual purpose of maintaining the mythos of American colonial exceptionalism regarding their colonised population and drug regulations as well as conveniently providing a foreign scapegoat for the ongoing difficulties enforcing prohibition which the US colonial state in the Philippine experienced. Harrison's strategy of incriminating the British is consistent in a colonial context with what David Bewley-Taylor refers to as the American tendency to 'locate the source of domestic problems beyond the boundaries of American society'.[46]

British acceptance of the opium trade in North Borneo is understandable in light of revenue statistics from 1920. Of the colony's total revenue for that year, 70 per cent came from Customs and Excise, to which opium sales contributed a significant amount.[47] Harrison claimed that much of this found its way into American-controlled Mindanao and Sulu, and that during the preceding year 'about six million pesos' worth of opium, Sandakan price, was sold for smuggling into the Philippines'.[48] By 1920, Harrison asserted that 'in British North Borneo the opium trade has become a positive scandal ... two successive English [sic] chief justices of that colony were said to have resigned because of the duplicity with which the officials there were conducting the opium traffic'.[49]

Harrison complained to his superiors in Washington, asking them to 'invoke the good offices of the Government of Great Britain to the end that the Government of British North Borneo should show some respect for our laws and some consideration for our institutions and people'.[50] This resulted in the US ambassador to Great Britain, John W. Davis, lodging a protest in Whitehall, to no avail. In fairness to Harrison, there was a precedent for acrimonious exchanges between the British and American colonial officials in the Philippines. His predecessor, W. Cameron Forbes, had privately complained in regards to a separate dispute that 'it would have taken a stick of dynamite to blast those foolish Britons into action'.[51]

The establishment of the League of Nations hindered the ability of the United States to act unilaterally regarding international action on drugs diplomacy in the manner they had previously enjoyed. When the overtures of Ambassador Davis failed to produce results, Harrison approached President Woodrow Wilson about organising another international convention on the opium trade but was told that this was now a 'matter reserved for the League of Nations'.[52] Given Wilson's support for the League of Nations, he was presumably hesitant to take action that might be seen to undermine the League's prerogative on issues of narcotics trafficking.[53] This had the effect of safeguarding the League's standing but also blunting Harrison's attempts to pressure British North Borneo into cooperation regarding smuggling between their territory and the Philippines. The early 1920s thus marked a shift from international drug diplomacy largely spearheaded by an American agenda rooted in colonial policy to a more genuinely multilateral approach through the League of Nations.

Despite corruption plaguing drug control efforts in the Philippines, the earlier efforts of reformers like Hamilton Wright in Shanghai to tackle smuggling had still focused primarily on supply control, and this policy continued to dominate American involvement in drug control deliberations. After representing the United States at Shanghai and The Hague, Wright had died relatively young in 1917. His widow, Elizabeth Washburn Wright, was determined to carry on his legacy in American international diplomacy. She served on the League Advisory Committee on the Traffic in Opium and other Dangerous Drugs in the capacity of an assessor, beginning in 1920. She was at odds almost immediately with her contemporaries, with one official in the British Foreign Office describing her as 'incompetent, prejudiced, ignorant, and so constituted temperamentally as to afford a ready means of mischief-making'.[54] While sexism undoubtedly constituted part of this gendered assessment, the conflict was more deeply rooted in conflicting colonial agendas, in a nearly identical fashion to Francis Harrison's ongoing disputes with the Government of British North Borneo.

March 1921 marked Harrison's departure from office in the Philippines, as his tenure ended with the inauguration of Republican President Warren Harding. Despite Harrison's removal from power, the American belief in the supply control model was unchanged. This ideological commitment was highlighted by ongoing US actions regarding the Philippines at the beginning of the new decade. At a meeting of the Advisory Committee on the Traffic in Opium and other Dangerous Drugs of the League of Nations in May 1921, Elizabeth Wright featured once more in an advisory capacity as a delegate of the United States. She addressed the committee as follows:

> Since the war, opium abuses [in the Philippines] had generally increased and the situation was further aggravated by the enormous increase in the use of morphine ... If any effective work was to be done, the cultivation of the poppy must be restricted ... It was extremely regrettable that the Committee had not approached the question on its essential and vital side. If the League of Nations could not succeed in the task it had undertaken, a Conference would have to meet.[55]

This statement was not made to universal acclaim, as implied by Harrison's earlier description of the overtures of Ambassador Davis in London. The Committee's deliberations featured a letter from the International Anti-Opium Association petitioning for the abolition of the opium monopolies in Hong Kong and Singapore, which was of particular interest to the United States given the frequent illicit trafficking from Hong Kong and the Straits Settlements to the Philippines.[56] Wright's declaration that 'the United States, though not a Member of the League, were watching with the keenest interest for some definite and effective action ... when the results of the work of the Committee were known there would be keen disappointment in America, where radical measures were expected' failed to spur the other Committee members forward.[57] In response to the letter from the International Anti-Opium Association, Malcolm Delevingne merely proposed the Committee 'refer the letter to the British Government and ask for its observations'.[58]

Undaunted, Elizabeth Wright stated to the media that 'the opium traffic of the East must be eventually abandoned, that the tax based on the monopoly is a mode of taxation that is unethical'. In order to substantiate this argument, she 'pointed to the example of the United States, which gave up the opium monopoly on taking over the Philippines'.[59] She subsequently published a lengthy editorial in the *New York Times* in July entitled 'Opium Evil Up to League: Challenge as to Whether Real Control is to be Exercised Follows Geneva Report'.[60] Wright cited the precedent of prohibition in the

Philippines again, this time as the reason that the United States had initially been 'drawn irresistibly into the maelstrom of discussion that for a hundred-odd years had agitated the Far East'.[61] As the title implies, Wright criticised the League of Nations for failing to take more drastic measures regarding supply control and claimed 'as for the recent meeting of the Opium Committee held in Geneva, there is a feeling that the League failed to take advantage of the great opportunity presented'.[62] The editorial did not mention Delevingne by name but did attribute the League's supposed failure to 'a determined effort on the part of the Committee to restriction the [Hague] convention to a most rigid interpretation'.[63] Wright's conclusion exemplified the American ideological commitment to supply control in that 'there is but one solution to the opium problem – the suppression of the cultivation of the poppy save for medicinal purposes'.[64]

Elizabeth Wright's belief in supply control and call for further international action were shared by many of her American contemporaries in the post-war era. In the years following the Treaty of Versailles, the sense of a new era brought about through the cataclysm of the First World War inspired a number of reformers to push for additional measures on the part of the international community regarding the opium trade, including Thomas Pelletier. Pelletier was then the District Attorney for Suffolk County, Massachusetts, and an advocate for suppression of narcotics trafficking. Pelletier stated in his privately published work *Opium: A World Menace* in 1921 that the International Opium Commission of Shanghai in 1909

> was called primarily because of the interest of the United States in the Philippines; now, we are even more justified, in behalf [sic] of *humanity* [emphasis in original], to demand a conference on the present opium situation ... in the changed world of to-day, newborn amid the blood and horror of a war ... so great a moral appeal cannot fail to arouse a spirit of national right thinking on this question.[65]

Moreover, the narrative previously constructed by US officials in the Philippines regarding colonial drugs policy and American exceptionalism clearly took hold in public discourse within the metropole during the post-war era, as evidenced further by the writings of Ellen N. LaMotte. The role of public opinion itself had by then become a significant internationalist idea, as Robert Laker's essay in this volume establishes. LaMotte was a nurse, suffragette and author, who claimed (incorrectly) in *The Opium Monopoly* that upon conquering the Philippines 'our first act was to eliminate the opium traffic, which had been established there by our predecessors ... but we immediately set about to abolish it'.[66] LaMotte claimed the decision of the United States to forgo opium revenues was the primary evidence of 'enlightened' rule, as 'we might have cut in half the cost of our Philippine budget had we followed the example set by other nations ... But we refrained from treating our Filipinos in this manner.'[67] LaMotte argued this was particularly noteworthy given that 'we have seen that certain British colonies, Hongkong and the Straits Settlements, for example, derive from one-third to one-half of their upkeep expenses from this traffic', without specifying what 'upkeep' or other uses of these funds entailed.[68] Aside from what LaMotte viewed as the moral failing inherent in these operations, legal opium sales in Hong Kong and the Straits Settlements posed a practical difficulty to the Philippines, as a report in 1921 from the American Consul in Amoy (Xiamen) indicated. The Consul's report noted that 'the great centers for distribution are Singapore and Hongkong ... Manila also offers a large field for opium'.[69] Moreover, 'in respect to the Philippines, it is stated that as much as 85 pesos ($42.40) or thereabouts are readily paid to anyone who will place a 5-tael tin of opium in Manila'.[70] This partially ad hoc system of trafficking made it difficult to track down distributors, and the 'profit is so extraordinarily large that those who traffic in this product can well afford to pay the amount'.[71]

The US and the League of Nations Advisory Committee on the Traffic in Opium, 1922–24

Despite the myriad of complaints regarding the opium traffic from various American observers, official reports from the United States were in short supply. The minutes from the League of Nations Committee on the Traffic in Opium meeting in April 1922 pointedly noted 'nor has any information been received from the United States of America, which is one of the largest importing and manufacturing countries. A general review of the traffic in opium and other dangerous drugs is therefore not yet possible.'[72] The lack of information from the United States was re-emphasised in another section of the minutes, which stated even more markedly that

> the statistical information, which ... has not yet been furnished, would be of the greatest value, and ... the Committee venture to express the hope that means may be found before long by which the co-operation of the United States in the work of giving full effect to the provisions of the Opium Convention of 1912, of which they took so large a part, may be secured. The Committee feel that they cannot emphasize too strongly that it is only by the fullest international co-operation that a traffic which is world-wide in its ramifications can be effectively controlled.[73]

Elizabeth Wright claimed that this was simply 'owing to a misunderstanding' and that further information would follow forthwith.[74] In the meantime, she lectured the Committee that 'the way to rid the world of the curse of opium – is to reduce its cultivation'.[75]

The League of Nations Advisory Committee noted once more in the minutes of the January 1923 meeting that they had not received any reports from the United States with regards to the drug control situation outside the metropole; 'no statistics nor information on conditions in any colony, possession or leased territory are given'.[76] The League reiterated that information 'on the methods adopted for the effective suppression of the opium traffic in the Philippine Islands would have been valuable'.[77] Despite the lack of reports on the subject, representatives of the United States, particularly Elizabeth Wright, continually referred to the Philippines as evidence of the merits of supply control. Wright clashed once more with other members of the Advisory Committee on the issue of the gradual limitation of opium production, of which producer states were naturally more in favor. Wright insisted that 'public opinion did not demand the limitation or the regulation of the opium evil but its suppression'.[78] More specifically, 'public opinion in the United States was demanding the restriction of cultivation to medicinal needs'.[79] This was substantiated by the claim that 'America had so recognized that the use of opium was an evil for which no financial gain could compensate that she had brought the opium trade in the Philippines to a termination at the end of five years, without financial disaster to that country.'[80] This exchange alludes to the tension between American nationalist insistence on its exceptionalism regarding colonial drug policy and its dependency regarding enforcement on internationalist efforts to cooperate on drug control.

Further information received by the League on the subject later that year came not from any official reports from the US government but instead from Brent appearing before the League Advisory Committee to testify in person in May 1923. This was obviously not a report attempting impartiality, however, but an impassioned personal defence of prohibition. Brent made the case to the League Advisory Committee on the Traffic in Opium that the surrounding colonies in southeast Asia should adopt the measures against the opium trade that the United States had taken previously in the Philippines. To substantiate this, Brent provided statistics demonstrating that opium imports had fallen from 224,115 pounds in 1900 to 235 pounds in 1918 and 77 pounds in 1921. The duties paid on these imports had correspondingly decreased from $81.5 million in 1900 to approximately $4,000 in 1921.[81] There was obviously a glaring flaw to this argument, namely, that these statistics only showed the opium legally imported into the Philippines for medicinal purposes and thus failed to take into account the amount of opium and other drugs smuggled in during the same timespan. The same League Committee meeting noted that opium shipped to British North Borneo from India 'was an important question to the United States, as it was [illegally] re-exported to the Philippines'.[82] Moreover, the Philippine Bureau of Health report for 1923 reported treating nearly 200 individuals in the Bilibid Prison Hospital for 'opium indulgence'.[83] This was not an appreciable decrease from previous years, indicating rates of recidivism for drug-related offences remained high.

In addition to Brent's statistical information on the Philippines, he also came armed with a unanimous resolution passed by the US Congress earlier in March of 1923. *The Traffic in Habit-Forming Narcotic Drugs: Statement of the Attitude of the Government of the United States with Documents Relating Thereto* essentially reiterated the commitment of the United States to supply control as the best method of implementing the Hague Convention protocols. It also related to another ongoing controversy regarding the definition of 'legitimacy' in the use of opiates. These were summarised as follows:

1. If the purpose of The Hague Opium Convention is to be achieved according to its spirit and true intent, it must be recognised that the use of opium products for other than medical and scientific purposes is an abuse and not legitimate.
2. In order to prevent the abuse of these products it is necessary to control the production of raw opium in such a manner that there will be no surplus available for non-medicinal and non-scientific purposes.[84]

The Traffic in Habit-Forming Narcotics Drugs frequently referred to the Philippines in order to substantiate this argument. In particular, the

> United States of America, in dealing with the traffic in habit-forming narcotic drugs within its own territory and possessions, notably in the Philippine Islands … has always been committed, without regard to revenue, to a program for the complete suppression and prohibition of the production of and traffic in them, except for strictly medicinal and scientific purposes.[85]

The Geneva Convention, 1924–25

However, by the mid-1920s, The Hague Convention agreement had failed to meaningfully reduce the available opium supply and curb illicit trafficking. As a result, further international diplomacy on drugs regulations was deemed necessary. The 1924 congressional hearings on funding for the US delegation to Geneva revealed the ongoing significance of the Philippines to the vision of the United States for an international drugs regulatory regime, and, moreover, how the United States viewed its own role in its development. Congressional proceedings reiterated that continued international cooperation was necessary if prohibition was to be effective. In short, 'unless the nations stand together it is virtually impossible for any people to be free from the opium addiction'.[86] The overall significance of the Philippines to the US drug-control efforts was summarised as follows: 'There can be no doubt that the wider interest of the United States in the international opium problem was one of the results of the occupation of the Philippines.'[87]

Despite these sentiments in favour of international cooperation, American involvement in the Geneva Convention proceedings in 1924 and 1925 was not characterised by a willingness to compromise. The ideological commitment of the United States to immediate supply control within ten years put them at odds with producer states who favoured an approach of gradual limitation. European imperial producer states sought to broaden the focus of the convention from opium to pharmaceuticals such as cocaine and morphine. Illicit trafficking of these substances was also a matter of concern for customs officials in the Philippines. Nonetheless, the US delegation eventually walked out. The *New York Times* claimed that 'the fumes of opium had permeated so deeply into the physiological habits of the East, and the business and political habits of European Colonial offices, that the program offered by the United States was regarded as impossibly idealistic'.[88]

More clashes on an international stage followed after the submission of the 1926 report from the United States to the League of Nations Advisory Committee on the Traffic in Opium. This was met with opposition from other Committee members, in particular the report's allegation that 'the situation in the Philippine Islands, even under the most pessimistic view, will compare most favorably with a like situation in any other island possession in Southern or South-Eastern Asia'.[89] The representative from the Netherlands, W. G. van Wettum, stated bluntly in April 1928 that he 'did not understand on what basis this opinion had been founded'.[90] John Caldwell, the US representative at the Committee meeting, conceded that

> the aim of the passage was not ... to express, after thorough examination, a definite opinion regarding the situation in the Philippine Islands as compared with that in other islands possessions, such as the Netherlands Indies, but to state that, from the information available, the position in the Philippine Islands was believed not to be worse than elsewhere.[91]

The United States also clashed with the British on the issue of prohibition, as Malcolm Delevingne cited the numerous statements regarding opium smuggling in the Philippines in the abovementioned 1926 report by the

United States. Delevingne noted in particular the report's admission that 'it cannot be denied that smugglers succeed in bringing into the Philippine Islands large quantities of opium and morphine' and that 'these difficulties were exactly the same as those encountered by the British Government'.[92] Delevingne claimed that this 'justified the view expressed in 1925 that prohibition was only one way of dealing with the problem and that it was not a decisive way'.[93] Moreover, he admonished that it 'was not and could not, under present conditions, be equivalent to suppression'.[94]

The US and British representatives on the Committee did eventually come to agree on one issue, however, regarding smuggling between British North Borneo and the Philippines. By the late 1920s, both were in agreement that the issue had been largely resolved, regardless of conflicting reports from external observers.[95] At the April 1928 meeting of the League Advisory Committee, Malcolm Delevingne raised the question of British North Borneo's inclusion in the most recent report on drug control in the Philippines. Delevingne asserted that 'during the last few years the authorities of British North Borneo had exercised the greatest vigilance and the Government of the United States on enquiry had found that no opium coming from British North Borneo had been seized for at least two years'.[96] John Caldwell replied that

> there had been correspondence with the British Government and the Governor-General of the Philippine Islands and the latter had stated that, during the last two years, there had been no evidence of smuggling into the Philippine Islands from British North Borneo ... the report of the Government of the United States had been completed at too early a date to show the inclusion of this statement.

Delevingne was recorded as thanking Caldwell for this explanation, ending, at least on the surface, a long-running conflict between the colonial powers.[97]

While this one particular regional conflict was considered to have been resolved, the League continued to further attempt to determine the extent of opium smoking in southern and eastern Asia, including in the Philippines.[98] In 1930, the League's Commission of Inquiry on Opium Smoking in the Far East visited a number of countries in Asia, as well as the Philippines. The report on their findings further belied the insistence of the colonial authorities in the Philippines that narcotics smuggling was now inconsequential. These findings were reiterated by Elizabeth Wright, who visited the Philippines in spring 1931 and wrote a long report on the subject of drug control to Federal Bureau of Narcotics chief Harry Anslinger in DC. Wright stated that 'the use of smoking opium has not been suppressed in the Philippine Islands ... a great deal of opium enters the Islands primarily through the ports of Manila and Cebu ... and through Jolo, Bongao and other islands to the South'. She attributed this state of affairs to 'a definite and well-organized ring with limitless funds' operating between mainland China and the Chinese diaspora in the Philippines as well as 'many individual and petty smugglers'.[99] Wright also claimed, 'I believe my visit wakened a new interest in the opium question and a realization of how important is the part played by the Philippines in the solution of the problem.'[100]

The Bangkok and Geneva Conventions, 1931

Following the findings of the League's Commission of Inquiry on Opium Smoking in the Far East, the Bangkok Convention of 1931 was called to deal with the ongoing issue of illicit traffic and consumption of opium in Asia. However, the United States was represented merely by an observer, John Caldwell from the League Advisory Committee, rather than a plenipotentiary delegation. Similarly to previous international conferences and his statements at League meetings, Caldwell cited US colonial drug policy in the Philippines as evidence of the merits of prohibition. Caldwell noted that the United States had considered an opium monopoly system and referred to Taft's original proposal in 1904. He nonetheless hastened to emphasise that 'this proposal insofar as it related to government monopoly was rejected and the principle of absolute interdiction of the traffic was adopted by the Congress of the United States'.[101] Despite the evidence to the contrary, Caldwell also claimed that the 'result of enforcement of complete prohibition of the use of opium for purposes other than medicinal is considered to have proved satisfactory in the Philippine Islands'.[102] The Bangkok Convention was largely considered ineffectual by observers and the *New York Times* reported that no consensus was reached.[103] Despite the presence of the United States at the Conference, the State Department later noted 'it will be recalled that the Government of the United States was represented at the Bangkok Conference by an observer only, is not a party to the agreement signed at that Conference, and did not sign the Final Act of the Conference'.[104]

Elizabeth Wright's tenuous claims of 'a new interest in the opium question and a realization of how important is the part played by the Philippines in the solution of the problem' were contradicted further by the fact the United States did send a plenipotentiary delegation to another convention on drug control that year.[105] At the 1931 Convention for Limiting the Manufacture and Regulating the Distribution of Narcotics in Geneva, John Caldwell featured once more as a representative of the United States. In this instance, he was joined in Geneva by California Senator Sanborn Young,

Assistant Surgeon-General Dr Walter Lewis Treadway and, most importantly, Commissioner of Narcotics Harry J. Anslinger. In addition to sending plenipotentiary rather than observational representatives to this round of international drugs diplomacy, the United States also actually signed the agreement of the Convention. This came with several caveats, however. The United States reserved the right to enforce 'measures stricter than the provisions of the Convention'.[106] The United States in signing did not implicitly acknowledge the Governments also signing the Convention as the legitimate governing bodies of their respective polities if they had not already recognised them as such, or were obligated in any way to a country's unrecognised government as a result of the Convention's agreement. The United States also took issue with administrative procedures of the League of Nations, stating that the 'Government ... finds it impracticable to undertake to send statistics of import and export to the Permanent Central Opium Board short of sixty days after the close of the three months' period to which such statistics refer'.[107]

Despite the presence of the US delegation and the rather extensive list of caveats, the Philippines were not represented or mentioned in any capacity in the agreement. This was a telling omission regarding the shift in American priorities regarding drug control. Instead of the prominence of the Philippines in earlier conventions on drug regulations, American concerns were focused on the metropole and drug control efforts there. Anslinger, rather than Brent, was directing American regulatory negotiations now and colonial prohibition was an afterthought rather than a driver of diplomatic priorities. The lack of reference to the Philippines was nonetheless decidedly not because enforcing prohibition there had ceased to be a challenge for the colonial government, or due to a lack of an illicit supply of manufactured narcotics in the archipelago. The smuggling, sale and consumption of illicit manufactured drugs such as cocaine and morphine continued to vex colonial authorities.[108] Although the Philippines would not be fully autonomous until 1935 and independent until 1946, the United States was already preparing to divest itself of its perceived colonial burden and the responsibility of enforcing prohibition there.

Conclusion

American attempts to confine opium and manufactured pharmaceuticals to medicinal and scientific use in their new colony developed into a global restrictive approach to the regulation of psychoactive substances, establishing an international drugs regulatory regime based on controlling supply. This was achieved through multilateral summits, during which the United States sought to convince foreign producer and manufacturing states of the need to restrict exports of drugs to countries permitting their entry and to work towards restricting their use to medical purposes. This led to the agreements of the 1909 Shanghai Commission, the 1912 Hague Convention, the 1924–25 Geneva Convention and the 1931 Bangkok and Geneva Conferences. Despite the importance of the Philippines to the United States in earlier multilateral agreements, by the early 1930s American drug diplomacy was centred on the metropole, in large part due to the difficulty of enforcing prohibition in the colonial context. But the precedent remained. The clearest marker of the colonial legacy of these multilateral summits for drug control was the delegation from the independent Republic of the Philippines at the Single Convention on Narcotic Drugs in 1961 in New York City. Eduardo Quintero testified the country's primary issue in confronting criminalised narcotics was 'the illicit traffic in opium, which was smuggled in from the mainland of China via Hong Kong and North Borneo'.[109] His colleague, Mrs S. D. Campomanes, the head of the Narcotic Drugs Division of the Bureau of Internal Revenue, claimed that 'excessive supply was one of the principal causes of illicit drug traffic'.[110] E. D. Espinosa – Chief Drug Inspector for the Bureau of Health – asserted that despite the 'illicit traffic', the prevalence of drug addiction in his native country was not unduly concerning. Espinosa also stated that the Philippine Government was nevertheless committed to furthering 'the interests of international co-operation' regarding drug control.[111] Similarly, the Philippines permanent representative to the UN and plenipotentiary delegate F. A. Delgado rather grandly declared that 'although his country did not produce or manufacture drugs, he would vote in favor of the Convention in the interests of all mankind'.[112] While these diplomatic exchanges took place nearly fifteen years after the official declaration of the independence of the Philippines from the United States, the enduring colonial legacy of prohibition is clear. The claims of the Philippine representatives that drug addiction posed little threat to the archipelago but that they were nonetheless prepared to forgo potential revenue given the importance of drug control worldwide echoed similar statements from former colonial officials. So, too, did the characterisation of illicit narcotics as an external threat from the surrounding nations rather than an internal problem, which made supply control imperative in order to stem the flow of illegal drugs from without the Philippines – the result of the profoundly transformational approach to drug regulation by the US colonial state and its usage of multilateralism.

Notes

1 Steffen Rimner, *Opium's Long Shadow: From Asian Revolt to Global Drug Control* (Cambridge, MA: Harvard University Press 2018) pp. 170, 176.

2 Anne Foster, 'Prohibition as Superiority: Policing Opium in South-East Asia, 1898-1925', *The International History Review* 22:2 (2000), 253-73.
3 Ibid., 272.
4 Anne Foster, 'Models for Governing: Opium and Colonial Policies in Southeast Asia, 1898-1910', in *The American Colonial State in the Philippines: Global Perspectives* (Durham, NC: Duke University Press, 2003), p. 94.
5 Alma Bamero, 'Opium: The Evolution of Policies, the Tolerance of the Vice, and the Proliferation of Contraband Trade in the Philippines, 1843-1908', *Social Science Diliman* 3:1-2 (2006), 49-83.
6 Jessica Kuperavage, 'Petitioning Against the "Opium Evil": Economic Policy as Humanitarian Intervention in Early Antidrug Rhetoric', *Southern Communication Journal* 79:5 (2014), 369-86.
7 John Collins, 'Imperial Drug Economies, Development, and the Search for Alternatives in Asia, from Colonialism to Decolonisation', in Julia Braxton, Mary Chinery-Hesse and Khalid Tinasti (eds), *Drug Policies and Development: Conflict and Coexistence, International Development Policy Series* (Leiden: Brill Nijhoff, 2020), p. 55.
8 Tim Madge, *White Mischief: A Cultural History of Cocaine* (London: Mainstream, 2001), p. 92; William McAllister, *Drug Diplomacy in the Twentieth Century* (London: Routledge, 2012), p. 27; Arnold H. Taylor, 'American Confrontation with Opium Traffic in the Philippines', *Pacific Historical Review* 36:3 (1967), 307-24.
9 David Musto, *The American Disease: Origins of Narcotic Control* (Oxford: Oxford University Press, 1973, 1987, 1999), p. 25; David Courtwright, *Dark Paradise: A History of Opiate Addiction in America* (Cambridge, MA: Harvard University Press, 2001), p. 79; Tim Madge, *White Mischief*, p. 98.
10 McAllister, *Drug Diplomacy*, p. 27.
11 Carl Trocki, *Opium, Empire, and the Global Political Economy: A Study of the Asian Opium Trade, 1750-1950* (London: Routledge, 1999), p. 155.
12 Philip F. Victoria, '"The Most Humane of Any That Could Be Adopted": The Philippine Opium Committee Report and the Imagining of the Opium Consumer's World in the Colonial Philippines, 1903-1905', in Portia L. Reyes (ed.), *Towards a Filipino History: A Festschrift for Zeus A. Salazar* (Quezon City: Bagong Kasaysayan, 2015), p. 90.
13 Foster, 'Prohibition as Superiority', 254.
14 For more background on the British empire and opium, see John F. Richards, 'Opium and the British Indian Empire: The Royal Commission of 1895', *Modern Asian Studies* 36:2 (2002), 375-420; and Virginia Berridge, *Opium and the People: Opiate Use and Drug Control Policy in Nineteenth and Early Twentieth Century England* (London: Free Association Books, 1999).
15 John Collins, 'Imperial Drug Economies, Development, and the Search for Alternatives in Asia, from Colonialism to Decolonisation', *International Development Policy* 12 (2020), 54.
16 'Correspondence respecting the Opium Question in China', No. 2, Sir Edward Grey to Sir Mortimer Durand, 17 October 1906, Foreign Office, FO 415:

Correspondence Respecting Opium, PRO., 6 vols (Wilmington: Scholarly Resources, 1974).
17 Foreign Office, United Kingdom, 'Correspondence respecting the Opium Question in China', No. 2, 17 October 1906.
18 Ibid.
19 Ibid.
20 Collins, 'Imperial Drug Economies', 54.
21 Jerry Mandel, 'Protestant Missionaries: Creators of the International War on Drugs', in Jefferson M. Fish (ed.), *Drugs and Society: US Public Policy* (Lanham, MD: Rowman & Littlefield Publishers, 2006), p. 24.
22 Musto, *American Disease*, p. 26.
23 Courtwright, *Dark Paradise*, p. 80.
24 Marcel de Kort, 'Doctors, Diplomats, and Businessmen: Conflicting Interests in the Netherlands and Dutch East Indies, 1860–1950', in Paul Gootenberg (ed.), *Cocaine: Global Histories* (London: Routledge, 1999), p. 132.
25 Courtwright, *Dark Paradise*, p. 202.
26 Library of Congress, Manuscript Division, Washington D.C., USA, Charles Henry Brent (CHB) Papers, Conferences on Opium, *Report of the International Opium Commission: Shanghai, China, February 1 to February 26, 1909*, Vol. I p. 26; Box 38, Folder 2.
27 *Barrier Miner*, New South Wales, Australia, 'Opium Smuggling in the Philippines: Traders Also Sell Rifles to Natives', 4 April 1910.
28 LOC CHB, *Opium Problem: Message from the President of the United States, Transmitting a Report from the Secretary of State on the International Opium Commission and on the Opium Problem as Seen Within the United States and its Possessions, Prepared by Mr. Hamilton Wright on Behalf of the American Delegates to the Said Commission, Held at Shanghai in February, 1909*, p. 4, Box 41, Folder 10.
29 Ibid.
30 *New York Times*, 'Move Against Opium Trade: Bishop Brent Presses on Britain Carrying Out of Shanghai Agreement', 9 July 1910.
31 Ibid.
32 LOC CHB, *Importation and Use of Opium: Hearings Before the Committee on Ways and Means of the House of Representatives, 61st Congress, 3rd Session on H.R. 25240, H.R. 25241, H.R. 25242, and H.R. 28971,* January 11, 1911 (Washington: Government Printing Office) p. 79, Box 41, Folder 12.
33 *New York Times*, 'Opium Conference To-day: Twelve Countries Represented in the Deliberations at The Hague', 1 December 1911.
34 Ibid.
35 Ibid.
36 See *The United States v. Louis T. Grant and William Kennedy* (29 December 1910) G.R. No. L-5786 (Supreme Court of the Philippines, 1910); *The United States v. Valeriano de los Reyes and Gabriela Esguerra* (16 November 1911) G.R. No. L-6800 (Supreme Court of the Philippines, 1911); *The United States v. Pow Sing et al.* (12 November 1912) G.R. No. L-7424 (Supreme Court of the Philippines, 1912).

37 LOC CHB papers, *Memoranda on the manufacture of and traffic in morphine and cocaine in the United States and the Philippine Islands, with statement as to opium, in continuation of Senate Document No. 377, 61st Congress, 2nd Session: Memorandum in amendment of statement on 'Opium Problem in the Philippine Islands', pages 26–29) Senate Document No. 377, 61st Congress, 2nd Session*, p. 13. Box 41, Folder 12.
38 Ibid.
39 Ibid.
40 *International Opium Convention Signed at The Hague January 23, 1912*, League of Nations Treaty Series, Vol. VIII.
41 McAllister, *Drug Diplomacy*, p. 39.
42 *New York Times*, 'Special to the New York Times', 23 October 1912.
43 Ibid.
44 *Report of the governor of Mindanao and Sulu* (Manila: Bureau of Printing, 1916).
45 Francis Harrison, *The Cornerstone of Philippine Independence: My Seven Years in the Philippines* (New York: The Century Company, 1922), p. 337.
46 David Bewley-Taylor, *The United States and International Drug Control, 1909–1997* (London: Continuum, 2001), p. 6.
47 Ellen N. LaMotte, *The Ethics of Opium* (New York: The Century Company, 1924).
48 Harrison, *Cornerstone*, p. 336.
49 Ibid., p. 333.
50 Ibid., p. 337.
51 Library of Congress, Manuscript Division, Washington D.C., USA; William Cameron Forbes Papers, Diaries, Set B, Vol. I, p. 184.
52 Harrison, *Cornerstone*, p. 337.
53 It is unclear from Harrison's discussion whether this exchange took place before or after the United States refused to join the League.
54 British National Archives, Kew, London, United Kingdom, 'Minute by Basil Cochrane Newton', 5 March 1925, Foreign Office [FO] 371/10966.
55 League of Nations Records, Category XI, *The Traffic in Opium and Other Dangerous Drugs*, Andersonian Library, University of Strathclyde, Glasgow, Scotland, C.77.M.39. 1921 [XI] pp. 22–3.
56 LN C21/68/105 [XI] p. 1.
57 LN [C.77.M.39. 1921 [XI] p. 22.
58 Ibid., p. 12.
59 *New York Times*, 'League Aid Asked to Curb Opium Evil: Restriction of Poppy Growing the Only Cure, Says Mrs. Hamilton Wright', 29 May 1921.
60 *New York Times*, 'Opium Evil Up to League: Challenge as to Whether Real Control is to Be Exercised Follows Geneva Report', 3 July 1921.
61 Ibid.
62 Ibid.
63 Ibid.
64 Ibid.
65 Thomas Pelletier, *Opium: The World Menace* (Massachusetts: self-published, 1921), p. 13.

66 Ellen N. LaMotte, *The Opium Monopoly* (New York: The MacMillan Company, 1920), p. 75.
67 Ibid., pp. 75–6.
68 Ibid., p. 75.
69 Chief, Division of Customs, to the Chief of the Bureau of the Insular Affairs, 6 August 1921, United States National Archives and Records Administration, College Park, Maryland, USA; Record Group 350, Records of the Bureau of Insular Affairs (BIA), Entry 5, Box 200, File 1023/236.
70 BIA, Entry 5, Box 200, File 1023/236.
71 Ibid.
72 LN A.15.1922 [XI] p. 2.
73 Ibid.
74 C.416.M.254.1922.XI.
75 Ibid.
76 LN C.52.M.20.1923.XI p. 7.
77 Ibid.
78 LN C.155.M.75.1923 p. 42.
79 Ibid.
80 Ibid.
81 *New York Times*, 'Geneva', 30 May 1923.
82 *New York Times*, 'Formosa the Centre of Opium Trade in East; League Notes Big American Exports', 29 May 1923.
83 *Report* [1923] Philippines Bureau of Health (Manila: Bureau of Printing), p. 19.
84 *The Traffic in Habit-Forming Narcotic Drugs: Statement of the Attitude of the Government of the United States with Documents Relating Thereto* (Division of Printing: Washington DC, 1923), p. iii.
85 *The Traffic in Habit-Forming Narcotic Drugs*, 1923, p. vii.
86 Hearings before the Committee on Foreign Affairs, House of Representatives, *The Traffic in Habit-Forming Narcotic Drugs* On H.J. Res 195, 1924, p. 103.
87 Ibid., p. 243.
88 *New York Times*, 15 February 1925.
89 *Minutes of the Eleventh Session, Advisory Committee on the Traffic in Opium and Other Dangerous Drugs, Held at Geneva from April 12th to 27th, 1928; Seventh Meeting April 17th, 1928*, p. 39, BIA, Entry 5, Box 202, File 1023/338.
90 Ibid, p. 41.
91 Ibid.
92 Ibid.
93 Ibid.
94 Ibid.
95 See the report by Herbert May, *Survey of Smoking Opium Conditions in the Far East* (New York: Foreign Policy Association, 1927).
96 *Minutes of the Eleventh Session, Advisory Committee on the Traffic in Opium and Other Dangerous Drugs, Held at Geneva from April 12th to 27th, 1928; Sixth Meeting April 16th, 1928*, p. 31, BIA, Entry 5, Box 202, File 1023/338.

97 Ibid.
98 *New York Times*, 'Bishop Brent', 28 March 1929.
99 Elizabeth Wright to Harry J. Anslinger, 8 May 1931, BIA, Entry 5, Box 205, File 1023/401.
100 Ibid.
101 'Statement by Mr. Caldwell, Observer of the Government of the United States of America, at the 3rd Meeting on November 11th, 1931', *Conference for the Suppression of Opium-Smoking Convened Under Article XII of the Geneva Opium Agreement, League of Nations, Bangkok, November 11th, 1931, Traffic in Opium and Other Dangerous Drugs*. BIA, Entry 5, Box 205, File 1023/415C(6).
102 'Statement by Mr. Caldwell', 1931, BIA, Entry 5, Box 205, File 1023/415C(6).
103 *New York Times*, 'Opium Conference Counted a Failure: Meeting at Bangkok Reached No Decision on Main Points, Geneva Hears', 20 December 1931.
104 'Statement by Mr. Caldwell', 1931, BIA, Entry 5, Box 205, File 1023/415C(6).
105 BIA, Entry 5, Box 205, File 1023/401.
106 *Convention for Limiting the Manufacture and Regulating the Distribution of Narcotic Drugs*, 13 July 1931, Geneva, League of Nations, C.69(a).M.35(a).1932.XI. p. 15.
107 Ibid.
108 *Traffic in Opium and Other Dangerous Drugs with Respect to the Philippine Islands for the Six Months' Period from July 1–December 31 1928 and for the Calendar Year 1929* (Division of Printing: Washington D.C., 1929); *Traffic in Opium and Other Dangerous Drugs with Respect to the Philippine Islands for the Calendar Year 1930* (Division of Printing: Washington DC, 1930).
109 *United Nations Conference for the Adoption of a Single Convention on Narcotic Drugs, New York, 24 January–25 March 1961, Official Records*, New York, United Nations, 1964 (Volume I; Volume II, UN E/CONF 34/24; E/CONF/34/24(1), Vol. I, p. 16.
110 *Single Convention on Narcotic Drugs, 1961*, Vol. I, pp. 56–7.
111 Ibid.
112 Ibid., p. 216.

7

In the eyes of the world: media oversight and diplomatic practices at the League of Nations Assembly

Robert Laker

Introduction

As the Third Assembly of the League of Nations drew to a close, so too did the diplomatic career of Winifred Coombe Tennant. As the first woman to represent the United Kingdom at the League, she had arrived in Geneva without diplomatic experience, excited to play her part in a great experiment in internationalism. Here her path would cross with both elder statesmen and young evangelists, as the foundations of the old international order collided with emerging ideas to create a unique moment in multilateralism. While being a newcomer in international circles at times proved at times to be a disadvantage, it also positioned her to observe with incisive clarity both the mechanisms of power which underpinned League diplomacy and the contradictions inherent to them. Writing in her diary at the end of the month, she reflected on these experiences: 'once I leave here the curtain will fall and I shall be reduced to the level of the ordinary newspaper reader – and how low that is I have only been able to judge as a result of the experience this month'.[1]

Coombe Tennant's insider account exposes disparities between the ideal and reality of public oversight of the League, inviting questions about the complicated nature of the relationship between the media and diplomats at the Assembly. Her experiences provide an insight into the role of the media in establishing 'open' diplomacy at the League and the changing diplomatic practices which instrumentalised this relationship. As Coombe Tennant would come to find, the Assembly brought to a confluence many of the forces which quietly governed multilateral diplomacy at the League, from imperial rivalries to new moral norms, optimistic idealism to entrenched great power politics. Her observations as a novice diplomat, thrust unprepared into a new world of subtle diplomatic conventions and strategies, serve to illuminate the role of the Assembly within both the League and the wider diplomatic system which emerged from the fires of the First World War.

At the time Coombe Tennant attended, the Third Assembly the League of Nations was still a relatively new innovation in state relations. Set up at the Paris Peace Conference in 1919 to facilitate international cooperation, the League was a multilateral organisation founded as a safeguard against another devastating global conflict. For decades it was defined by its failure to prevent this outcome, but more recently scholars have begun to re-examine the League in earnest, exploring its wider impact during the interwar years.[2] This wave of historiographical investigation has now advanced perceptions of the League beyond binary discussions of the success or failure of its institutions on paper, exploring instead the nuance involved in the daily functioning of League diplomacy. It has been shown that the media, for example, was integral to the League's approach to projects such as disarmament, as journalists were considered vital to the establishment of what Heidi Tworek has termed 'new discursive norms of peace'.[3] Historians such as Glenda Sluga, meanwhile, have argued that the League created opportunities for a range of previously excluded actors to participate in international affairs.[4] By showing how the League's headquarters in Geneva became a nexus of international encounters, with many charities, political groups and non-governmental organisations setting up a permanent presence in the city, scholars have tracked the emergence of the informal international system which developed in both geographical and ideological proximity to the League.[5]

These historical analyses have also examined the interplay of wider global forces such as nationalism at the League, placing it back within its broader context. Susan Pedersen, for example, has explored the intersection of internationalism and European empires in the 'mandates system', examining the League as an evolution in imperial governance which in varying ways both undermined and reinforced imperial authority.[6] This system charted a path to self-determination for many imperial possessions, acknowledging their right to (eventual) independence and autonomy. Yet it also served to reinforce the established hierarchical perceptions of race which had underpinned empire, categorising civilisational development through a Western lens and consequently denying colonies access to varying markers of interwar statehood.

At the heart of the League was the Assembly, a nominal parliament of the world which, alongside the Council and the Secretariat, was one of the three principal organs of the League of Nations. Designed as a conference of all the League's member states, the Assembly was arguably one of the most radical innovations of the Geneva system. Its very structure implied that nation-state status (rather than relative global or local power and influence) was the prerequisite for legitimate diplomatic opinion on any given issue. Therefore, while the Assembly's direct authority was limited, sharing with the League's

Council an official remit which was defined as 'any matter within the sphere of action of the League or affecting the peace of the world', the Assembly represented a brand new institution within international relations.[7] It convened once a year – usually in September – allowing each member state one equally weighted vote on each of the wide-ranging issues which might be brought before the League. As a result, while the Assembly's full sessions often concerned themselves with administrative duties relating to the League itself, they were important as a space for grievances to be publicly put before the international community.

A typical conference of the Assembly would unfold as follows: during its first week, the Assembly would concern itself with pressing administrative issues ranging from the annual election of its president to the admission of new member states. The second week of proceedings usually involved a formal review of the League's previous year of work, before the Assembly split off into public committees – designated the 'First Committee' and so on – which would debate and prepare legislation on six broadly defined areas.[8] As the conference drew near to its conclusion, elected rapporteurs would then formally present each committee's reports to the full Assembly to be voted upon, which, in almost all cases, led to the recommendations being passed and thus entered into official League policy. Many of these meetings – most notably the grand plenary sessions – were explicitly public, providing a focal point for observers of the Assembly to showcase the new approaches to diplomacy upon which the League was predicated.

Many international histories have tended to evaluate the Assembly on the basis of its inability to wield hard power, citing its constitutional deference to the Council as evidence for its supposed impotence. It is assumed that all real political manoeuvring at the League occurred in the Council, or else behind closed doors. Yet such accounts neglect to sufficiently factor the broader context of the Assembly's role within the Geneva system into their analysis. One such example is Mark Mazower, who argues that, as the Assembly lacked law-making capabilities, it was in reality simply a space for public deliberation, encouraging 'theatrics rather than serious policymaking'.[9] Zara Steiner, meanwhile, has characterised the Assembly as a public forum designed to mobilise world opinion 'rather than as the initiator of positive action'.[10] This chapter seeks to add nuance to these characterisations by exploring the relationship between the media and diplomatic practices within the Assembly, showing that theatrics and policymaking, or indeed public deliberation and positive action, could in fact be co-dependent processes within the Assembly's forums.

To achieve this, this chapter will make four connected claims about the relationship between media oversight of the Assembly and diplomacy at the League. Firstly, by exploring recent historiographical arguments about the importance of the media and public opinion within international history, it will be shown that public engagement was of pivotal importance to the ideological construction of the League. The First World War had brought the consequences of conflict to homes across Europe and the world, changing perceptions about the importance of the outcomes of diplomacy to regular citizens and broadening the expectations of public participation. These new expectations about the League's obligations to public opinion meant that mechanisms for transparency were built into its architecture, enshrining the importance of 'open diplomacy' in the organisation's work.

This chapter shall also demonstrate that the Assembly was one of the key channels through which the League sought to engage with international public opinion. Media oversight of the Assembly was deliberately cultivated by the League, which invested substantial resources into ensuring that its public forums would facilitate interactions between diplomats and public opinion. Media oversight transformed a full plenary conference of the Assembly into a highly visible global stage, from which displays of open diplomacy could demonstrate the League's successes to the world. In this way, the Assembly was a platform which provided not for true transparency but for projection, promoting monodirectional communication with a nebulously defined global public. Publicity could obscure as much as reveal, and so the Assembly helped legitimise the League as a whole by promoting its most ideologically palatable manifestation, while allowing older diplomatic processes to continue behind closed doors.

Out of this visibility new diplomatic practices were born, as diplomats and other actors began to instrumentalise the Assembly's visibility to exert influence and authority in new ways. Diplomats quickly became adept at practising what this chapter will term 'performative diplomacy' – the use of the Assembly's public sessions to act or re-enact privately made diplomatic agreements as live diplomatic debate. Though the public misrepresentation of private statecraft is not necessarily unique to the League or its chronological bounds, the interwar years nonetheless represent a unique ideological moment in which these practices could be reinvented to provide new opportunities. For as long as the League drew its power and legitimacy from public opinion, diplomats could leverage unique influence through public performance. This created intricate international practices which relied on both dinner-party discussions and public performance in equal measure.

Finally, taking these points together, it will also be argued that the Assembly's relationship with the media created a point of convergence between 'open' and secret diplomacy. The use of these two opposing, seemingly incompatible, diplomatic practices in complementary ways allowed skilful diplomats working in the Assembly to confer unparalleled legitimacy on bilateral (or even unilateral) initiatives by providing a vital demonstration of apparent openness. In this fleeting interwar context, when the ascendant power of public opinion reached its symbolic zenith, the Assembly provided a controlled environment in which these co-dependent practices could be deployed to great effect.

Public opinion, media and open diplomacy at the League

Underpinning this new approach to internationalism was the League's relationship with 'public opinion', a force which has only relatively recently been seriously interrogated in a diplomatic context by scholars of international history.[11] The influence of public opinion as an idea had been slowly infiltrating foreign policymaking since the mid nineteenth century, but it was not until the end of the First World War that the concept was brought to the forefront of international affairs.[12] It was popularly believed that secret alliances, decided by elites without the knowledge of their citizens, had been the cause of the conflict, and so visions of a post-war world which involved the public in international affairs quickly grew in popularity, particularly after their endorsement by President Woodrow Wilson in his famous Fourteen Points. As Stephen Wertheim has shown, Wilson's decision to adopt the concept of public opinion played a critical role in the early development of the League. It positioned it to ultimately become the linchpin of the League's Covenant and so tied the new organisation's legitimacy to its ability to differentiate itself from pre-war diplomatic practices.[13] The idea that public outcry could prevent governments from acting with bellicosity was therefore at the core of the League's ideological foundations, leading it to rely upon the force of public opinion as a key sanction for safeguarding peace.[14]

If the force of world opinion was to function as an effective counter to state warmongering, however, it was reasoned that public opinion needed to be sufficiently informed of diplomatic agreements. One of the essential purposes of diplomatic transparency, therefore, was to make diplomats theoretically accountable to the public by broadening participation in international affairs.[15] It is for this reason that, as Pedersen has argued, the League was 'founded on the principle of public openness', deriving much of its legitimacy from the power of assumed public consent.[16] This new 'open diplomacy' was deeply rooted in the founding mythology of the League, appealing to the desires of those who wished for diplomats to be accountable to the people they represented without actually 'democratising' international affairs. In other words, as Wertheim argues, the League's notional adherence to open diplomacy allowed internationalists to speak on behalf of public opinion without being bound by the constraints of public sentiment on any particular issue.[17] In this regard, the selective integration of the media into the Assembly's activities should be understood as an important demonstration of the League's claim to represent informed public consent.

To maintain this relationship with public opinion, the League dedicated much of its resources to publicising its activities. At the centre of these efforts was the League's Information Section. The Section was, as Emil Seidenfaden has argued, founded upon the principle that publicity was essential to legitimising diplomatic interaction.[18] Its duties were wide and varied, but can be roughly broken down into two broad areas: supporting journalists and educating the public. Examples of the latter included producing pamphlets and educational resources to be sold internationally, as well as developing home-grown media outlets for the League. In 1932, for example, the section launched the League's own radio station – *Radio Nations* – intended to provide a commentary on international and League affairs for the international public.[19] Much of the section's day-to-day work, however, revolved around supporting the journalists and established media professionals who flocked to Geneva from across the world. It was the administrative link between diplomats and the press, liaising with news agencies, providing accreditation for press correspondents and organising pigeonholes for journalists, which were kept updated with League publications and proceedings.[20] The section also sponsored multiple conferences of press experts, telegraph officials and journalists throughout this period, encouraging discussions which in many ways anticipated modern debates about media disinformation.[21] Their job was to be, as one observer put it, 'journalists among diplomats and diplomats among journalists'.[22]

Despite the League's emphasis on the importance of public opinion, exactly who or what this referred to was generally left ambiguous. Seidenfaden has shown that even the League's Information Section, which had been specifically created to manage public opinion, rarely chose to define its parameters, and that when definitions were advanced, they often proved fleeting or contradictory.[23] This did not mean that the potential influence offered by public opinion was not taken seriously in interwar Geneva, however.[24] In fact, it was the very intangibility of public opinion which allowed it to become such an important figurative concept. As Tomoko Akami has argued, the League treated public opinion less as a sum of prevailing national moods and more as the will of an actively cultivated yet ambiguously defined 'international society'.[25] This can be best understood as an example of what Daniel Hucker has termed 'residual public opinion' – a series of preconceptions and embedded assumptions about the commonalities and collective values shared by a particular group of people.[26] In the case of the League, it was assumed that international public opinion – conceived as it was as emerging from an international society – was inherently peace-loving and internationalist and that, provided it was educated and informed of the League's work, its support could be automatically assumed. As a result, the League's claims to represent public opinion bore little relation to any articulated political preferences, instead taking on a largely allegorical function grounded in a series of whiggish beliefs about modern democratic societies. For diplomats at the League, therefore, public opinion was primarily symbolic concept for which the presence of media at the League – as ambassadors of open diplomacy – was sufficient to presume public support.

This emphasis on the influence of public opinion meant that the involvement of the media was crucial to the League of Nations. The media allowed the League to enshrine 'open diplomacy' within its structure, a process which effected, as Tworek has argued, a 'revolutionary change' in the relationship between diplomats and the public.[27] For advocates of the League, the press was seen as not only a channel for relaying information to the public but as a critical instrument of moral disarmament.[28] Such was this belief that a committee dedicated to exploring the 'cooperation of the press in the organisation of peace' was constituted at the World Disarmament Conference in 1932. Discussing the issue, Lord Robert Cecil, rapporteur of the committee, publicly argued that without the media as a 'means of appealing to the public opinion of the world' the League would be, if not totally powerless, then certainly 'far less useful and effective than it was at present'.[29] The task of fostering cooperation between the journalists and the League was therefore 'a vital matter to the success of the League'.[30] In this way, engagement with the press was at the heart of the League's peacekeeping mission, conferring upon the League the mantle of transparency and allowing it to actively engage with the public.

Media oversight and the Assembly

While engagement with public opinion underpinned the League more widely, the Assembly was central to this relationship, acting as an amplifier of sanctioned information by virtue of its visibility. The importance of this function can be seen in the Assembly's physical layout, for though it was twice relocated to reflect changes in the League's capabilities and requirements, key features remained constant across each building which housed it. Looking at the Salle de la Réformation, for example, which hosted the Assembly between 1920 and 1932, a number of characteristic features can be observed. Plenary sessions were held in a room not dissimilar from a concert hall in architecture and layout: public galleries spanning three of the hall's four walls overlooked rows of benches which, arranged in alphabetical order, provided a seat for every country in the League. These benches looked towards a raised platform at the front of the room, upon which the President of the Assembly, an annually elected public figure, presided as Speaker. Behind the Speaker, their subordinates sat at tables along the back of the stage, transcribing and assisting. Rather than speaking from their benches, delegates would be invited by the President to address the Assembly from a podium in the centre of the stage – the focal point of the entire room – from which microphones would project their voice to the galleries and beyond. In this way, the Assembly's plenary sessions should be understood as a space designed more to facilitate a series of public addresses than live diplomatic negotiations.

Yet other delegates were not the only audience for these speeches, nor perhaps even the principal ones. Crowds of journalists, typically numbering between three and five hundred per major session, filled the galleries which overlooked proceedings on the Assembly floor.[31] These correspondents, sent to observe and report on the Assembly, represented newspapers from across the world, extending the body's reach even to non-member states like the United States of America. Furthermore, a number of tourists, inhabitants of Geneva and other interested members of the public were also allowed to observe the proceedings, providing a direct, if ultimately symbolic, demonstration of the Assembly's public accessibility. From 1925 onwards, the spectators in the galleries were also joined by listeners in homes across Europe, as the League began to experiment with live radio broadcasts of the Assembly's sessions.[32] In this way, media oversight provided a medium through which the public could be made passive participants in the Assembly – a supposedly inarguable demonstration of the 'open diplomacy' upon which the League's legitimacy was primarily built.

Such was the importance of media oversight to the Assembly, that the League provided dedicated facilities to support these reporters. In the Salle de Réformation, much space was devoted to providing services for correspondents covering the League, including the large press room.[33] Here journalists were provided with telephones, office space and telegraph facilities, as well as regularly maintained postal services.[34] Downstairs, teams of translators, stenographers and editors reproduced the Assembly's proceedings in real time, creating publications and resources to be widely disseminated to the press before the next meeting.[35] The League also employed a team of technicians and sound specialists, whose job was to monitor technical aspects of the Assembly, such as microphones and lighting, further optimising the experience for those in the galleries. These hidden aspects of the Assembly, to which significant resources were dedicated, constituted part of an attempt to facilitate the involvement of media correspondents, whose presence was as important to the success of this body as the diplomats themselves.

These arrangements were an integral part of the Assembly and, although the building in which it was housed changed during this period, the

Figure 7.1 Photograph of the Seventh Assembly in the Salle de la Réformation, 1926.

architecture of the rooms and the integration of the media remained constant throughout the lifespan of this institution. Such architectural designs were not merely coincidental but were in fact conscious design choices. A visitor to the Assembly Hall in the Palais des Nations (the room that had been purpose-built to house the Assembly) in 1936 would have found that it had incorporated many of the same features previously found in the Salle de Réformation. Unlike some conference rooms, this hall was not curved; instead, diplomatic benches were arranged in rows which faced towards a stage at the front of the room. Large balconies again dominated three of its four walls and provided seating from which journalists or other onlookers could observe proceedings. This was, furthermore, the first room in the world to be equipped for simultaneous translation, employing technology as a medium of amplification for its speakers. Like previous Assembly rooms, therefore, it was a room configured for monodirectional communication rather than active debate, positioning the stage as the focal point of a room which architecturally demarcated spaces for speakers and listeners.

The cumulative product of such arrangements, therefore, created a uniquely visible stage upon which nations and diplomats could interact with the international public. Speeches and debates in these arenas were not performed solely for the benefit of fellow diplomats but also for the often tightly packed galleries, through whom the words of delegates would disseminate across continents. Inside this room, displays of strength, conciliation or egalitarianism could be amplified to a global audience, providing a stage upon which diplomacy could be conducted in the eyes of the world. As Max Beer, a journalist at the 1932 Assembly, put it: 'they do not want lake or sky to look in on them; for their walls of stone or wood will in any case be more transparent than glass, and their horizon wider than that of the Geneva landscape'.[36] It was this visibility, facilitated by a carefully cultivated relationship with the media, which allowed the Assembly to be presented as an example of the League's transparency.

The Assembly's visibility achieved more than just a demonstration of openness, however, for it also provided an eye-catching focal point through which the League could project an idealised image of itself. This could be seen in the Assembly not only in the fulfilment of liberal promises for international inclusion, but also its informal designation by League officials and observers alike as a nominal 'Parliament of the World'.[37] Although the Assembly itself adopted a report at its very first conference that argued that it was 'impossible' to seriously consider itself a parliament in any legal or constitutional sense, the idea nonetheless proliferated that it was in some way a democratic institution.[38] Educational material produced by organisations such as the League of Nations Union often directly described the

Figure 7.2 Photograph of a delegate speaking at the First Assembly in the Salle de la Réformation, 1920.

Figure 7.3 Photograph of the Eighteenth Assembly in the Palais des Nations, 1937.

Assembly's relationship with the Council as analogous to that of a parliament and a government in national contexts.[39] The International Federation of League of Nation Societies, meanwhile, argued that delegates were not ambassadors of governments but of whole peoples, lobbying for national delegations to be politically diverse and demographically representative.[40] It was this focus on broad representation that contributed to the successful campaigns in Britain and the Scandinavian countries to include women in Assembly delegations. This served to reinforce the perception that the Assembly was in some undefined sense a democratic body, thereby making it more appealing to those who wanted public accountability in diplomacy. For as long as the Assembly was the most visible manifestation of the League, therefore, its mythologisation conferred legitimacy upon the entirety of the organisation's work.

The conscious use of media oversight of the Assembly to project a favourable public image is apparent in early discussions at the League. Internally circulated minutes show that, in 1921, senior officials believed that concentrating publicity efforts on the work of the Assembly, rather than the Council, would help produce a favourable international impression of the League. The American public in particular, one document contended, was naturally wary of the Council, and so focussing attention on its work was consequently proving counterproductive. It was reasoned that 'America is far more suspicious of the Council as an instrument of evil than of the Assembly', and that, as such, shifting publicity towards the Assembly might help bring the United States into the League.[41] To rectify this, the document proposed that journalists should have access not only to the Assembly's plenary session but also to its committee meetings, and that their presence in both these forums should be actively promoted in an attempt to direct attention away from other apparatuses of the League's machinery. Soon after the circulation of these proposals, which were personally reviewed by the League's Secretary-General, changes were implemented which allowed journalists to observe committees for the first time at the 1922 Assembly. As this example illustrates, media oversight of the Assembly was consciously used to project an idealised version of the League as a whole, aligning its public image with that of the Assembly, rather than the Council, in order to make it more palatable to both national and international public opinions.

The Assembly therefore served a legitimising function for the League of Nations. It provided an example of 'open diplomacy' in action, an arena in which the presence of hundreds of journalists appeared as self-evident proof of its public accessibility. In addition to this, the abundance of publicity which media oversight provided made the Assembly the most prominent and recognisable organ of the League, positioning it as a significant public relations machine for the organisation. Considering these together, it can be seen that media oversight transformed the Assembly into a globally visible stage upon which a carefully curated, idealised version of League diplomacy could be projected across the world. The Assembly's potential to amplify favourable narratives in this way was key to its function.

Instrumentalising media oversight

The ability to control media oversight was not exclusive to League officials, however, for this publicity could be used to amplify the voice of any actor operating in the Assembly. Such was the unparalleled platform which the Assembly was perceived to provide that, in 1936, it even witnessed a Czech journalist end their life in an attempt to even fleetingly command its attention. Štefan Lux, whose death at the Assembly made headlines around the world, had hoped that turning a gun on himself on this global stage would draw attention to the rise of Nazism in Germany, making tangible its deadly potential in an attempt to reframe public debate.[42] While the use of the Assembly's platform by non-state actors like this was certainly atypical, it nonetheless serves to emphasise the visibility which it provided to those able to access it and the extreme, in this case tragic, lengths which could be taken to achieve this access by those who did not. The Assembly was seen as a forum with a unique international reach which could allow even individuals to influence international affairs. For diplomats, the ability to selectively leverage public attention in this way as a tool in everyday international politics quickly came to shape diplomatic practices at the Assembly.

The importance of access to the Assembly in this context is further underscored by the inverse of this relationship, for any institution that provides an exclusive platform of power to some actors must, by its very nature, deny it to others. In this way, like many elements of the League, the Assembly also functioned as an instrument of imperial control. By providing the legitimacy of representation to countries such as Czechoslovakia, while simultaneously denying it to peoples such as Native Americans or 'mandates' such as Palestine and the Cameroons, the Assembly reinforced embedded racial and civilisational hierarchies which underpinned imperial hegemony and further delegitimised non-Western governmental practices. For those represented, the Assembly afforded emerging countries an otherwise unachievable diplomatic presence and yet, as it has been widely noted, this influence was largely contingent on their ability to conform to Western conceptions of modern statehood.[43] National groups which fell too far outside this definition were excluded from this forum of nations and were therefore denied a crucial path to legitimisation.

For those with direct access to this platform, however, its visibility provided a way of achieving international recognition for the issues, causes or nations which they represented. As the Assembly developed, it increasingly attracted political (and occasionally even religious) leaders, rather than career diplomats. For small or emerging states in particular, sending to the Assembly a representative whose name or title could command international attention became an established way of pursuing national foreign policy objectives.[44] Impassioned oratorical performances were often an effective strategy in the Assembly, for resulting media coverage could raise the public profile of a given cause or issue. To some degree, this tailoring of public performances was even encouraged by the League, for the Information Section published and delivered daily reviews of press opinions to the hotel rooms of Assembly delegates every evening.[45] These reports, which by 1928 contained extracts from over two hundred newspapers from across the world, were genuinely international (if unevenly so) and provided a summary of how the Assembly's proceedings were being reported worldwide. This allowed delegates to gauge the mood of their media observers and, if necessary, moderate their performances upon the global stage.[46]

The Assembly's work extended far beyond its plenary sessions and public committees, however, its debates percolating from these foundational forums down into a series of informal sub-committees, secret conferences and private parties at which international politics could be frankly conducted. In an excoriating first-hand account of the League's inner workings, Beer despaired that the need for conversation among diplomats seemed 'so insatiable that they call on each other between sessions at their hotels, lock themselves in their dining-rooms, have luncheons and dinners in groups, and arrange banquets and receptions in each other's honour', producing the effect of a 'second League Assembly'.[47] The distinction between these 'two Assemblies', however, was often hazy. In a month when delegates from many nations were often housed in the same hotel, public diplomacy frequently spilled over into social interaction, punctuating lunches and evening drinks, and dominating conversations during recreational weekend car rides or days out with old friends. It was this labyrinthine web of public and private encounters which, functioning as a single sprawling international entity, defined diplomacy at the Assembly.

It is well established that serious diplomatic negotiations rarely occurred within the public eye at the League – the informality of private conversations allowing delegates to speak frankly – yet this did not mean that public sessions were less important to the diplomatic process. This was observed at the time by Charles Howard-Ellis – author of the 'standard work' on the League of Nations during its existence and himself an accredited press correspondent at the Assembly.[48] In his 528-page analysis of the League, Howard-Ellis revealed that agreements reached in the Assembly's various forums were 'binding in, roughly, the same proportion as their publicity'.[49] This meant that delegates were required to operate in a variety of spaces in order to effectively discharge their responsibilities. The volume illustrated this process as follows:

> (1) private conversations between individual delegates over a cup of tea or more substantial fare are purely informal and preliminary, but may (2) pave the way for a secret conference between two delegations which will determine the attitude of their representatives at (3) a private sub-committee whose deliberations provide a basis for discussion at (4) the public full committee, whose conclusions are (5) almost invariably endorsed as a matter of course in the Assembly.[50]

In other words, even though the formality of public debate precluded true diplomatic discussion, there nonetheless existed at the Assembly a direct relationship between the openness of diplomacy and the legitimacy of its products. In this fissiparous network of discussions, blurred by private sub-committees and ad hoc press-conferences held by delegates in the streets of Geneva, it was the presence or absence of journalists which defined a conversation's character.[51] Diplomatic practices at the Assembly therefore relied upon both secret and open diplomacy to operate, evolving in a way which created a convergence of these supposedly antithetical approaches to international politics.

Though meetings of the full Assembly were indeed, as Beer observed, 'a vast revolving stage' designed to present proposals to the public, the illusion of open diplomacy still required that the discussions which preceded policy occurred in public.[52] In the full committee meetings dedicated to drafting proposals, diplomats therefore often engaged in what can be termed 'performative diplomacy' – the enactment or re-enactment of private debates for the benefit of the media with the explicit goal of entering diplomatic discussion or legislation into the public consciousness. Since publicity was so essential to entering legislative proposals into official League policy, previously resolved debates were often in a literal sense performed by delegates to their audience. In these clearly defined spaces which allowed media oversight, diplomats led observers through artificial points of contention, which would often be 'resolved' by adopting a pre-agreed policy presented as a compromise. This aspect of diplomatic practice, while not necessarily historically unique to the League, was encouraged by the Assembly's fluid structure and acute relationship with public opinion, allowing delegates to fulfil their obligation to open diplomacy while still keeping disagreements out of the public eye.

Spotlights and shadows

The impact of the integration of the media into the Assembly, and the way in which this enabled the above-outlined diplomatic practices, is exemplified by the League's contentious early attempts to tackle the international 'trafficking' of pornographic material. In 1922, it was proposed that the League should outlaw the production and distribution of 'obscene publications' – photographs, literature and other materials of a sexual nature – on a worldwide scale. As historians have extensively argued, moralist discourse 'dominated' international attempts to tackle social issues through the League, tying them to the civilisational discourse which underpinned the organisation.[53] As the League developed, its purpose evolved to become an organisation which would not only act to avert war but also to shape peace, blending with more deeply ingrained ideas about civilisational hierarchy and Western moral paternalism.[54] Involvement in social initiatives therefore became particularly contentious during this period, as they provided a way for the League, and the great powers which led it, to demonstrate leadership and enhance their international prestige. It was common, for example, for Britain and France to condemn one another's failings on what was known as 'white slave trafficking' and opium trafficking respectively during this time in an attempt to assert themselves as the principal champion of international law.[55]

The campaign against the traffic in obscene publications, like other international social initiatives taken up by the League, was right at the centre of these debates. These materials were seen, as the Third Assembly's report would later state, as a key source of moral contamination.[56] Understood as a product intended to 'gratify the passions of depraved persons', this material was viewed by many primarily as a phenomenon originating in colonial territories which spread through a network of international criminals to spread 'corruption' among young people in Western European societies.[57] It was also widely believed that this material was being distributed by the same international criminals responsible for trafficking women, children and drugs across continents.[58] Attempts to address the trade in obscene publications were therefore imbued with the urgency both of humanitarian crisis and imperial anxiety which set the stage for a diplomatic clash.

It is in this setting which a set of anti-trafficking proposals were put on the agenda for the Third Assembly by the British government, prompting a struggle with France for prestige during what was already a nadir in Anglo-French relations.[59] Bringing this proposed bill before the League was Winifred Coombe Tennant, who was tasked with piloting it from first reading to its eventual passing in a plenary session of the Assembly. Along the way, the legitimacy of the proposals would be fought at every step, as diplomats sought to disrupt a process of escalating publicity, outlined above by Howard-Ellis. As with other bills, the obscene publications proposals began its journey through the Assembly in public. It was placed on the agenda at the beginning of the conference and formally submitted to the fifth committee for discussion by Coombe Tennant, who was unanimously elected as the rapporteur on the issue. In this role, she took on the responsibility of shepherding the bill through the Assembly, navigating the complicated network of forums and invested parties before unveiling the report for scrutiny at a plenary session.[60] As a newcomer at the Assembly, Coombe Tennant began this process by receiving procedural advice from key figures at the League, such as Dame Rachel Crowdy, head of the League's Social Section, and Secretary-General Eric Drummond, as well as seasoned diplomats such as Arthur Balfour.[61] These individuals coached Coombe Tennant on her role as rapporteur, providing expert insight on the informal process which she would be required to navigate.

Having informally discussed the bill with such figures in a social setting, the next step of this process was to convene a secret, undocumented conference. Here Coombe Tennant brought to the table delegates from Britain, France and Greece, as well as Crowdy. The purpose of this meeting was to work out compromises which would make the proposals acceptable to all parties. For delegates supporting the bill, it was important for it to be introduced to the media without blemish or controversy, so addressing grievances in private helped to ensure that no serious objection would be raised in the committee hearing. As Coombe Tennant recorded in her diary, a private compromise was easily reached and the delegations 'thrashed everything out clearly. Questionnaire – Summary – Committee of Experts – Draft Convention – Protocol'.[62] This meeting took less than two hours – a testament to just how routine such conversations had become even in 1922 – and at this stage no objections were raised. After this, all parties were given an advanced copy of the agreement and allowed four days to examine it further and raise objections.[63]

When the Fifth Committee eventually turned its attentions to a public debate on obscene publications, therefore, Coombe Tennant was understandably confident. As instructed, she introduced the agreed proposals which, in the presence of attending journalists, were lauded by various committee members for their humanitarian contribution. When the turn came for the French delegation to speak, however, its representative (a politician and later prime minister, Paul Reynaud) blocked the proposal despite the informal private agreement, citing a constitutional technicality. Were the League to convene such a conference, Reynaud argued, it would set a precedent which would be at odds with the powers outlined by its architects in the Covenant.[64] The resolution, therefore, was to be sent to the First Committee for legal review before any further progress could be made. As a result, although all parties had publicly stated their support for the substance of the proposals, the bill had been indefinitely delayed by what Coombe Tennant considered to be French duplicity: 'such volte face I have never before beheld', she would later complain in her diary.[65]

Reynaud's change of heart is best understood in the context of the Assembly's relationship with public opinion – as the first of a number of attempts to use differing messaging in public and private spaces to influence the outcome of these negotiations. As outlined above, controlled public interaction was a vital part of the diplomatic process at the Assembly, because open diplomacy, represented by the presence of media observers, was critical to the legitimisation of diplomacy. This was after all the reason why Coombe Tennant, supported by veteran diplomats, had invested such time into bringing the French delegates on board before the discussion phase had even officially begun. By waiting to raise these objections in a public committee meeting, therefore, the French delegation disrupted the diplomatic process far more effectively than they would have in a private spat. Coombe Tennant was undoubtedly shocked by this development, but as the more experienced diplomats in her delegation informed her, this was actually common practice at the Assembly.[66] In fact, an almost identical sequence of events had happened the previous year when, for similar reasons, the French delegation had stalled proposals tackling the traffic in women and children.[67] The practice of privately making agreements and, when necessary, publicly breaking them was recognised and accepted (if begrudgingly) at the Assembly.

By disrupting rather than challenging proceedings, the French delegation had therefore publicly placed the onus upon Coombe Tennant to resolve the matter quickly. Any delays were a potential source of embarrassment to Britain – particularly given the accusation of inadequate drafting – and as private minutes from within the British delegation show, there was a serious worry that the French would delay the bill for a year by stalling until the closing of the Assembly.[68] Public disruption threatened the chances for success, allowing the French delegation to control the pace of negotiations. It was a move which forced quick action by the British delegation who, as Coombe Tennant noted in her diary, felt they were being outmanoeuvred at every turn by France's 'mastery of the press'.[69] In this way, media oversight was used as a subversive instrument of international order, allowing diplomats to leverage the symbolic influence of public opinion to undermine rivals in private diplomatic negotiations.

The success of this strategy can be further seen in the events which followed as, within hours of the disruption, a private meeting had been convened between the two delegations in an attempt to reach a swift resolution.[70] Held in Crowdy's private office, this was undoubtedly intended to be secret, and consisted of only six participants: Crowdy representing the League's Humanitarian section, Coombe Tennant and two lawyers from the British delegation, and Reynaud and a lawyer representing the French government. It was only here, in this meeting, that the true nature of the objection was outlined. The proposals which the British Government submitted to the League were based on a series of recommendations drafted in 1910 at an international conference on the obscene publications problem in Paris. These had been amended upon their revival, however, to suggest that, given both the supposed neutrality of international organisations and the global nature of the trade, the international response to this threat should be taken up by the League. The French government, while supportive of the bill's substance, therefore objected because it feared that ceding leadership of the initiative to the League would undermine its credibility as a champion of (Western) progress and morality. Instead, France sought to see the bill stipulate that the resulting conference would be convened by the French government in Paris, rather than the League of Nations in Geneva.

The discussion in Crowdy's office saw every detail of the proposal fiercely contested from its administrative organisation to the constitutional ramifications of the decision for the still nascent League. In the end, however, it was decided that the international conference in question would in fact be convened in Paris by the French government, but formally 'under the auspices of the League'.[71] In return, the French delegation agreed to make vague promises that this was a special case which would not affect the powers of the League to lead in future initiatives (a promise which itself further implied that Reynaud's original objection was not simply one of constitutional procedure).[72] France, it seems, also promised to publicly thank Britain for bringing the issue back to their attention, ensuring that they too would receive appropriate approbation. These were minor concessions from the French government's perspective and the deal provoked objections from both Crowdy and Coombe Tennant, who worried about the 'unfortunate precedent' which this might set for the League. These qualms, however, were ultimately overruled by those present who favoured a solution which credited both parties with initiating action.[73]

Media oversight would continue to play a crucial role in progressing these negotiations, however. In order to legitimise this new agreement – hammered out and signed in secret by six people in a small office – it had to be portrayed as a product of open diplomacy. The solution, therefore, arranged between Britain and France, was a carefully crafted display of conciliation in the next meeting of the public committee. The following day, the meeting was opened by Coombe Tennant, who tabled the newly amended proposals which, though largely unchanged in substance, now recommended a special case should be made for the French government 'in recognition of the interest previously taken' on this issue.[74] Next spoke Reynaud who, thanking Coombe Tennant for the proposals, praised Britain for reviving international interest in French efforts. Reynaud also informed the public committee that it was no longer necessary for 'recourse to the advice of the First Committee' as the new wording of the amended proposals had settled any 'question of principle' previously raised.[75] In this way, the narrative presented to the media became one of public conciliation rather than private negotiation.

This exhibition of performative diplomacy was then consolidated by a public 'debate' which presented the bill as a product of international cooperation. Though Coombe Tennant privately believed French policy to be 'very strange' – noting that prior to this Assembly they had attempted 'absolutely nothing' since the 1910 conference – she actively praised their previous efforts to the committee and its observers.[76] The debate was further interspersed with thick praise from the (English) representatives of New Zealand and South Africa, who too paid 'tribute to the work previously done' by the French government in tackling the trade.[77] Finally, after an afternoon of placid discussion, an agreement identical to that decided in Crowdy's office was publicly reached and, although the delegate from Yugoslavia is noted to have 'wondered whether procedure which had been followed had been quite in order', the proposal was eventually passed by the committee.[78]

It can be seen here that, by performing conciliatory discussion, the two delegations were able to present what was in reality a hard-fought diplomatic process – fraught with secrecy and deception – as the product of open and cooperative diplomacy. To an outside observer, there was little indication that the obscene publications proposals had provoked anything more serious than a swiftly retracted procedural query in an otherwise conciliatory discussion amongst nations. In this way, media oversight had created the conditions for a false relationship with international public opinion that appeared to satisfy the requirements of open diplomacy. Its presence in certain forums was therefore critical to this diplomatic process. It had allowed Coombe Tennant and her fellow delegates to use performative diplomacy to ensure the legitimacy of their final agreement and to ultimately pass her bill. Within days of this debate, the revised recommendations were adopted and submitted to a plenary session of the Assembly. The final report would later note that the Fifth Committee was of the 'unanimous opinion' that France should host the event.[79]

The case of the obscene publications bill showcases the ways in which media oversight of the Assembly created defined public forums of publicity, as well as how these forums, and the practices which they facilitated, were crucial to the legitimacy of diplomacy at the League. The instrumentalisation of media oversight had shaped this process from the start. At first, as a newcomer to the Assembly, Coombe Tennant's inexperience had allowed more seasoned diplomats to control the pace of negotiations, using public scrutiny to disrupt the performance of open diplomacy. Here the case illustrates how diplomats would come to rely on the ability to leverage both open and secret diplomacy through the instrumentalisation of media oversight. Public transparency may well have been understood as an illusion by Coombe Tennant and her fellow delegates, but the very process of maintaining this façade ultimately forced her to compromise to secure the legitimacy of her proposals. Success in a secret conference could decide the terms of a proposal, but only successful public engagement could transform a private agreement into a sanctioned initiative. This co-dependence between supposedly incompatible diplomatic approaches placed the Geneva system in a unique moment, caught between the dominance of great power politics which preceded it and the rejection of public opinion as a primary mechanism for peacekeeping which would follow.

Ultimately, however, it was this same practice of performative diplomacy which also allowed Coombe Tennant to present this compromise, born of tense negotiations, as an uncontroversial initiative. By guiding the bill through this series of discussions, each only as binding as it was public, she was able to confer legitimacy on the bill as a product of open diplomacy. Furthermore, from the partially obscured perspective of the media, the impression formed by events in the committee was that an uncharacteristically collaborative debate had been enabled by the Assembly, further demonstrating its effectiveness at facilitating altruistic international cooperation. Summing up the origins of the obscene publications proposals ahead of the resulting Paris conference in 1923, the *Times* would later report to its readers that 'the defective character of international machinery before the League was established is well illustrated in the manner in which this question has been handled'.[80] This journalist may have falsely interpreted displays of open diplomacy as proof of the death of great power politics, but the Assembly did nonetheless alter the conduct of diplomacy at the League. While diplomats were not always transparent in their engagements with public opinion, the importance of acquiring its symbolic capital disrupted old approaches to diplomacy because it forced collaboration and compromise. The need to engage with media observers therefore directly created new diplomatic processes which rewarded a more collaborative (if not necessarily conciliatory) approach to international affairs.

Conclusion

Built on the ideological foundations of open diplomacy, the Assembly allowed performances of diplomacy to be conducted under the scrutiny of as much of the world as cared to look, appearing to satisfy the demand for public accountability in international affairs. The sanctification of the relationship between diplomats and public opinion had created a new symbolic force which focused the internationalisation of the media around spectacle and pageantry of the Assembly. This intense focus on these plenary sessions was core to the Assembly's function and helped to amplify this perception of transparency. It also played an important role in legitimising the League by directing the gaze of observers towards the apparently open – and even at first glance democratic – organ of international society. The brighter the spotlights shone on the stage where well-rehearsed actors performed, the less anyone noticed the activity in the shadowy wings.

Though this visibility was primarily intended to operate at an institutional level, the platform which this created provided unique opportunities for the actors it hosted to develop new diplomatic practices. In this way, media oversight of the Assembly, as a manifestation of open diplomacy, was a key instrument of international order. As Coombe Tennant's experiences show, this instrument would come to define the course and substance of diplomacy at the League, allowing diplomats to create their own public narratives through rehearsed displays of openness. Though performative diplomacy could be disruptive to the Assembly's progress, it ultimately relied on the public perception of unity. Here the requirement of transparency, achieved through a prescribed pattern of escalating publicity, itself had the inadvertent effect of forcing international cooperation into the back-rooms where 'real' diplomacy continued to unfold. In this way, the Assembly provided a point of convergence for two seemingly diametrically opposed diplomatic methods. In the myriad forums of the Assembly, diplomacy was shaped by a relationship between transparency and power, the publicity given to a discussion determining both the frankness of its participants and the legitimacy of its outcomes.

The broader international norms which facilitated these diplomatic practices would, however, be short lived. By the end of the Second World War, a broader loss in faith in public opinion as a safeguard against war had begun to cause a shift in the way in which 'open diplomacy' and secret statecraft were viewed, refracting a perceived dichotomy along multiple axes: of pre- and post-war, of illusion and truth, of idealism and realism. Yet as this chapter has demonstrated, in the short-lived yet unique context of the Assembly these would prove to be co-dependent practices. Engagement with the public as part of international affairs was certainly not unique to the interwar years, but for diplomats who derived their legitimacy from public opinion rather than direct representation or state authority alone, this would prove uniquely effective. In this context, though open diplomacy was undoubtedly performative, the impact it had on diplomatic practices should not be understated. On the great world stage that was the Assembly, neither theatrics and policy-making, nor public deliberation and positive action, could exist in isolation.

Notes

1 West Glamorgan Archive Service, Swansea, D/DT3978, Winifred Coombe Tennant, 'Geneva Diary', 3 September–3 October 1922, p. 50.
2 Susan Pedersen, 'Back to the League of Nations', *The American Historical Review* 112:4 (2007), 1091–1117.
3 Heidi J. S. Tworek, 'The Press and Moral Disarmament through the League of Nations', *Medien und Zeit* 25:4 (2010), 16–28, 22.
4 Glenda Sluga, *Internationalism in the Age of Nationalism* (Philadelphia, PA: University of Pennsylvania Press, 2013), p. 57.
5 Daniel Gorman, *The Emergence of International Society in the 1920s* (Cambridge: Cambridge University Press, 2012).
6 Susan Pedersen, *The Guardians: The League of Nations and the Crisis of Empire* (Oxford: Oxford University Press, 2015).

7 Covenant of the League of Nations, https://avalon.law.yale.edu/20th_century/leagcov.asp (accessed 23 July 2021).
8 C. B. Fry, *Key-Book of the League of Nations* (London: Hodder and Stoughton, 1923), p. 26.
9 Mark Mazower, *Governing the World: The History of an Idea* (London: Penguin Books, 2012), pp. 136, 142.
10 Zara Steiner, *The Lights That Failed: European International History, 1919–1933* (Oxford: Oxford University Press, 2005), p. 353.
11 Daniel Hucker, 'International History and the Study of Public Opinion: Towards Methodological Clarity', *The International History Review* 34:4 (2012), 778–9.
12 Ibid., 780.
13 Stephen Wertheim, 'Reading the International Mind: International Public Opinion in Early Twentieth Century Anglo-American Thought', in Nicolas Guilhot and Daniel Bessner (eds), *The Decisionist Imagination: Democracy, Sovereignty, and Social Science in the 20th Century* (New York: Berghahn Books, 2019), p. 37.
14 Carolyn N. Biltoft, *A Violent Peace: Media, Truth, and Power at the League of Nations* (Chicago, IL: University of Illinois Press, 2021), p. 6. Wertheim, 'Reading the International Mind', p. 27.
15 Gaynor Johnson, 'Lord Robert Cecil as an Internationalist: A Mental Map', in Gaynor Johnson (ed.), *Peacemaking, Peacemakers and Diplomacy, 1880–1939: Essays in Honour of Professor Alan Sharp* (Newcastle: Cambridge Scholars Publishing, 2010), p. 192.
16 Pedersen, *The Guardians*, p. 10.
17 Wertheim, 'Reading the International Mind', p. 29.
18 Emil Eiby Seidenfaden, 'Message from Geneva: The Public Legitimization Strategies of the League of Nations and Their Legacy, 1919–1946' (PhD thesis, Aarhus University, 2019), 16–19.
19 Simon J. Potter, *Wireless Internationalism and Distant Listening: Britain, Propaganda, and the Invention of Global Radio, 1920–1939* (Oxford: Oxford University Press, 2020), p. 4.
20 Seidenfaden, 'Message from Geneva', pp. 56, 59.
21 Tworek, 'The Press and Moral Disarmament', 23.
22 Max Beer, *The League on Trial: A Journey to Geneva*, trans. W. H. Johnston (London: George Allen & Unwin, 1933), p. 367.
23 Seidenfaden, 'Message from Geneva', p. 18.
24 Wertheim, 'Reading the International Mind', p. 47.
25 Tomoko Akami, 'The Emergence of International Public Opinion and the Origins of Public Diplomacy in Japan in the Interwar Period', *The Hague Journal of Diplomacy* 3 (2008), 108.
26 Hucker, 'International History and the Study of Public Opinion', 787–8.
27 Tworek, 'The Press and Moral Disarmament', 23.
28 Ibid., 17.

29 United Nations Archives, Geneva, Conf.D/143, report by R. Cecil, 'Cooperation of the Press in the Organisation of Peace', 1 November 1932.
30 Ibid.
31 Charles Howard-Ellis, *The Origin, Structure and Working of the League of Nations* (London: Allen and Unwin, 1928), p. 136.
32 Potter, *Wireless Internationalism and Distant Listening*, p. 32.
33 Seidenfaden, 'Message from Geneva', p. 61.
34 West Glamorgan Archive Service, Swansea, D/DT4016, 'Third Assembly of the League of Nations, Official Guide', September 1922.
35 Biltoft, *A Violent Peace*, p. 18.
36 Beer, *The League on Trial*, p. 376.
37 Pedersen, *The Guardians*, p. 5.
38 United Nations Archives, Geneva, R1359, 26 9051 1184, report by R. Viviani and N. Rowell, 'Report on the Relations between, and Respective Competence of, the Council and the Assembly', 1 December 1920.
39 'The League of Nations: Its Achievements and Machinery' (London: League of Nations Union, 1921), p. 3.
40 Norbert Götz, 'On the Origins of "Parliamentary Diplomacy": Scandinavian "Bloc Politics" and Delegation Policy in the League of Nations', *Cooperation and Conflict* 40:3 (2005), 274.
41 United Nations Archives, Geneva, R1367, 26 15393, memo by P. J. Baker, 'Publicity for Assembly Commissions', 26 August 1921.
42 For more information see Biltoft, *A Violent Peace*, pp. 89–112.
43 Alison Adcock Kaufman, 'In Pursuit of Equality and Respect: China's Diplomacy and the League of Nations', *Modern China* 40:6 (2014), 611–4.
44 See Biltoft, *A Violent Peace*, p. 30. Daniel Laqua, *The Age of Internationalism and Belgium, 1880–1930: Peace, Progress and Prestige* (Manchester: Manchester University Press, 2013), pp. 159–60.
45 'Third Assembly of the League of Nations, Official Guide', p. 2.
46 Seidenfaden, 'Message from Geneva', pp. 59–60.
47 Beer, *The League on Trial*, p. 388.
48 James Cotton, '"The Standard Work in English on the League" and Its Authorship: Charles Howard Ellis, an Unlikely Australian Internationalist', *History of European Ideas* 42:8 (2016), 1089–1104.
49 Howard-Ellis, *The Origin, Structure and Working of the League of Nations*, p. 137.
50 Ibid.
51 Beer, *The League on Trial*, p. 389.
52 Ibid., p. 388.
53 Daniel Gorman, 'Empire, Internationalism and the Campaign against the Traffic in Women and Children in the 1920s', *Twentieth Century British History* 19:2 (2008), 209.
54 Gorman, *The Emergence of International Society in the 1920s*, p. 108.
55 Karen Gram-Skjoldager and Haakon Ikonomou, 'The Construction of the League of Nations Secretariat: Formative Practices of Autonomy and

Legitimacy in International Organizations', *The International History Review* 41:2 (2017), 270.
56 West Glamorgan Archive Service, Swansea, D/DT4032, Robert Cecil, 'Obscene Publications: Report of the Fifth Committee to the Third Assembly', 26 September 1922.
57 'Obscene Publications: Report of the Fifth Committee to the Third Assembly'.
58 Paul Knepper, 'International Criminals: The League of Nations, the Traffic in Women and the Press', *Media History* 20:4 (2014), 403–4.
59 Steiner, *The Lights That Failed*, p. 116.
60 West Glamorgan Archive Service, Swansea, D/DT4023, 'Journal of the Third Assembly of the League of Nations, No. 18', 23 September 1922.
61 'Coombe Tennant diary', pp. 15, 17, 23. Gorman, *The Emergence of International Society in the 1920s*, pp. 60–5.
62 'Geneva Diary', p. 31.
63 West Glamorgan Archive Service, Swansea, D/DT 4032, memo by Winifred Coombe Tennant, 'Obscene Publications', 21 September 1922.
64 'Journal of the Third Assembly', p. 186.
65 'Geneva Diary', p. 38.
66 Ibid.
67 Ibid.
68 West Glamorgan Archive Service, Swansea, D/DT3978, memo by Winifred Coombe Tennant, 'Note to Balfour', 21 September 1922.
69 'Geneva Diary', p. 32.
70 West Glamorgan Archive Service, Swansea, D/DT4032, memo by Winifred Coombe Tennant, 'Meeting in Dame Rachel Crowdy's Room', 21 September 1922.
71 Ibid.
72 West Glamorgan Archive Service, Swansea, D/DT4032, memo by Winifred Coombe Tennant, 'Point raised by the French delegation on Obscene publications', 22 September 1922.
73 Ibid.
74 'Obscene Publications: Report of the Fifth Committee'.
75 'Journal of the Third Assembly', p. 218.
76 'Note to Balfour'.
77 Ibid.
78 'Journal of the Third Assembly', p. 219.
79 United Nations Archives, Geneva, R655, 12 23883 13827, report by T. Tsai Fou, 'Trade in Obscene Publications', 2 October 1922.
80 'Traffic in Obscene Publications', *Times* (31 August 1923), p. 7.

8

The League of Nations and the advisory opinion of the Permanent Court of International Justice as 'preventive adjudication'?

Gabriela A. Frei

The architects of the peace in 1919 designed a post-war order founded upon international law and the League of Nations (LoN) and the Permanent Court of International Justice (PCIJ) stood as its guarantors.[1] The Covenant of the League of Nations stated in Article 14 that a Permanent Court of International Justice 'shall be competent to hear and determine any dispute of an international character [...] (and) may also give an advisory opinion upon any dispute or question referred to it by the Council or by the Assembly'.[2] The latter clause provided the basis for the creation of a new instrument in international politics, bringing the newly founded League of Nations and the Permanent Court of International Justice in close interaction with each other. An advisory opinion is a non-binding interpretation of the law, whereas a court's judgment in a case is binding.[3] Precedents could be found in domestic law of Great Britain and France and in the national courts of the United States, Colombia, Sweden and other countries.[4] For instance, in Great Britain, the House of Lords could consult the judges and ask for advice in any legal matter.[5]

Introducing this instrument to a newly founded international court opened up ways for the Court to provide its legal expertise to international politics. The American jurist Manley O. Hudson excitedly wrote about the advisory function that

> we have become accustomed to thinking of courts only as machinery for handling conflicts between opposing individuals or groups after they have come into clash. [...] But we have made slow progress toward developing what might be called preventive adjudication, and the notion widely prevails that the judicial branch of the legal profession must necessarily confine itself to ripened conflicts.[6]

Thus, the advisory function was seen as a tool of conflict prevention, which significantly expanded the scope of the court and the judges' competencies.

The existing literature treats the advisory opinion almost exclusively from the perspective of the development of an international jurisdiction. The latest research on the PCIJ by Malgosia Fitzmaurice and Christian J. Tams provides a broad assessment of its achievements but also its failures.[7] Ole Spiermann's study offers probably the most exhaustive and in-depth analysis of the workings of the PCIJ and also deals with the advisory opinion.[8] Other researchers focus on the continuation of the instrument of the advisory jurisdiction in the twentieth century.[9] For instance, Michla Pomerance and Gleider I. Hernandez compare the period of the League of Nations with that of the United Nations (UN).[10]

This chapter explores the advisory opinion of the Permanent Court of International Justice from a historical perspective, relating the position of the PCIJ to that of the League of Nations and how this new international organisation made use of the advisory opinion as a new instrument in international politics. Hudson described the PCIJ as 'pioneering' and that with it 'new paths may have to be blazed, unfamiliar tools may have to be tried, and our ancient conceptions of judicial function may have to be re-moulded'.[11] This experimental character of the advisory opinion will be at the heart of this chapter. In fact, there is a large literature that describes the period of the League of Nations as an experiment, as Jean d'Aspremont has highlighted most recently.[12] Between 1922 and 1935, when the PCIJ gave its last advisory opinion, the Court issued twenty-seven advisory opinions, compared to twenty-nine judgments. This chapter will first examine how the advisory jurisdiction was developed as part of the Court's Statute. A second part will analyse the scope of the advisory opinion by describing various case studies to show how the advisory jurisdiction worked in practice, what the motivation was for the LoN to request advice from the Court, who the parties were and what the advice served for. The third and final part will assess the advisory opinion as an instrument in international politics, whether it fulfilled the expectations hoped for and more broadly what legacy it produced.

Origins of the advisory jurisdiction

The foundation of the World Court, as the PCIJ was often called, was a significant achievement in the development of an international jurisdiction, which had started to take shape with the foundation of the Permanent Court of Arbitration (PCA) in 1899. While the PCA was quite limited in terms of cases, the World Court could deal with all aspects of international law.[13] Attributing an advisory function to the World Court was an absolute novelty and provocative at the same time. Yet it was up to the drafters of the Statute of the PCIJ to outline a procedure which would define how the advisory opinion would look in international jurisdiction and how it would work in practice. Article 14 of the Covenant laid the basis for the PCIJ, describing its functions in relation to the League. This double function of an international court was extraordinary and demanded creative legal skills to imagine how this function of an international court could be useful.

The British jurist Lord Walter Phillimore was closely associated with the idea of an advisory jurisdiction.[14] The British government had appointed Phillimore during the First World War to compile the various suggestions of post-war orders and how an international jurisdiction could be an essential part of it.[15] In the Phillimore plan of 1918 the idea of an advisory jurisdiction was clearly expressed and later incorporated into the Cecil plan (named after the British diplomat Lord Robert Cecil). The British draft of the Covenant was then discussed by the Allies.[16] The plan for the Covenant, which Woodrow Wilson, Léon Bourgeois, Robert Cecil and Vittorio E. Orlando presented at the Paris Peace Conference in February 1919, intended that the future PCIJ should be 'competent to hear and determine any matter which the parties recognized as suitable for submission to it (PCIJ) for arbitration'.[17] This vague statement needed refinement in later discussions. Lord Cecil proposed to replace 'matter' with 'any dispute or difference of an international character',[18] but as David Hunter Miller, one of the American drafters of the Covenant, highlighted in his memoirs, that wording was considered too broad. Miller feared that by broadening the scope, it would go 'the whole road to compulsory arbitration'.[19] According to the diary of Lord Cecil, the question of compulsory arbitration was one of the key obstacles in the negotiations with the United States.[20] The French delegate, Fernand Larnaude, also supported the idea of an advisory opinion. The redrafting of Article 14 avoided compulsory arbitration and instead introduced the idea of advisory opinion. In fact, the drafters separated the advisory opinion from the judiciary function of the proposed court.[21] Accordingly, the final draft of the Covenant stated in Article 14 in a separate sentence that 'the court may also give advisory opinion upon any dispute or question referred to it by the council or by the assembly'.[22]

The Covenant provided the legal framework within which the LoN had to operate. Thus, when the Council began its work in February 1920, it announced an Advisory Committee of Jurists, which would be responsible for drafting the Statute of the PCIJ, and where the advisory function could be outlined more precisely.[23] The discussions in the drafting committee offer a good starting point to understand how the drafters outlined the advisory opinion as an instrument in international politics. Eminent jurists were chosen to serve on the committee with Edouard Deschamps as head of the committee and Albert de Lapradelle as rapporteur. Other members of the committee were the American jurist Elihu Root, the Brazilian jurist Raul Fernandes, the Dutch judge Bernard Loder, the British jurist and Privy Councillor Lord Phillimore, the Japanese jurist Mineichiro Adatci, the Spanish historian and jurist Rafael Altamira, the Norwegian jurist and politician Francis Hagerup and the Italian jurist Arturo Ricci-Busatti. They were not only leading figures in their field but also experienced diplomats or judges, having served prior to the war as delegates at the Hague Peace Conferences or as judges at the Permanent Court of Arbitration.[24]

The advisory committee met at The Hague Peace Palace on 16 June 1920, where they were greeted by an enthusiastic crowd as the *New York Times* wrote.[25] The speech of Léon Bourgeois as delegate of the League's Council reminded the committee members of the role of the future PCIJ in the post-war order. Not only was it intended as a permanent body, but its task was 'the organisation of international justice'.[26] Moreover, Bourgeois linked the LoN and the PCIJ as pillars of 'international life' and emphasised that 'the independence of the judicial authority vis-à-vis the political power appears more and more one of the essential guarantees of liberty and internal peace'.[27] The Hague was chosen as the seat of the PCIJ, which symbolised its continuity with the Permanent Court of Arbitration.[28] The discussions of the advisory committee mostly revolved around how to make the PCIJ distinct from the existing Permanent Court of Arbitration. Most of the work was done by Root and Phillimore, who seemed to offer the most convincing draft scheme of the Statute of the PCIJ.[29]

The members of the committee struggled with the idea of the PCIJ's advisory function. Root regarded the advisory jurisdiction in case of existing disputes as a 'violation of all juridical principles'.[30] Lapradelle, on the other hand, argued that Article 13 of the Covenant gave the Council the power to send 'any case' to the Court for consideration.[31] The draft scheme of the Statute of the PCIJ outlined in Article 36 the procedure for advisory opinions. It distinguished between disputes and questions. While the former described an actual dispute and should be treated like a contentious proceeding, the latter was of theoretical nature and should only be considered by a group of judges rather than the full Court.[32]

The committee's report, which accompanied the draft scheme, gives some more details as to how the advisory jurisdiction should work in practice, outlining some safeguards for the Court which had been of concerns in the committee's discussion. First, the disputes and questions had to be of 'international character' in accordance with Article 14 of the Covenant of the League of Nations. Second, the advisory opinions were not binding upon the Council or the Assembly as the Court 'merely advises'. Third, should a dispute that had been treated as an advisory opinion return to the Court as a contentious matter, the Court 'must not be bound by this (prior) opinion'. Moreover, recurring disputes had to be evaluated by different judges.[33] Giving the parties the choice of an arbitrary and a conciliatory procedure, they may decide for the latter because of its non-binding character but nonetheless requiring a unanimous vote in the Council for requesting an advisory opinion in the first place. Moreover, the Court's 'decision would nevertheless have the moral force attaching to all its decisions; and, if the Council or Assembly adopt it, it would have the same wholesome effect on public opinion'.[34] The advisory opinion should be treated the same as any contentious case, which meant that the contesting parties were allowed to have a judge on the bench as well as present their arguments and proofs.[35]

When the draft scheme of the Statute of the PCIJ was sent in late 1920 to the League's Council and Assembly for consideration, a subcommission of the Assembly, consisting of lawyers, discussed the draft scheme and made recommendations prior to the Assembly's vote. In their discussions, Article 36, which outlined the advisory function of the Court, was contested.[36] The French jurist Henri Fromageot suggested dropping Article 36 as it went too far into detail and referred to Article 14 of the Covenant, which defined the Court's dual function.[37] The commission unanimously voted in favour of dropping Article 36 and the Council and Assembly followed their proposal.[38] This suggestion was, however, not a rejection of the idea of advisory jurisdiction as the Council 'recognized the need for advisory opinions in connection with its attempts to realize the aims and purposes of the League of Nations'.[39] Moreover, the subcommission had also clarified that the future World Court would also deal with all matters arising from the International Labour Organisation (ILO), rejecting the suggestion of its Director-General, Albert Thomas, who wanted to establish a separate court. Importantly, the ILO could also make use of the new instrument of the advisory opinion.[40] In the end, the Assembly approved the Statute of the PCIJ on 13 December 1920 without Article 36.[41] As a result, the advisory jurisdiction would be determined in the rules and procedures of the Court.

In January 1922, the judges of the PCIJ convened in The Hague, where they first had to determine the rules and procedures of the Court.[42] The advisory jurisdiction was again on the agenda and a committee prepared questions for discussion. They concerned the secrecy of advisory opinions, whether the Court could reject abstract questions and how the Court could withhold an advisory opinion until a concrete case occurred.[43] The American jurist John Bassett Moore, who had been elected as judge of the PCIJ, advised again against introducing an advisory jurisdiction to the PCIJ as he thought that it would undermine the PCIJ's primary judicial function 'to end disputes by deciding them'. Moreover, advisory opinions lacked 'authority'[44] and therefore belonged, according to Moore, to the settlement of private disputes or legal advice to governments. In essence, an advisory jurisdiction would rob the Court of 'one of its primary functions – that of contributing, through its jurisprudence, to the development of international law'.[45] Moore's advocacy against an advisory jurisdiction has also to be seen in the context of the United States' opposition to the World Court, prominently displayed in the Senate debates, which revealed the fear that the Court could voice an opinion on subjects which the United States did not want to raise in the first place.[46]

Yet Lapradelle and others won the argument and Articles 71, 72, 73 and 74 of the rules and procedures of the PCIJ provided the framework for the PCIJ's advisory opinion.[47] The articles outlined that the requests must be made in writing and accompanied by all relevant documentation for the judges to study. Most importantly, Article 72 stated that 'the request shall contain an exact statement of the question upon which an opinion is requested'. The Court would immediately publish the request and inform all relevant bodies of the LoN about it. The Statute made no distinction between a dispute and a question. Moreover, all judges of the Court would decide on the advisory opinion and all opinions would be 'printed and published in a special collection' of the PCIJ. Dissenting opinions could also be included in the advisory opinion and published. In fact, the advisory opinion was treated like a decision of the Court, as the procedural steps included written statements of the parties involved as well as public hearings at the Court.[48] The adoption of the same rules as applicable for decisions at the PCIJ meant that advisory opinions were held to the same standard. In essence, the rules and procedures of the PCIJ strengthened the newly created instrument for the Court by defining clear safeguards. It also gave the LoN and its members a clear legal framework for requesting an advisory opinion. This opened the opportunity to explore the advisory jurisdiction as an instrument in dispute resolution in the interwar period.[49]

Scope of the advisory jurisdiction

The PCIJ issued in total twenty-seven advisory opinions in the interwar period.[50] The requests covered broad aspects: the competence of international organisations and special commissions, treaty interpretations (minority treaties in particular) and obligations and frontier disputes. Seventeen requests concerned actual disputes. All of the requests for an advisory opinion were submitted by the Council.[51]

In the early years of the PCIJ and the League, there was room for experimentation with the instrument of advisory opinion. It is noticeable, though, that both organisations were careful in expanding or limiting its scope. They

The League of Nations and 'preventive adjudication' 183

tried to keep within the given framework of the rules and procedures of the PCIJ outlined above. The Eastern Carelia[52] opinion of 1923 provided one of the key cases of this early period. In November 1921, the Finnish government approached the Council seeking advice in the question of Eastern Carelia, a region in the northeast of Europe. In the Peace Treaty of Tartu (also known as Dorpat) of 1920 between Finland and Soviet Russia, the two parties agreed to separate the region of Carelia into a Western and Eastern part. The former became part of Finland, while the latter became part of Soviet Russia. The treaty further regulated that Finnish troops had to withdraw from Eastern Carelia and that the 200,000 ethnically Finnish locals living in Repola and Porajärvi would be granted an autonomous status within Soviet Russia. In a Declaration, the Russians further granted the Carelians the right to self-determination, internal autonomy, preservation of their language and continuity of their economic life. The Finnish government argued, however, that these stipulations were never fulfilled from the Soviet side.[53]

As a result, Finland turned to the Council and asked for a clarification on the Peace Treaty of Tartu. Other neighbouring countries – Poland, Latvia, Lithuania and Estonia – had also urged the Council 'to find a peace settlement' as the dispute affected the entire region. The local population of Eastern Carelia had also petitioned the Council in 1921, while, at the same time, they started an insurrection against Soviet Russia, in which they demanded their independence.[54] As a result, Soviet Russia accused Finland of supporting the insurrection.[55] In January 1922, the Council discussed the case and agreed to assist in the matter but also addressed the 'interested States', by which they meant the neighbouring countries, to help negotiate in the dispute.[56] When the Estonian government approached the Soviets, the latter denied their consent, arguing that the dispute was an internal matter. As a non-member of the LoN, Soviet Russia did not acknowledge the PCIJ. As a result, the Council felt that it had no power to bring Moscow to the negotiating table.[57] Nevertheless, the Council continued collecting material on the question of Eastern Carelia. Since the Council did not act, Finland tried to get the ball rolling in the Assembly in February 1923, but its request was rebuffed, bringing the issue back to the Council. In the meantime, the Finnish government had successfully lobbied jurists to support their case, among them Charles De Visscher, Mikael H. Lie, Knud Berlin, W. van der Vlugt, Lage Staël von Holstein and Karl Strupp.[58] Three Finnish jurists from the University of Helsinki also prepared a memorandum, pleading for an advisory opinion from the PCIJ.[59]

In March 1923, the Finnish government formally proposed that the Council seek an advisory opinion from the Court. Supporting this suggestion, the Council submitted on 21 April 1923 a request for an advisory opinion to the PCIJ. The Council's rapporteur, Antonio Salandra, justified the decision by arguing that 'the Council has undoubtedly [sic] the right to refer this question to the Court'. He further reassured that this was 'within the competence of the League', which had 'the duty [...] to help its Members, through its institutions to maintain good relations [...] and facilitate the peaceful settlement of disputes'. At the same time, he warned that Soviet Russia was neither a member of the League nor of the Court, which meant that it was not bound by any decision, and Finland had to respect that. Yet the Council hoped, despite Russia's continued hostility towards the LoN, that the Court could clarify the matter and that the Soviets would respect the PCIJ as a body 'of the most complete impartiality, of eminent jurists'. In fact, the Council was confident that the PCIJ would not object to the request as the question was 'based entirely on the interpretation of the Treaty of Dorpat [Tartu] and of the general principle of international law'. The Council hoped that the PCIJ would be more successful in gaining consent from Moscow than the Council had been.[60]

The Court opened the case and invited the two parties to submit pleadings. As expected, the Soviets rejected the invitation on the grounds that it constituted 'an intervention in its domestic affairs'. Since the LoN had not even recognised the Soviet regime, they were concerned whether the LoN or the PCIJ would be 'impartial'.[61] With this outright rejection, the Court used the case instead for clarifying the scope and limitation of the advisory opinion. Although the question before the Court concerned the interpretation of a treaty, the Court feared that their opinion would have had an effect on an 'actual dispute'. Without Soviet Russia's consent to the procedure, no material could be gathered for forming an opinion and, as a consequence, the Court decided on 23 July 1923 that it could not give an advisory opinion because it was 'well established in international law that no State can, without its consent, be compelled to submit its disputes with other States either to mediation or to arbitration or to any other kind of pacific settlement'.[62] The decision of the Court was narrow. Judges Anzilotti, Finlay, Huber and Moore, as well as Deputy-Judge Wang, were against giving an advisory opinion. Judges Altamira, de Bustamente, Nyholm and Weiss dissented from the majority.[63] The fact that the PCIJ rejected giving an advisory opinion signalled to the Council that it was not willing to overstep its competencies. Its independence was paramount to the PCIJ, and the judges wanted to protect it. It also established the principle of the consent of the disputing parties.[64] Judge Moore later admitted that he feared that the Court could have been used for political purposes, which he thought was wrong. Yet Judge Altamira suggested in the aftermath of the Eastern Carelia opinion that the advisory function of the PCIJ should be treated differently from its judicial function. In fact, he thought that the advisory opinion should be secret.⁶⁵ The discussions in the aftermath of the Eastern Carelia opinion illustrate that the judges were much more concerned with the protection of the judiciary function than with dispute resolution in thinking about how to develop the Court's advisory function.⁶⁶

The Council had accepted the PCIJ's decision in the Eastern Carelia case and subsequently treaded more lightly in requesting an advisory opinion from the Court. In the same year, the Council dealt with a dispute between Romania and Hungary about the Hungarian minority in Romania. Hungary demanded the Council request an advisory opinion from the PCIJ in the matter. However, Romania opposed such a course, because Hungary's question was not a judicial but a political one. As a result, the Council refrained from getting further involved. Yet the dispute was again placed before the Council in 1927, and the Council's rapporteur, Sir Austen Chamberlain, suggested writing a report with the help of the two parties in an attempt to resolve the dispute.⁶⁷ Neither the Hungarians nor the Romanians, however, accepted the conditions outlined in the report. Only in 1930 did both sides sign an agreement which resolved the dispute.⁶⁸ The case illustrates that the Council, and in particular the rapporteur, tried to find alternative means of conflict resolution to the PCIJ.

In 1926, Greece demanded an advisory opinion to deal with a question regarding the Maritza or Evros River and the delimitation of its Thracian frontier with Turkey.⁶⁹ The matter had been brought to the Council in February 1926, since Greece was not satisfied with how the Delimitation Commission, established after the Treaty of Lausanne in 1923, dealt with the question. Turkey, however, refused to consent to an advisory opinion since it doubted the Council's competence to deal with the question. Instead, it reassured the Council that it would recognise the Delimitation Commission and that it 'would accept any resolution to settle the question that might be adopted by majority of the Delimitation Commission'.⁷⁰

In the Council meeting of 16 March 1926, Greece and Turkey presented their respective points of view. The Greeks doubted the competency of the Delimitation Commission and did not trust its decisions.⁷¹ They cited a Delimitation Commission minute in which the Chairman, Lt Col F. Backer from the Netherlands, said that he would not 'forbid the Greek Government to have a recourse to the Court at The Hague, which was constituted to interpret treaties and to prevent any conflicts between the peoples which might have serious consequences'. He assured that the Delimitation Commission would respect any decision or opinion of the Court but he also made clear that the Commission would render an 'impartial decision'.⁷² The Turkish delegate reiterated Ankara's position, arguing the question was of 'striking simplicity' and that the Commission should continue its work. In fact, the Commission had not even decided on the issue and the Turkish delegate reminded the Council of its own resolution of 24 January 1924, which required the Council to reject proceeding with the request, since the issue was already under legal consideration by another body created under the auspices of the League.[73]

In dealing with the Greek request, the Council's rapporteur, Afranio de Mello Franco from Brazil, suggested that the Council consult 'two to three lawyers' present in Geneva on the question, which seemed to him about the Court's competence and subsequent treaty interpretation. The choice of the lawyers would be upon the rapporteur's consultation with the Secretary-General.[74] The jurist committee, consisting of Cristobal Botella, J. P. Kremer and Henry Rolin, came to the conclusion that it was in the power of the Delimitation Commission to consider the case in the first place and that

> it is only when the Commission has exhausted all these sources of information and announced that it has such serious doubts that it is unable to decide on these questions, or if it has flagrantly exceeded its power, that the parties would be justified in attempting to reach a settlement of such difficulties in accordance with international law.

Since the three lawyers were not convinced that all means had been exhausted to settle the dispute within the Commission, they recommended that the Council decline taking the question to the PCIJ for an advisory opinion. Both parties accepted this opinion.[75]

The Maritza question illustrates how the Council found another way to receive legal counsel without bringing the question to the PCIJ. Interestingly, the jurists chosen to enquire about the Greek question did not refer the case to the League's Legal Section but instead to the representatives of the Assembly. This suggests that the close relationship between the LoN and the PCIJ envisaged by the drafters of the Covenant turned out in practice quite differently, and that in the end they became two separate bodies. Moreover, it shows that the Council needed legal counsel to deal with the many and sometimes complex questions concerning treaty interpretation from the peace treaties after 1919.[76]

Nonetheless, the majority of cases were submitted by the Council upon the request and with the consent of the disputing states or parties.[77] In the border dispute between Poland and Czechoslovakia about the region of Spisz (Jaworzina, today part of Slovakia), the two states approached the Council to request an advisory opinion on the question of the delimitation of the frontier. Initially, the border had been determined by the Inter-Allied Conference of Ambassadors in July 1920 and was renegotiated in 1921, and was again scrutinised in 1923 when locals from both sides of the borders disputed the decision.[78] On 21 August 1923, the Polish Foreign Minister,

Maurice Zamoyski, urged the Conference of Ambassadors to seek an advisory opinion via the Council for 'the political and economic stabilisation of Central Europe' as he feared that further delay 'would stir up public opinion in Poland, which would be justly aroused in regard to the fate of the local population, which had been pending for three years'.[79] The President of the Conference of Ambassadors had just reached out to the Council two days earlier to request a judicial clarification.

After the Council meeting of 20 September, which agreed to take on the case, the rapporteur of the Council, Jose Maria Quinones de Léon, approached the two disputing parties, which both agreed to submit the request of an advisory opinion to the PCIJ. The rapporteur even pushed the Court to call for an extraordinary meeting of the Court so that the question could be addressed without delay.[80] The two parties submitted documentation to the PCIJ to support their claims with regard to the border region of Jaworzina. After careful assessment of the documents, the Court invited the parties to give oral statements on 13 and 14 November 1923. Based on the written and oral evidence presented to the PCIJ, the judges issued their advisory opinion on 6 December 1923, in which they stated that the decisions of the Delimitation Commission of the Conference of Ambassadors, and of the procedures leading to those decisions, were executed in accordance with the arrangement made in the peace treaty. Only in the case of Spisz did the Court object and decided that the Commission needed to provide new proposals based on the peace treaty.[81]

In the meeting of the Council on 13 December 1923, the members voted unanimously in favour of adopting the advisory opinion. It was noted that 'the Court leaves no doubt on the point that the modifications of the frontier' were required. In a conversation with the two parties, the rapporteur noted that the two parties 'fully recognised the importance of the Court's opinion'. Subsequently, the Council suggested entrusting the Delimitation Commission with the implementation of the required changes to the Polish-Czechoslovakian border.[82] The Delimitation Commission presented a new border proposal in Spisz in February 1924 and the Conference of Ambassadors endorsed the changes that March.[83] The Council also agreed to the proposed border changes in its meeting of 12 March 1924, which provided the basis for the protocol, which was signed in Cracow by Poland and Czechoslovakia on 6 May. The protocol regulated in detail the economic relations of the regions, the customs rules and the domicile of inhabitants, as well as the property rights.[84]

The case illustrates how efficiently the PCIJ operated in this matter, providing an advisory opinion within three months, also thanks to the rapporteur, who had pushed for a quick solution. The swift action helped significantly to deescalate the dispute in the Jaworzina region. The inhabitants on both sides of the border accepted the Court's opinion, as did their governments. Despite the non-binding character of the opinion, nobody doubted or questioned the authority of the Court's opinion. This was true for the governments, which sought advice, but it was also reassuring for locals, who were most directly affected by the decision.

The revision of the PCIJ's Statute in 1929 (and adopted in 1936) assimilated the Court's practice of the advisory procedure to that of the contentious procedure in Article 68.[85] The discussions had taken place during the negotiations of the United States' accession to the Court in 1929. One of the major objections was the Court's advisory jurisdiction. The Americans feared that the Court's legal advice could interfere with internal matters of the United States without its consent.[86] The Greek lawyer Nicholas Politis justified the suggested changes to the Court's advisory function as giving it a 'more permanent character'.[87] The assimilation of procedure received mixed reviews from the legal community. Hudson welcomed this assimilation because 'the judicial character of the Court should be safeguarded in the rendering of advisory opinions'. Moreover, the advisory opinion received an 'authoritative' sanction which bolstered 'the prestige of the Court'.[88] The Belgian jurist Charles de Visscher, on the other hand, thought that the Court had missed an opportunity to develop the instrument of the advisory opinion into something distinct from the Court's judiciary function. The fact that the advisory opinion was non-binding never undermined its authority. On the contrary, the parties consenting to request an advisory opinion also accepted its outcome.[89]

Conclusion: successful instrument?

The advisory opinion was a popular instrument that states used to explore options for dispute resolution at an early stage, before a dispute had escalated. Its non-binding character proved particularly useful because it gave the parties the freedom to adhere or not. Most importantly though, it lowered the bar to seek such an opinion in first place.[90] The public character of the Court's procedure was another reason why the advisory opinion was popular. It not only raised the prestige of the Court itself, but also helped build on the idea of 'public jurisdiction'.[91] In all cases discussed, the rapporteur of the Council had considerable influence on how the Council dealt with requests for an advisory opinion. Rather than operate in the limelight, he operated in secret.[92] In fact, a study by Solomon Nkiwane suggests that the rapporteur had considerable influence in choosing the appropriate instrument to resolve disputes quickly.[93] If the rapporteur thought a preliminary legal counsel was necessary for the Council to make an informed decision, it was up to the rapporteur to select the lawyers with the approval of the Secretary-General, as the Maritza question illustrated. The selected committee of jurists then prepared a recommendation for the Council to consider in the case put before them. This informal legal counsel proved to be an important step in evaluating the request for an advisory opinion. The practice developed out of the PCIJ's reluctance to give an advisory opinion in the Eastern Carelia case, which set the standard and signalled to the LoN that the World Court would act independently in assessing whether to accept or reject requests for advisory opinions.

Most cases, though, were submitted for an advisory opinion with express wishes from the disputing parties through the League's Council. The parties hoped for a quick solution and accepted the Court's advice as the Jaworzina case illustrates. The parties' willingness to accept a non-binding advisory opinion was seen as a great success. In 1927, the annual report had highlighted that

> such prestige as the Court to-day enjoys as a judicial tribunal is largely due to the amount of its advisory business and the judicial way in which it has dealt with such business. In reality, where there are in fact contending parties, the difference between contentious cases and advisory cases is only nominal.[94]

In one point though, the advisory jurisdiction did not meet the expectations of the drafters of Article 14 of the Covenant. The advisory function should have brought the LoN and the PCIJ in close interaction, yet the Court often refused to give an opinion, as the Eastern Carelia case showed. As a result, the LoN, or rather the Council, developed the practice of seeking legal counsel from lawyers of the Assembly, creating a more informal tool.[95] The Council explored various ways to gain legal expertise to fulfil the LoN's function in conflict resolution. The advisory opinion proved a useful tool for the Council to deal with disputes and clarify legal contexts. Moreover, it also showed the 'efficient functioning of international institutions'.[96] Most importantly, it offered disputing parties an alternative to a formal arbitration or a judgment from the PCIJ.[97] In fact, several special treaties and statutes created after 1919, such as the Statute on Freedom of Transit (1921), the Statute on the International Régime of Railways (1923) or the Opium Convention (1925) also successfully introduced an advisory jurisdiction.[98] Hudson concluded that the advisory opinion seemed to meet the desire of the states and other private parties to 'informalize the settlement of differences'.[99]

After 1945, the International Court of Justice (ICJ), the successor of the PCIJ, adopted the advisory jurisdiction, albeit with some hesitation.[100] In a report of the Informal Inter-Allied Committee on the Future of the

Permanent Court of International Justice of 1944, it was noted that the advisory opinion 'tended to encourage the use of the Court as an instrument for settling issues which were essentially of political rather than of a legal character'. At the same time, the report stressed that the Council needed legal advice as the 'League experience has shown the necessity of having an authoritative standing tribunal to which, in suitable cases, questions of this (advisory) kind can be referred to for an opinion'.[101] As a result, two significant changes transformed the character of the advisory opinion. First, the advisory opinion was considered only as a question, and no unanimity of the United Nations Security Council (UNSC) was required. Second, besides the Security Council and the Assembly, other UN bodies could also seek an advisory opinion.

The changes, though, did not lead to an increase in advisory opinion. They rather deterred the UN and its various organs from making use of the advisory opinion in extenso. Only twenty-six advisory opinions have been issued since 1945. The American jurist Grant Gilmore welcomed the restrictions put on the ICJ's advisory jurisdiction since he did not believe that the instrument was of any use during the period of the PCIJ, not least because of the Council, 'which was never notable for its capacity to meet difficult issues squarely', making explicit mention of the Eastern Carelia case.[102] Several factors explain the discrepancy of how the advisory jurisdiction worked in the period of the LoN and the UN. The PCIJ acted swiftly on the matter and issued advisory opinions on average within four months compared to the ICJ's twenty-four months. The requests submitted to the PCIJ were precise, which allowed the Court to give a concrete advisory opinion. In contrast, the requests submitted to the ICJ were rather vague in formulation and sometimes even biased. Finally, the advisory opinions of the PCIJ were unanimous and thus carried authority, despite their non-binding character. The ICJ's advisory opinions did not need to be unanimous and resulted in offering dissenting opinions, which was and is not in the interest of the Court. As a result, the advisory jurisdiction was not an effective tool in helping de-escalate disputes between parties.[103] Other international courts have taken up the idea of an advisory jurisdiction but only in a very limited and narrow scope. The European Court of Human Rights (ECHR) and the International Tribunal of the Law of the Sea (ITLOS) provide examples which include an advisory jurisdiction, though the legal community is rather hesitant in developing the tool much further.[104]

This brings us back to Manley O. Hudson, who had called the development of an international jurisdiction an 'experiment'. Indeed, advisory jurisdiction is still an experimental field today. The drafters of the Covenant, and later those behind the Statute, rules and procedures of the PCIJ, had many different visions of how an international jurisdiction would work. The idea of an advisory jurisdiction was novel. It empowered the World Court to actively work with the LoN. Yet from the beginning, the judges were hesitant in embracing this new instrument, as they feared too much involvement in the political sphere. As a result, this led to a much more conservative approach to developing international jurisdiction, as the revision of the Court's Statute in 1929 illustrates. The judges of the PCIJ were careful in protecting their independence and integrity, which may explain why the Court pursued a very conservative interpretation of the advisory opinion and did not push for the creation of a more powerful instrument. More progressive voices in the lawyer community saw it as a missed opportunity. Hudson, one of the advisory opinion's few American supporters, pleaded for more creativity, when he said that

> it is not a matter of choosing a gadget which will fit into a particular place. It calls for exercise of highly creative faculties. Standards and principles and rules of law do not often apply themselves automatically in particular disputes. A nexus of direct contact to concrete situations must be forged, and the task requires both discrimination and judgment.[105]

Notes

1 Jane A. Hofbauer, '1918: The League of Nations as a "First Organized Expression of the International Community" and the Permanent Court of International Justice as its Guardian', *Austrian Review of International and European Law* 23:1 (2020), 1–21; Marcus M. Payk, *Frieden durch Recht? Der Aufstieg des modernen Völkerrechts und der Friedensschluss nach dem Ersten Weltkrieg* (Oldenbourg: De Gruyter Oldenbourg, 2018); Ole Spiermann, *International Legal Argument in the Permanent Court of International Justice: The Rise of the International Judiciary* (Cambridge: Cambridge University Press, 2005), pp. 3–33.
2 Covenant of the League of Nations, Paris, 28 June 1919.
3 Manley O. Hudson, *The Permanent Court of International Justice 1920–1942: A Treatise* (New York: The Macmillan Company, 1943), pp. 511–12.
4 Manley O. Hudson, *The Advisory Opinions of the Permanent Court of International Justice* (New York: Carn. End. for Intern. Peace, 1925), pp. 352–66. See also Marika Giles Samson and Douglas Guilfoyle, 'The Permanent Court of International Justice and the "Invention" of International Advisory Jurisdiction', in Malgosia Fitzmaurice and Christian J. Tams (eds), *Legacies of the Permanent Court of International Justice* (Leiden: Martinus Nijhoff Publishers, 2013), pp. 41–68, here: 43.
5 Van Vecten Veeder, 'Advisory Opinions of the Judges of England', *Harvard Law Review* 13:5 (1900), 358–70.

6 Manley O. Hudson, 'Advisory Opinions of National and International Courts. I. National Courts', *Harvard Law Review* 37:8 (1924), 970–1001, here: 971–2.
7 Malgosia Fitzmaurice and Christian J. Tams (eds), *Legacies of the Permanent Court of International Justice* (Leiden: Martinus Nijhoff Publishers, 2013).
8 Spiermann, *International Legal Argument*.
9 Dharma Pratap, *The Advisory Jurisdiction of the International Court* (Oxford: Oxford University Press, 1972); Stephen Schwebel, 'Was the Capacity to Request an Advisory Opinion Wider in the Permanent Court of International Justice Than It Is in the International Court of Justice?' *British Year Book of International Law* 62:1 (1992), 77–118.
10 Gleider I. Hernandez, *The International Court of Justice and the Judicial Function* (Oxford: Oxford University Press, 2014); Michla Pomerance, *The Advisory Function of the International Court in the League and UN Eras* (Baltimore, MD: John Hopkins University Press, 1973).
11 Hudson, *Advisory Opinions*, p. 8.
12 Jean d'Aspremont, 'The League of Nations and the Power of "Experiment Narratives" in International Institutional Law', *International Community Law Review* 22 (2020), 275–90.
13 Andrei Mamolea, 'Saving Face. The Political Work of the Permanent Court of Arbitration (1902–1914)', in Ignacio de la Rasilla and Jorge E. Vinuales (eds), *Experiments in International Adjudication. Historical Accounts* (Cambridge: Cambridge University Press, 2019), pp. 193–210; Mary Ellen O'Connell and Lenore VanderZee, 'The History of International Adjudication', in Cesare P. R. Romano, Karen J. Alter and Yuval Shany (eds), *The Oxford Handbook of International Adjudication* (Oxford: Oxford University Press, 2013), pp. 42–60; Anneliese Quast Mertsch, 'The Relationship between the Permanent Court of Arbitration and the Permanent Court of International Justice, and its Significance for International Law', in Christian J. Tams and M. Fitzmaurice (eds), *Legacies of the Permanent Court of International Justice* (Leiden: Martinus Nijhoff Publishers, 2013), pp. 243–67; Spiermann, *International Legal Argument*, pp. 3–7, 13–14.
14 David Hunter Miller, *The Drafting of the Covenant* (New York: G.P. Putnam's Sons, 1928), p. 52. See also Leland M. Goodrich, 'The Nature of the Advisory Opinions of the Permanent Court of International Justice', *American Journal of International Law* 32:4 (1938), 738–58, here: 739.
15 Walter Phillimore, *Schemes for Maintaining General Peace* (London: HM Stationery Office, 1920).
16 Gerry Simpson, 'Walter Phillimore, The Phillimore Plan, 20 March 1918 (Draft Convention), 1918', in Jill Barrett and Jean-Pierre Gauci (eds), *British Contributions to International Law, 1915–2015. An Anthology Set* (Leiden: Brill, 2021), pp. 1547–52; The Austrian jurist, Heinrich Lammasch, had also described the advisory function of a world court in 1918; see Heinrich Lammasch, *Der Völkerbund zur Bewahrung des Friedens* (Olter: W. Trösch, 1918), p. 13.

17 *Constitution of the League of Nations. Text of the Plan Presented to the Peace Conference at Paris and the Addresses Delivered before the Conference by President Wilson, M. Leon Bourgeois, Lord Robert Cecil, Premier Orlando* (New York, 1919), p. 7.
18 Miller, *Drafting*, p. 328.
19 Ibid., p. 329.
20 'Formation of the League of Nations, 1919. Lord Cecil's Diary of the British Delegation, Paris, 6 January–10 June 1919', Papers of Lord Robert Cecil, AD MSS 51131, British Library, London.
21 Miller, *Drafting*, pp. 391–3, 406.
22 *Comparison of the Plan for the League of Nations. Presented by Mr. Pittman, 20 May 1919* (Washington, DC: US Government Printing Office, 1921), p. 19. See also Ruth B. Henig, *The League of Nations* (London: Haus Publishing, 2010), pp. 25–53; Hudson, *Advisory Opinions*, pp. 9–14.
23 Hudson, *Advisory Opinions*, pp. 11–12.
24 James Brown Scott, *The Project of a Permanent Court of International Justice and Resolutions of the Advisory Committee of Jurists* (Washington, DC: The Endowment, 1920); For biographies of the committee members, see P. Sean Morris (ed.), *The League of Nations and the Development of International Law: A New Intellectual History of the Advisory Committee of Jurists* (London: Routledge, 2021).
25 'Jurists Begin Work on League's Court', *The New York Times*, 17 June 1920, p. 6.
26 'Discours pronocé par M. Léon Bourgeois, The Hague, 16 June 1920', in Comité consultatif de juristes, *Procès-verbaux des séances du comité, 16 juin–24 juillet 1920 avec annexes* (The Hague: Van Langenhuysen frères, 1920), pp. 5–11, here: 7.
27 Ibid., p. 8.
28 Ibid., pp. 1–19.
29 Ole Spiermann, '"Who Attempts Too Much Does Nothing Well": The 1920 Advisory Committee of Jurists and the Statute of the Permanent Court of International Justice', *British Year Book of International Law* 73:1 (2003), 187–260.
30 Comité, *Procès-verbaux*, p. 584.
31 Ibid., p. 585.
32 'Draft Scheme', in Jurists, *Procès-verbaux*, pp. 673–85, here: 80. See also Panos Merkouris, 'The Advisory Jurisdiction of the Permanent Court of International Justice in Practice: A Tale of Two Scopes', in Malgosia Fitzmaurice and Christian J. Tams (eds), *Legacies of the Permanent Court of International Justice* (Leiden: Martinus Nijhoff Publishers, 2013), pp. 69–85, here: pp. 74–6.
33 'Rapport du Trente-Quatrième Séance, La Haye, 24 juillet 1920', in Comité, *Procès-verbaux*, pp. 693–749, here: 730–1.
34 Ibid., p. 731.
35 Ibid.

36 'Fifth Meeting, 29 November 1920', in Assembly. Third Commission (Court of International Justice). Minutes of the Meetings of Sub-Commission, 1920, 1–5, R1362, 26/8885/8540, League of Nations Archives, Geneva (hereafter LNA).
37 'Henry Fromageot in Ninth Meeting, 4 December 1920', in Assembly. Third Commission (Court of International Justice). Minutes of the Meetings of Sub-Commission, 1920, 7, R1362, 26/8885/8540, LNA.
38 Hudson, *Advisory Opinions*, pp. 331–3; Giles Samson and Guilfoyle, 'Invention', pp. 51, 58–9.
39 Hudson, *Advisory Opinions*, p. 333.
40 'Eighth Meeting, 2 December 1920', in Assembly. Third Commission (Court of International Justice). Minutes of the Meetings of Sub-Commission, 1920, 1–9, R1362, 26/8885/8540, LNA.
41 Resolutions of the First Assembly, 2 August 1920, R1361, 26/8537/8537, LNA.
42 The judges were elected on 14 September 1921. Under Article 21 of the Court's Statute, the judges needed to be leading figures in their field; see Spiermann, *International Legal Argument*, pp. 134–40.
43 'Questions to be Submitted for Discussion at a Full Meeting of the Court, 7 February 1922', in *Publications de la cour permanente de justice internationale. Série D: Actes et Documents relatifs à l'organisation de la cour. No. 2. Préparation du Règlement de la Cour. Procès-verbaux, avec annexes, des séances de la session préliminaire de la Cour (30 janvier–24 mars 1922)* (Leiden: A.W. Sijthoff, 1922), pp. 289–92, here: 292.
44 'Memorandum by John B. Moore on the Advisory Question, 18 February 1922', in *Publications de la cour. Série D. No. 2*, pp. 383–98, here: 383.
45 'Memorandum by John B. Moore on the Advisory Question, 18 February 1922', in *Publications de la cour. Série D. No. 2*, pp. 383–98, here: 398.
46 Michael Dunne, *The United States and the World Court, 1920–1935* (London: Continuum International Publishing Group Ltd, 1988), 104; Giles Samson and Guilfoyle, 'Invention', pp. 44–7, here: 45.
47 *Cour Permanente de Justice Internationale. Règlement de la Cour. Adopté par la Cour le 24 mars 1922* (The Hague: Cour permanente de justice internationale, 1922).
48 Michla Pomerance, *The United States and the World Court as a 'Supreme Court of the Nations': Dreams, Illusions and Disillusion* (The Hague: Brill, 1996), pp. 74–7.
49 Giles Samson and Guilfoyle, 'Invention', p. 53; Hudson, *Advisory Opinions*, pp. 334–7.
50 Hudson, *PCIJ: A Treatise*, pp. 513–22.
51 Goodrich, 'Nature of the Advisory Opinions', 744–7; Hudson, *PCIJ: A Treatise*, pp. 486–8.
52 The spelling of the geographical terms is retained throughout the text to reflect the terms used in the source material.
53 W. Keynäs, 'Soviet Russia and Eastern Carelia', *The Slavonic and East European Review* 6 (1928), 520–8, here: 520–5.

54 Nick Baron, *Soviet Karelia: Politics, Planning and Terror in Stalin's Russia, 1920–1939* (London: Routledge, 2008), pp. 20–7.
55 Eastern Carelia – Communique Copy of the Green Paper containing the Documents Concerning the Carelian question, 1922, R560, 11/27723/1387, LNA.
56 Eastern Carelia – Council of the League of Nations – Sixteenth Session of the Council, Geneva, 10–14 January 1922, R559, 11/18628/1387, LNA.
57 Spiermann, *International Legal Argument*, pp. 160–74.
58 Keynäs, 'Soviet Russia', 526.
59 Wilhelm Chydenius, R. Erich and R. Hermanson, 'Pour quelles raisons et sur quels points la question de la Carélie Orientale est-elle susceptible d'un avis consultatif de Cour Permanente de Justice internationale', Helsinki, 12 March 1923, R560, 11/27715/1387, LNA.
60 'Eastern Carelia. Report by M. Salandra and Resolution Adopted by the Council, 21 April 1923', *League of Nations Official Journal* 4 (1923), 663–4.
61 'Georgi W. Tchitcherin (Russian People's Commissary for Foreign Affairs) to PCIJ (Telegram), 11 June 1923', in *Statut de la Carelie orientale. Avis consultatif, PCIJ, 23 July 1923*, 12–14.
62 Permanent Court of International Justice. Third Ordinary Session, The Hague, 23 July 1923, 27. See also Hudson, *Advisory Opinions*, pp. 341–3. Although the statement above could be interpreted as a *quasi*-acknowledgement of the Soviet Union as a state, Salandra made it clear in his report that this was not the case, see 'Eastern Carelia. Report by M. Salandra and Resolution Adopted by the Council, 21 April 1923', *League of Nations Official Journal* 4 (1923), 663.
63 Permanent Court of International Justice. Third Ordinary Session, The Hague, 23 July 1923, 22–9.
64 Schwebel, 'Capacity', 96.
65 Spiermann, *International Legal Argument*, pp. 161–6.
66 Philip Burton, 'Searching for the Eastern Carelia Principle', *ESIL Reflections* 8:1 (2019), 1–9, here: 4.
67 Dispute between Romania and Hungary Concerning the Mixed Romanian-Hungarian Arbitral Tribunal. Report of the Committee of the Council, 17 September 1927, R 614, 11/61980/28470, LNA.
68 Pomerance, *Advisory Function*, pp. 173–4, 184–97.
69 Loukas Kanakaris-Roufos (Greek Minister of Foreign Affairs) to Secretary-General, Telegram, 24 February 1926, R626, 11/49710/49710, LNA.
70 Tewfik Roushdy (Turkish Minister of Foreign Affairs) to Secretary-General, Telegram, 8 March 1926, R626, 11/49710/50008, LNA.
71 'Fourth Council Meeting (Public), Geneva, 16 March 1926', *League of Nations Official Journal* 7 (1926), 511–13.
72 'Minute of the Delimitation Commission, 27 December 1925', *League of Nations Official Journal* 7 (1926), 513. See also Minute of the Delimitation Commission, Alexandroupolis, 12 December 1925, R626, 11/49710/50283, LNA. See also Communiqué aux Membres du Conseil. Délimitation de la

frontière entre la Grèce et la Turquie. Question de la Maritza, Geneva, 8 March 1926, C.142.1926. VII, LNA.
73 'Fourth Council Meeting (Public), Geneva, 16 March 1926', 513–15.
74 Ibid., 516.
75 Botella, Kremer, Rolin, Legal Opinion on the Maritza Question, Geneva, 16 March 1926, R626, 11/49710/50024, LNA; For a broader analysis, see Antonis Klapsis, 'Attempting to Revise the Treaty of Lausanne: Greek Foreign Policy and Italy during the Pangalos Dictatorship, 1925–1926', *Diplomacy & Statecraft* 25:2 (2014), 240–59.
76 Pomerance, *Advisory Function*, 274–6.
77 *Fourteenth Annual Report of the Permanent Court of International Justice, 1937–38, Series E, No. 14* (Leiden, 1938), pp. 72–3. See also Schwebel, 'Capacity', 77–118, here: 81.
78 *Receuil des avis consultatifs. Affaire de Jaworzina (Frontière Polono-Tchécoslovaque). Série B. No. 8, 6 December 1923* (Leiden, 1923), 5–19; For maps, see No. 8: Question of Jaworzina. Delimitation of the Czechoslovak-Polish Frontier, 1923, CRID 13/206/123, LNA.
79 Maurice Zamoyski to Conference of Ambassadors, Telegram, Paris, 21 August 1923, R615, 11/30526/30604, LNA.
80 *Receuil des avis consultatifs. Affaire de Jaworzina (Frontière Polono-Tchécoslovaque). Série B. No. 8, 6 December 1923* (Leiden: Permanent Court of International Justice, 1923), p. 18.
81 Ibid., p. 57.
82 Report by Quinoses de Léon on the Resolution adopted by the Council Meeting of 17 December 1923, R616, 11/30526/32627, LNA.
83 Delimitation Commission to Conference of Ambassadors, Brno, 11 February 1924, R616, 11/34457/30526, LNA.
84 See, for more details, Protocol between Poland and Czechoslovakia regarding the Delimitation of the Two Countries, Cracow, 6 May 1924, R617, 11/30526/39148, LNA. See also Ludwig Spiegel, *Der Streit um die Javorina (Urgarten). Ein Beitrag zur Praxis des neuen Völkerrechts* (Vienna, 1924).
85 Pratap, *Advisory Jurisdiction*, 17–30. See also Giles Samson and Guilfoyle, 'Invention', 60; Merkouris, 'Advisory Jurisdiction', p. 77.
86 Committee of Jurists on the Statute of the Permanent Court of International Justice. Minutes of the Session held at Geneva, 11–19 March 1929, C.166.M.66.1929.V, LNA. See also The United States and the Permanent Court of International Justice. Documents relating to the Question of American Accession to the Court (Washington DC, 1930).
87 'Report of M. Politis to the Assembly, 14 September 1929', in *Sixth Annual Report of the Permanent Court of International Justice, 1929–1930, Series E, No. 6* (Leiden, 1928), 87.
88 Hudson, *PCIJ: A Treatise*, p. 509.
89 Charles de Visscher, 'Les avis consultatifs de la Cour permanente de justice internationale', *Recueil des cours* 26 (1929), 58–9.
90 Giles Samson and Guilfoyle, 'Invention', pp. 56–7.

91 Ibid., p. 51.
92 Pomerance, *Advisory Function*, p. 57.
93 Solomon Nkiwane, 'The Role of the Rapporteur in the League of Nations' (Doctoral Thesis, McGill University, Montreal, 1975), 242–55.
94 *Fourth Annual Report of the Permanent Court of International Justice, 1927–28, Series E, No. 4* (Leiden, 1928), 76.
95 Committee of Jurists on the Statute of the Permanent Court of International Justice. Minutes of the Session held at Geneva, 11–19 March 1929, 15, C.166.M.66.1929.V, LNA.
96 Hudson, *PCIJ: A Treatise*, p. 523.
97 Ibid., p. 524.
98 Hudson, *Advisory Opinions*, pp. 367–70.
99 Ibid., p. 370.
100 Mohamed Sameh M. Amr, *The Role of the International Court of Justice as the Principal Judicial Organ of the United Nations* (The Hague: Brill, 2003); Hernandez, *International Court of Justice*, 74–85; Schwebel, 'Capacity', 100–18.
101 Report of the Informal Inter-Allied Committee on the Future of the Permanent Court of International Justice (1944), Cmd. 6531, Para. 65 and Para. 67.
102 Grant Gilmore, 'International Court of Justice', *The Yale Law Journal* 55:5 (1946), 1049–66, here: 1055.
103 Giles Samson and Guilfoyle, 'Invention', pp. 62–5. See also Pomerance, *Advisory Function*, pp. 368–71.
104 Tom Ruys and Anemoon Soete, '"Creeping" Advisory Jurisdiction of International Courts and Tribunals? The Case of the International Tribunal for the Law of the Sea', *Leiden Journal of International Law* 29:1 (2016), 155–76; Giles Samson and Guilfoyle, 'Invention', pp. 65–7.
105 Manley O. Hudson, *International Tribunals. Past and Future* (Washington DC: Lawbook Exchange Ltd, 1944), p. 246.

9

With or without the metropole: deferred sovereignty as instrument of racial governance

Pablo de Orellana

An introduction to saving colonialism in the 1940s

To anti-colonial figures like the Vietnamese and Indian nationalists Hồ Chí Minh and Jawaharlal Nehru, the Allied Second World War charters appeared to extend the right to self-determination to 'subject peoples'. Even though such promises and their inclusion in the United Nations Charter were not binding,[1] the emergence of the principle as universal, rather than limited to Europe, as occurred with United States President Woodrow Wilson's First World War version, was key to informing and legitimising post-war claims to and efforts towards decolonisation.[2]

In response, the French empire reformed to resist decolonisation by making colonial arrangements appear consensual and endowed with their own sovereignty. In this strategy, resisting decolonisation was devolved to structures in hands of colonial settlers and governors,[3] allowing France to claim it respected self-determination and consequently sign agreements to this effect, such as the 1941 Atlantic Charter and the UN Charter of 1945, while in effect deferring it indefinitely. French leader Charles de Gaulle's 1944–45 imperial reforms targeted the triple threat of post-war international intervention, the demand – supported by the United States – for the self-determination of non-self-governing peoples, as well as anti-colonial and progressive liberals at home.[4]

These reforms radically changed how French colonial governance worked. The principles of this reform worked their way into the very practices of colonial government, its power in relation to the metropole, and ultimately also shaped the international order of its time. This chapter takes as its case study the post-war administration of Indochina, France's wealthiest and most populous colony, and its relationship to France. De Gaulle's reforms made Indochina superficially resemble India's All India Government of the 1920s to the 1940s, particularly insofar as it became a legal 'international person' in 1946, even though it remained fully a part of the French Empire. Hitherto known as French Indochina, the colony became the Indochinese Federation. It was granted its own elected assemblies, where only European colonists could vote, and included the 'federated governments' of the five 'associated states' of Indochina: Cambodia, Laos and the three territories into which Vietnam had been divided in 1881. Crucially for the analysis in this chapter, it was also given the prerogative to act as a state in many domains, for example sending its own high-level diplomatic delegations to international events such as the Philippine independence celebrations of July 1946, as well as prerogatives concerning military forces on its territory, which would from then on answer to Saigon as well as Paris.

Colonial organisations endowed with deferred sovereignty were not a new idea in the immediate post-war era. In 1945, the United Kingdom signed the UN Charter alongside a nominally legally sovereign India, just as the Soviet Union had the Byelorussian and Ukrainian Soviet Socialist Republics sign as actual states, and France had Syria and Lebanon (so-called mandates of the League of Nations). Likewise, deferred sovereignty, due to its capacity to indefinitely extend the 'unready' exception to self-determination while symbolically and legally acknowledging it, was used later too, for example by Rhodesia in its Unilateral Declaration of Independence in 1965, or Spain in its 1970s attempt to make Spanish Sahara and Equatorial Guinea into fully fledged Spanish provinces in order to comply with UN-mandated self-determination while preventing colonial subjects from fully participating due to their 'unreadiness'.

Thinking of these structures as international instruments, part of a repertoire of instruments of international order, is very helpful. The origin of these colonial quasi-state structures, together with the ideational discourse and practice assumption that they are to be co-governed between European colonists and the metropoles until natives are 'ready', lies in the nineteenth and early twentieth century, but subsequent iterations have been widely applied and have continued to shape international relations since. This means that we are looking at a concept and resulting set of specific practices, the origins of which need to be located in the context of the colonial and anti-colonial politics of the interwar period.

Crucially, this was an ulterior and further development of earlier colonial concepts, approaches and structures, such as the French '*code de l'indigénat*' (native code) that governed colonial subjects based on race and ethnic birth. That is, deferred sovereignty, and the institutional structures and practices it informed, are interwar developments that came to the forefront in the immediate post-war period. This is not only visible in the case of the reconquest of Indochina explored in this chapter. Deferred sovereignty is in fact an interwar international instrument that remains active in unresolved decolonisation cases like West Irian (late 1970s), Western Sahara (1975–present) and Chagos (1970s–present).

Researching these structures from the perspective of their conceptualisation as instruments defined by practice permits analysis to empirically focus on the specific practices, ideas, structures and relations that shaped them, their metropoles and their contribution to contemporary international relations, for inter-imperial (even intra-imperial) relations are international relations too and have decidedly shaped post-colonial international relations. Crucially, it allows historical and international political analyses to appreciate how colonial instruments of governance, born in the ethnogeopolitical historical international order of the nineteenth century and informed by its racial theories, were able to transform in the post-Second World War rights-based international order, which itself, however, also retained key imperial features and provisions.[5] They did this, I argue, by including colonies into norms of sovereign self-determination, while indefinitely deferring their application on the basis of the older racial hierarchies, which are thus revealed to have been fully retained and indeed act as the core idea of the instrument of deferred sovereignty, informing the constitution of its institutions, agents and doxa. In this way, treating the instrument of the colonial state as a structure of governance linked to but not always led by the metropole allows for detailed nuancing of the study of struggles over colonial hegemony and, crucially, their impact on the metropoles.

These quasi-state colonial structures are sometimes thought of as extensions of their respective coloniser states, responding precisely, even in the context of decolonisation, to instructions from policymakers in their metropolitan capitals.[6] It is widely assumed that colonial governments ultimately yielded to metropolitan ones – that, to put it in Schmittian terms, it is the metropole and not the colony that ultimately decides; this is a notion that probably survives to this day because it fits with the even more widespread and still deeply entrenched notion that one of the key attributes of state power is that it is centralised. The 1944 Brazzaville Conference, convened by de Gaulle to reform the French Empire, is commonly raised as an example of such a French colonial strategy that later developed into a national 'colonial consensus'.[7] Rather, this chapter argues that Indochinese colonial authorities worked against orders from Paris to retain the racial order of colonial governance, and when war broke out with Vietnamese rebels, they imposed a military-only strategic *fait accompli* onto divided French parliaments and governments with differing colonial policies. Examining the colonial state instrument from such a perspective therefore involves analysing not only the strategies and policies coming from the metropole, but also the actions, work and practices of a colonial elite that continually sought to force France to fight to retain its colonies by any means and avoid any reform of their racial order.

Examining the specific ideas and different threads of colonial discourse that dominated the Brazzaville conference[8] suggests that it reinforced policy goals long pursued by colonial, military and settler elites in many colonies, from the Union of South Africa to Algeria and Indochina, and which progressives in the metropoles had been trying to soften since the 1920s.[9] These included reinforcing legal inequality by race, rejecting admission of colonial subjects to French citizenship and conditioning any grant of autonomy, legislative power and sovereignty on restricting democratic, economic and legal participation to Europeans only.

These structures were frequently treated as legal international persons, which means they had the potential to wield significantly more agency than previous colonial structures.[10] There are some obvious ways in which their relative independence from metropoles and one another had significant contemporary and historical impact. At the very least, their administrative borders, as evident in Africa and Latin America, shaped future sovereign states and, less bureaucratically, contributed to the cultural, political and social particularisation of specific areas. In some cases, they even provided the basis for effective decolonisation, as is the case of India, where Nehru in 1945 forced the British to allow elected Indian representatives to take over the Government of India while partition and the final structures of independence were negotiated. In other cases, they proved to be farcical puppets; the State of Hatay was, for example, a legal fiction erected in 1938 for France to 'recognise' its particularity and then be legally able to cede it to Turkey without breaching the terms of its League of Nations' mandate over Syria. In many cases, however, these structures made significant far-reaching reforms of their own accord, sometimes independently of the metropole, as was the case of South Africa in 1910, which, after being granted sovereign powers on a similar basis which deferred the rights of non-Europeans, began to aggressively legislate to repress non-whites. Crucially, this included instances in which they contradicted, rejected or ignored British laws and provisions, as occurred in 1906 when the British Parliament repealed provisions targeting Black and Indian South Africans. Using the powers granted in 1910 to the Union of South Africa, South African governments reinstated those laws and began issuing the legislation that from the 1940s would become known as apartheid, and later sought to export it to other deferred sovereignty colonial instruments that were becoming states.[11]

What happens when the colonial instrument isn't just a tool of the metropole? In other words, how can we think of this instrument in relation to its metropole and the international? South Africa in the 1910s, like Indochina and Algeria in the 1940s, saw reforms that devolved vast powers from metropolitan capitals to colonial settlers and local administrators, which came to be invested in the retention of racial orders that established even more legal economic and violent power over non-European subjects and often led to conflicts with the metropoles. Where racialised orders and resistance to them have long been subjects of post-colonial international relations and history, this chapter proposes expanding this perspective beyond the ideas and laws to the institutional incarnation and practices that made and sustained colonial orders and hierarchies.[12]

Accounting for such dynamics requires thinking beyond the classical view of colonial government. Specifically, it calls for an exploration of how the deferred sovereignty instrument endowed colonial institutions with effective agency that made some colonial governments into quasi-independent international actors that were able to defy their metropoles. The post-war period is often seen as the very apex of territoriality and state power, but the account offered in this chapter shows that old imperialist practices of settler and conqueror independence continued, encased in and indeed propelled by new structures, practices and institutions, all informed by a novel rewriting of why, though now acknowledged to be sovereign, imperial subjects needed to remain under white rule. This is 'white man's burden' 3.0: a post-Nazi version for the twentieth century that preserves racial order. This, in turn, requires analysis of how in practice colonial instruments were able to work against the will of the metropole and, as we shall see in the case of Indochina, sought to force their capitals to keep fighting to maintain colonialism (as occurred in Algeria), or, when unable to do so, sought independence so as to be able to continue their preferred vision of colonial settler rule (as in Rhodesia) on the basis of deferred sovereignty. Such examples are vital, for they show that the instrument of deferred sovereignty, though initially intended to preserve colonies and their attachment to the metropole, could also serve to justify quasi or fully independent statehood.

How did this instrument work? This chapter takes the post-war history of the Indochinese Federation as a case study to examine deferred sovereignty. Specifically, it analyses how the instrument of deferred sovereignty was used by colonial administrations, how it informed their institutions and the practices of its governmental agents. Further, it also examines how deferred sovereignty allowed these colonial structures and practices to enact remarkable independence from the metropole, particularly when it came to contradicting mandates from colonial policymakers in the metropole. We could look at deferred sovereignty, it is found, as the sovereign reification and independence of the earlier colonial entrepreneurs – such as James Brooke in Sarawak – now made into spiritual and military guardians of the superiority of the metropole.

In its first move, in the next section, the chapter details the bureaucratic, diplomatic and power structure of the reformed French Union (Empire), and the Indochinese Federation within it,[13] to explore the ways in which the reforms affected relations between the metropole and the colony. The second move in our analysis, also in the next section, examines the practices of the Indochinese Federation through analysis of three key events in the history of the Vietnam Wars: the failure of the 1946 Franco-Vietnamese Da Lat and Fontainebleau negotiations; the outbreak of war in the so-called 'Hai Phong Incident'; and role of the colonial government and its personnel in persuading the United States to support the French war of colonial reconquest. Though the history of the latter has been studied very extensively, our focus here is on the extent to which it came not from Paris, which was mostly failing to persuade the United States to help, but rather from the colonial government.[14] It is found that the Federation had surprising independence, even when acting against France.

Where the earlier documentary analysis establishes that the colonial state had wide autonomy in relation to the French state, the third step in this analysis is conceptual, picking up on the historical and praxis insights of the previous section to extract the political ideas at the heart of these quasi-independent colonial institutions. It is found that the structures linking French Indochina and France as established by de Gaulle's 1944 reforms were not governmental. Tight institutional relations were replaced by military and ideological links, giving ample agency to individuals such as governors and generals, and effectively preventing Paris from promoting reform. Finally, the chapter explores the conceptualisation of this instrument of international order, which I call 'deferred sovereignty', and how its focus on racial order turned colonial institutions from extensions of the metropole into protectors of colonial racial hierarchies, even at the expense of their metropoles.

Deferred sovereignty, it emerges, is an idea of sovereignty: a legal, theoretical, and political device that prevents colonial subjects from wielding sovereignty on the basis of race, birth and gender. The concept produced legal structures where Vietnamese subjects could not vote in elections held in their name. It informed the constitution of institutions such as colonial states, armies, puppet states and even states like South Africa and Rhodesia that sought independence to preserve racial order. It shaped the doxa of agents such as governors or police that wielded the power of these institutions in the name of deferred sovereignty.

The Indochinese Federation: defending French colonialism against the world and France

This section firstly introduces the colonial administration reforms advanced by the 1944 Brazzaville Conference, focussing on how it re-established links between Free France and the colonies. The rest of this section is then devoted to analysis of three key episodes in the history of Indochina that serve as test cases for analysis of the powers of the Indochinese Federation and its range of independent action. These are: the collapse of the Fontainebleau conference in 1946 due to the opening of a rival conference at Da Lat; the 'Hai Phong Incident', which marked the outbreak of hostilities in 1946; and the drafting of the 'new Bao Dai Solution', a puppet monarchy arrangement used as proof of France's willingness to decolonise, which was key to persuading American diplomats that the war was about communism, not maintaining colonial rule, and securing US support for the reconquest of the colony.

The 1944 Brazzaville conference set out to reform the French Empire. Set in the context of the Second World War and the key role played by French colonies in rescuing, militarily substantiating and supporting de Gaulle's Free French movement, it placed vast importance on colonial decision-making and colonial military links to the metropole. This is unsurprising considering the key role played by colonial military commanders like Jean Decoux, who surrendered Indochina to the Japanese; or François Darlan, Vichy France's military leader and governor of North Africa, who then switched to the Allies in 1942 and had a very uncomfortable relationship with de Gaulle.

The impact of these events is evident in the structures established in Brazzaville. Equally evident is concern that the Allies, particularly the United States, which had expressed opposition to the restoration of French rule in Indochina, might establish some form of trusteeship or intervene in colonial affairs.[15] The most evident impact was administrative and symbolic: the Empire was to become the French Union, loosely attached to France through indirect structures of leadership rather than the previous mix of direct-rule colonies and indirectly ruled protectorates.[16] This saw tightly centralised colonies assembled from several territories apiece that aggregated them into macro-colonies such as West Africa, the Overseas Metropole (Algeria) or the Indochinese Federation studied in this chapter.[17] These organisations were invested with powers typical of statehood such as currency, diplomacy with other powers, justice and means of colonial repression.

Instead of direct rule from the Ministry of Colonies, the reform established assemblies in each colony, where French citizens of the colony elected representatives to send to the Assembly of the French Union, itself the colonial equivalent of the French Assemblée Nationale, together with which it formed the Assembly of the Republic. This in effect gave colonial settlers seats in the French Assemblée Nationale, but, vitally for our analysis, this fiction of democratic representation, similar to apartheid and other racial regimes, served to substantiate de Gaulle's case that 'qualified peoples' in these territories were being given a democratic voice to determine their futures.[18] The command structure of the colonial governments was loosened; governors were no longer tied to the French Parliament and cabinet, but rather became accountable to the Minister of Colonies and Prime Minister, as well as ad-hoc colonial committees convened by the Prime Minister and staffed by colonial civil servants. Colonial military commanders were further removed from parliamentary oversight and were expected to work with colonial governors. The conference rejected the possibility of granting native autonomy, let alone independence, to any colony, as 'the aims of France's civilising mission preclude any thought of autonomy or any possibility of development outside the French Empire'.[19] This is important and far more than symbolic; the French Union enshrined colonial ideas such as 'qualified peoples' into its constitution as administrative principles, meaning that these could potentially trump orders from Paris from anyone other than the Prime Minister.

The Conference also mooted giving more legal rights to the indigenous populations who had been subject to brutal measures ranging from forced labour and collective punishment to torture, expropriation and compulsory purchases of liquor and opium, and who, crucially, were not entitled to French rights and could be punished – even to death – by any French person at any time. The conference, however, voted to delay granting any legal or voting rights to indigenous populations as well as reforms to soften the exploitative nature of the relationship, essentially retaining the loathed *code de l'indigénat* and the racial order of the French Empire.[20]

The Brazzaville Conference, staffed entirely by French colonial civil servants, settlers and colonial military, could itself be considered an example of how colonial policy was influenced by the interests of the colonial settler and military elites and administrations rather than just central metropolitan government strategy. Though some natives also agreed with this policy, they were not invited to the conference.[21] In many ways, it could be seen as a move to free colonies form metropolitan control, mooted on the basis of Vichy's betrayal and de Gaulle's discourse that all the ills of France were due to parliamentary indecision and the Republic's lack of strong men endowed with constitutional power. Indeed, despite the progress made by French liberals like the civil servant Émile Bollaert in making the case for colonial reform, particularly some self-rule limited to domestic affairs, the

UNION FRANÇAISE

LIBERTÉ – ÉGALITÉ – FRATERNITÉ

Figure 9.1 Crest of the Union Française established by de Gaulle. Drawn by Tally de Orellana from 1945 archival document photos.

Brazzaville Conference – which did not include a single such reformer – explicitly rejected any such proposal.

This reform had a profound impact on Indochina and the events that would lead to the Vietnam Wars as well as the Algerian War. De Gaulle's reforms meant that the new Haut Commissaire (governor) he appointed in 1945, Admiral Thierry d'Argenlieu, had unprecedented powers and freedom of action. The new constitution of the Indochinese Federation was based on the Brazzaville principles with the addition of items designed to prevent US or international intervention, while France reconquered the colony after the Japanese occupation and the Viet Minh declaration of independence on 2 September 1945. It gave the High Commissioner control over all areas of government and administration and even constitutional powers – far more than any French politician in the metropole, and greater than the powers of comparable positions like the twentieth-century British Viceroy of India.[22] It furthermore granted d'Argenlieu control over the *Corps expéditionnaire français en Extrême-Orient* (Far East French Expeditionary Corps), which remained theoretically accountable to the head of the Army in Paris but had political oversight only from the High Commissioner.

From 1945, the High Commissioner of Indochina was in most respects a head of state with total control of administrative, military, political and constitutional affairs. He had a cabinet with Commissioners for Political, Economic, Diplomatic and Military affairs, who effectively acted as ministers. The High Commissioner no longer reported to the Cabinet and Assemblée Nationale; he reported to a special Interministerial Committee for Indochina called COMINDO (created 1946), chaired by the Prime Minister. COMINDO reported only to the Prime Minister's office, with the latter informing the Assemblée Nationale as well as the Colonial and Foreign Ministries as and when COMINDO deemed it necessary.[23] The COMINDO would turn out to be a serious problem in 1946–48. In practice, the High Commissioners reported to COMINDO, but the committee, if not actioned by the Prime Minister, lacked the authority to do anything, even pass reports onto other authorities. This meant that, if a friendly Prime Minister – like de Gaulle himself (until January 1946) or later Georges Bidault – was in office, COMINDO was only a fig leaf. In practice, when the High Commissioners needed action they wrote directly to Prime Ministers. COMINDO was in fact so detached from core government structures that its archives remain separate from those of the French Cabinet.[24]

Since the reform placed so much power and decision-making in the hands of the High Commissioner, it is worth briefly mentioning why d'Argenlieu was such an important choice. The naval officer had begun his career and earned the *Légion d'honneur* during the 1911–12 conquest of Morocco, was a Catholic priest and passionate advocate of the sacred mission of colonialism, had participated in the conquest of Morocco, had been involved

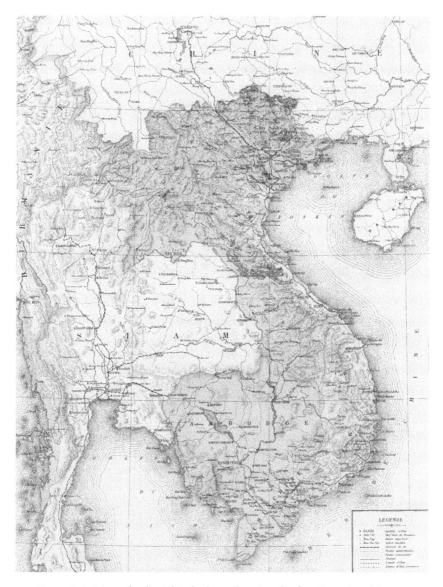

Figure 9.2 Map of colonial Indochina showing the five 'Associated States' that made up the Indochinese Federation. Bibliothèque Nationale de France, Wikimedia Commons.

in 'saving' the colony of New Caledonia during the Second World War and was a firm believer, like de Gaulle, that 'it is united to the overseas territories that she opened up to civilisation that France is a great power'.[25] Further, analysis of his personal and administrative files, as well as communications with his officials and the metropole, reveals a 'fervent' colonial and religious zeal, making him the 'ideal' candidate to preserve the colony, as de Gaulle noted when communicating the appointment.[26] Consideration of d'Argenlieu and the Brazzaville reforms suggests that the task of preserving and administering French colonies was passed from French ministries to officers steeped in colonial ideology.

The relative place of the colonial administration in relation to the metropole will now be examined empirically. For the purpose of this chapter's enquiry into deferred sovereignty, this is analysed through three key incidents that stand as major examples of how the instrument of deferred sovereignty allowed the colonial state to act with remarkable independence while seeking to determine French policy and force a military solution to the Vietnamese rebellion.

The instrument sabotages the metropole's negotiations: Da Lat vs Fontainebleau 1946

On 2 September 1945, Hồ Chí Minh declared the independence of Vietnam. The colony had surrendered to the Japanese during the Second World War, French troops were not in control, and the Viet Minh were able to take advantage of the Japanese surrender to declare independence. De Gaulle sent intelligence officer Jean Sainteny to negotiate with the Vietnamese rebels in their capital Hanoi, while British forces tasked with disarming the Japanese helped the French retake Saigon in the South. The Ho-Sainteny accords of 6 March 1946 established a truce that, awaiting direct Franco-Vietnamese negotiations, established a settlement based around the reunification of Vietnam – which had been separated into three separate 'states' called 'Ky' (see Figure 9.2) – and practical independence within a reformed French Union. In return, the Vietnamese Republic would allow French forces to return to the colony.

Negotiations were due to continue at Fontainebleau in France in July 1946. The talks, led by Vietnamese President Hồ Chí Minh and Minister of Colonies Marius Moutet, were initially hailed as a moment of progressive evolution in French relations with its colonies.[27] They opened on 6 July and focussed on a long-term arrangement not unlike the status of the Dominions within the British Commonwealth. Though they were frequently condemned as a French sham to distract the Vietnamese and enable a military reconquest,[28] my analysis suggests that this perspective tends to homogenise the French position and conceal divisions within the French nationalist and colonial political compacts.[29]

Many leading French figures did not agree with the premise of the talks. For de Gaulle, losing Indochina, France's 'balcony over the Pacific', meant no less than the collapse of French power and prestige – the loss of the only remaining proof of its *grandeur*.[30] His nationalist movement had been successful in politically linking the recovery of *grandeur* after the humiliation of the Second World War to a colonialism that proved French power. Analysis of French presidency, COMINDO, Colonial Ministry and the Indochinese Federation government files for the period reveals a great deal of disagreement and sleight of hand within the French side.

In July 1946, d'Argenlieu was ordered to travel to Paris and participate at the talks at Fontainebleau. He, however, remained in Saigon, lying to his superiors about being unable to travel due to 'a broken foot'.[31] His subsequent actions reveal a lot about the power and independence of the colonial state structure he governed. From Saigon, his regime took a dual-track strategy involving dutiful official communications with COMINDO, as well as private communications with Prime Minister Georges Bidault. In his formal reports to COMINDO, he and the colonial government argued that the Viet Minh rebels were nothing but Axis puppets, that Vietnam existed only 'in the dreams' 'of Vietnamese fascists', and that the Vietnamese were negotiating in bad faith. In his view, France needed to protect other Indochinese races from racist Vietnamese expansionism, which principally meant preventing the reunification of Vietnam with Cochinchina, the southernmost of the pieces into which Vietnam had been divided and the area of greatest French investment and settlement. His suggestion was to bring Cochinchina closer to France on a permanent basis by reinventing its own quasi-state structure to make it more akin to Algeria (which was 'an integral part of France') and thus prevent its reunification with Vietnam. He furthermore argued that Vietnam had never existed, that it was akin to Hitler's fantasies and that its very name should be banned from linguistic use.

Crucially for the analysis in this chapter about how the ideological instrument of deferred sovereignty changed and reified the colonial state, he passionately defended his claim – supported by de Gaulle and his orders for Indochina – that any and all negotiations between one of the 'associated states' of the Federation and France needed to go through himself.[32] The COMINDO did not agree and appeared sincere in its statements about granting reunification and quasi-independence to Vietnam within the French Union, rather than subsumed within the Indochinese Federation.[33]

To substantiate his case, d'Argenlieu had his administrators produce thousands of pages of spurious 'evidence' for COMINDO that the Viet Minh were but a terrorist criminal enterprise that should not be negotiated with.[34] In secret, d'Argenlieu also communicated privately with the French Prime Minister, his procolonial ally and fellow Gaullist loyalist Georges Bidault. In these communications there was no pretence of interethnic fairness: the main objective was retaining the colony and its status quo. They spoke of

Figure 9.3 Colonial power in practice: High Commissioner for Indochina Thierry d'Argenlieu at his desk sometime in 1945–46. Undated. Archive Sainteny.

a Viet Minh 'plot' to kick the French out of Indochina, and expressed fears that recognition of any sort – including the very act of establishing direct negotiations – at Fontainebleau would create a powerful enemy 'against us' and entail the permanent loss of wealthy Cochinchina and France's colonial 'achievements' in the Far East.[35] He suggested separating Cochinchina from Vietnam and making it another colonial substate under his authority.[36] There are no clear replies on file from Paris to d'Argenlieu's arguments other than vague requests to wait for negotiations at Fontainebleau to proceed.

D'Argenlieu disobeyed. On 1 June 1946, a month before the opening of Franco-Vietnamese talks at Fontainebleau on 6 July, d'Argenlieu convened a small conference at the High Commissioner's summer residence at Da Lat, where he declared that Cochinchina would be reformed as an 'autonomous associated state' within the Indochinese Federation. This meant Fontainebleau opened with a focus on a Vietnamese reunification that d'Argenlieu had already rendered impossible, although French diplomats insisted remained on the table. D'Argenlieu, however, implementing his new prerogative to negotiate with Indochinese subjects, finalised his Cochinchina plan on his own authority, calling a conference at Da Lat beginning on 1 August that concluded that Cochinchina would be raised to the status of 'associated state' (like Cambodia or Laos), entirely separate from 'Annam' (the French name for central Vietnam) but remaining within the Indochinese Federation. Remarkably, this was within his purview. Despite his misrepresentations to COMINDO, cabinet and the National Assembly, French Premier Bidault and the cabinet were unwilling to contradict d'Argenlieu; he was only reprimanded and remained in post. The Fontainebleau talks could no longer resolve the issue of reunification, and the Vietnamese delegation returned home empty-handed.

D'Argenlieu's actions sabotaged the last chance for a peaceful political settlement between the Vietnamese rebel alliance and the French Empire. In his memoirs, d'Argenlieu defended his actions, claiming that there was no such sabotage since the rebels were negotiating in bad faith. Tellingly for our interest in the instrument of deferred sovereignty, he claimed that his main enemy in the Da Lat affair was not Vietnamese, but rather unpatriotic French saboteurs who would destroy French grandeur by allowing its colonial empire to whittle away.[37] Crucially, it was the principle of deferred sovereignty – as idea, law and organisational practice – that allowed this agent and the institution he led to defy the metropole and force it to defend the colonial order.

Starting a war to save the instrument: the 1946 'Hai Phong Incident'

De Gaulle's 1944 colonial reforms, amplified in his 1945 arrangements for Indochina, granted unprecedented autonomy to colonial military leaders.[38] In 1945, de Gaulle, using his near-absolute Second World War powers, dispatched the French Second World War hero General Philippe Leclerc de Hauteclocque to reconquer Indochina as head of the Far East Expeditionary Corps. Crucially, Leclerc, like most colonial military leaders after de Gaulle's reforms, acquired total independence from the French Assemblée Nationale and cabinet, becoming accountable only to the Prime Minister and the colonial governments themselves.[39] The Assemblée did not initially contest this arrangement, which was approved together with the entirety of de Gaulle's provisional government arrangements,[40] and it limited the role of parliament to voting funds for the war, which it did in December 1946, with (to many surprisingly) enthusiastic Communist Party support.[41] This tactical independence would play a key role in the outbreak of hostilities in the First Vietnam War of 1946–54.

The only agreement to emerge from Fontainebleau was a modus vivendi that extended the ceasefire of the 6 March Hô-Sainteny accords, provided for the separation of armies, laid out zones of control to prevent forces from clashing, and allocated responsibilities for the Vietnamese and the French administrations, including customs policing, which was to be shared. In November 1946, tensions rose as the Expeditionary Corps' commander,

General Jean Valluy, accused the Viet Minh of smuggling weapons from China through Hai Phong harbour, which they controlled. For the time being, however, standing orders from Paris to avoid conflict held out. For example, when a shootout broke out on 20 November over French attempts to seize a trading vessel docking at Hai Phong, French officers declared an immediate ceasefire on the same day and reiterated their desire to respect the modus vivendi, leaving Hai Phong in Vietnamese customs control.

D'Argenlieu, in France to request more troops for the Expeditionary Corps, intervened immediately. On his own authority, he cabled Valluy, ordering him to use force to bring Hai Phong harbour under control. Valluy, in turn, ordered his commanders on the ground to issue an ultimatum to the Vietnamese, threatening military action unless they withdrew from the port. The Viet Minh did not withdraw and French forces started bombarding the city, beginning the First Vietnam War.[42] Concurrently, d'Argenlieu fought a rear-guard informational bureaucratic war against the French government; he lied to the cabinet and Assemblée Nationale about his and Valluy's role in the outbreak of hostilities, accusing the Viet Minh instead. This did not go unnoticed; in November 1946, a Presidential committee investigating d'Argenlieu's actions concluded that he was purposefully concealing communications and reports from the Presidency and Parliament, including last-ditch efforts by the Viet Minh to stave off hostilities, which were intercepted by the colonial government.[43]

D'Argenlieu's gamble paid off, however, and again went unpunished. Possibly inspired by his actions at Da Lat, his manoeuvres – though illegal and against French policy – forced upon Paris the military solution preferred by colonist and military elites. As the historian Stein Tønnesson finally established beyond doubt in 2010, the 'colonial triumvirate' of colonial officers (d'Argenlieu, his political Counsellor Pignon and Valluy) had successfully manipulated France into war while the French Government, particularly colonies minister Moutet, did not have the political consensus necessary to stop the conflict once it started. The instrument's vision of colonial order prevailed over and determined that of France itself.

Deferred sovereignty on the high seas of diplomacy: acquiring American assistance to fight Viet Minh and the 'new Bao Dai solution'

The greatest achievement of the Indochinese Federation was, however, its little-known role in involving the United States in the Vietnam war on the French side. The above episodes involved only the French government and its colonial state, but in 1947 the latter would play a truly historical role in French diplomatic communication with the United States.

Franco-American diplomatic interaction in 1945–49 has been studied extensively as the origin of the US Vietnam War,[44] with the latest research in this long tradition suggesting that the core of the case that persuaded US policymakers to support the French consisted of two key elements. Firstly, France had finally, after years of refusing to, decided to take an American-like progressive stance towards self-rule and eventually independence for colonies. Secondly, the British had corroborated French accusations that Viet Minh were Soviet puppets, which the Americans had until then treated with suspicion of French manipulation. In research published elsewhere, I examine in great detail – at some points cable by cable – how these two fabrications evolved from simplistic accusations easily dismissed by US diplomats to ever more elaborate descriptions that tried to address these two American concerns in order to gain US support for the reconquest of Indochina. And descriptions were all they were; between 1945 and 1948 there was no evidence whatsoever that the Viet Minh were Soviet stooges, controlled or even in communication with Moscow.

In this fluid, complex and subjective realm of political descriptions of global enemies, French diplomats set out to persuade their American counterparts that the Viet Minh were their enemies too. Early French attempts were crude, accusing the Viet Minh of being Japanese and Axis puppets from whom Indochina had to be 'liberated'. By early 1946, French policymakers had moved to a new argument: the Viet Minh were the communist agents of Stalin and Mao and part of a 'long-range plan to conquer all Southeast Asia', but this too was dismissed by US diplomats as a misleading 'raising of the Communist bogey'. The core reason for this distrust was the extent to which it was clear that the French had no intention of giving up the colony, which belied their claims of anti-communist concern and reinforced Viet Minh claims of a legitimate struggle for self-determination. These two descriptions were mutually dependent and would not work without one another; if the Viet Minh had legitimate claims, they could not be just communist stooges, while French refusals to consider independence demonstrated that the war was indeed colonial. By 1947, the latter was the last hurdle facing French efforts to obtain US assistance.[45]

By late 1947, American policymakers appeared satisfied that France's new plan for the colony's emancipation, dubbed the 'Bao Dai Solution', proved that the war was no longer purely colonial.[46] The 'solution' was a superficial rearrangement of the puppet Vietnamese Imperial protectorate arrangements in place in Indochina since 1881 (Bao Dai was the Vietnamese Emperor). Its descriptions and core documents, however, precisely echoed the liberal anti-colonial progressive tone of 1930s US anti-colonial discourse (and to some extent that in France too).[47] This language appeared consistently throughout French diplomacy from late 1947, and had a major impact on US diplomacy,[48] which found it to be a major breakthrough that would allow them to support a non-colonial and non-communist solution in Indochina.[49]

The colonial government once again played a vital role, one hitherto not retrieved by the literature on this war. The 'new' Bao Dai solution (d'Argenlieu had tried a similar arrangement, also based on Bao Dai, in early 1947) was the brainchild of Léon Pignon, Chief Political Counsellor of the Indochinese Federation since 1945, who in 1948 had been elevated to the position of High Commissioner of Indochina. Piecing together French Foreign Ministry and Presidency files (declassified as late as 2012) with those from the Indochinese Government, particularly Pignon's work as Chief Political Counsellor in Saigon and that of Chief Diplomatic Counsellor Achille Clarac, helps reconstruct the long journey of this description, revealing that it begins in Saigon, not Paris. In an indication of the quasi-statal role of colonial governments, French diplomacy in the Far East, including negotiations with China, Thailand or Asian colonies of European powers, was entrusted to the Indochinese administration.

In 1946, Pignon represented France at the ceremonies celebrating the US grant of independence to the Philippines. He meticulously collected all the press and propaganda materials issued by US and Philippine officials and examined American ideas about colonialism. Returning to Saigon, he reported his outrage at American ideas of 'enlightened colonialism' leading to independence. In one, he even wonders in despair whether France too will 'need to enthusiastically follow the suggestions of the parable of the fox that cut off its own tail'.[50] The main reason for this interest in the Philippines was Pignon's observation that the United States was vigorously assisting the Philippine government to repress 'a violent insurgent movement that has presented a number of parallels with the Indochinese and Indonesian uprisings', observing that the 'repression was enterprised by order of an autochthonous government, which has left the Americans, who have taken part, leaving a good impression in world opinion'.[51]

Between 1946 and 1948, as d'Argenlieu implemented his military solution to the Vietnamese problem, Pignon's suggestion that France should learn from the Philippine case was ignored both in Saigon and in Paris. However, as the war became too expensive for a ruined post-war France to sustain and US assistance became essential, efforts to persuade US diplomats by 'raising of the Communist bogey' failed due to the transparent insincerity of French colonial progressivism. Pignon was finally given a chance to implement his American insights in October 1948, when he was appointed High Commissioner. He immediately drafted his Bao Dai solution, which raised mixed responses: in Paris it was divisive, supported by liberals and reformists but opposed by conservatives, nationalists and de Gaulle.[52]

To bypass debates in Paris, Pignon convened a conference in Saigon, inviting foreign diplomats and press, to present his draft solution. It was met enthusiastically by US diplomats, who congratulated Paris on its forward thinking – essentially making the new Bao Dai solution another fait accompli by the Saigon government due to its success with US diplomats.[53] Pignon's 'new' Bao Dai solution used the exact language, down to entire phrases, expressions and logic, used by US diplomatic communications when America granted independence to the Philippines, with France as a 'shepherd guiding natives towards self-rule' and the explicit promise of a state called Vietnam that might 'eventually be ready' for independence.[54]

In 1949, Pignon congratulated himself, 'without too much optimism', that he had found a political solution satisfying all parties.[55] And indeed a solution it proved to be: US assistance climbed from an immediate 'emergency' $33 million in 1948 to a staggeringly generous financing of the French war effort so large that, by 1953, the US National Security Council cautioned that 'the United States would assume about 50 per cent of the 1954 budgetary expenditures ($829 million out of $1,676 million) and, if end-item aid is included, would be carrying about 61 per cent of the total financing' of the French war effort.[56]

This study of the role of the colonial government in conceiving and promoting the 'Bao Dai solution' highlights the vital role played by the concept of deferred sovereignty, its institutional practice by the post-1944 colonial governmentality it created and the actions of the agents created by this institution and informed by the concept. Firstly, the concept itself constituted the political momentum that led to this conflict, informing and supporting the preservation of French colonialism without concessions, as demonstrated by the Da Lat Conference and the 'Hai Phong Incident'. Secondly, these three cases demonstrate the extent to which the colonial institution, thanks to the reforms of 1944, was able to evade supervision from Paris, orders and even national policy without any consequences for the civil servants and military involved. Thirdly, the Hai Phong and Bao Dai cases also show that the colonial military played a central role, particularly leaders like Valluy, who started the war with d'Argenlieu's illegal support, as well as Generals Jean de Lattre de Tassigny and Raoul Salan, who followed as commanders of the French Far Eastern Expeditionary Corps (and in de Tassigny's case, also as High Commissioner) and were behind similar efforts between 1950 and 1953 to avoid political compromise and impose a military solution. These colonial generals, enacting de Gaulle's 1944 rejection of parliamentary oversight over colonial administrators and forces, managed to impose their policies on Paris – not a small feat for an instrument supposedly at the service of France but which, in these instances, revealed itself to be at the service of colonial rule.

More French than France: colonial instruments come home

What does this mean for the understanding of French colonialism and international relations? Over the 1940s and 1950s, France essentially lost control of its colonies to colonial and military elites deeply marked by their colonial mission. The above analysis established that the link between the metropole and the colony was now primarily ideological and military, unchecked by constitutional or administrative oversight from the metropole. Their idea of France necessitated the survival of colonial domination, particularly racial legal and political orders dominated by colonists – even at the expense of the French Republic. This analysis now enables conceptualisation of the international instrument of deferred sovereignty, its impact on institutions like colonial administrations and how it informed agents of these institutions like High Commissioner d'Argenlieu.

This section picks up on the insights provided by the analysis of how the colony was governed in relation to the metropole, particularly the dynamics of practice identified. These empirical insights are, firstly, re-explored in relation to the colonial discourses of the time to analyse how this instrument constituted, in political theory and legally, a particular form of sovereignty constructed on the basis of racial hierarchy and governmentality. This makes it, secondly, possible to understand how institutions constituted on the basis of this sovereignty, such as the colonial government, could turn against their metropoles when the latter begun to decolonise. It emerges that, ultimately, deferred sovereignty is an instrument not of the metropole but of colonialism itself as a racially structured political, economic and social order.

The core ideological conceptualisation of colonial order is known in post-colonial studies as 'deferred humanity'.[57] Homi Bhabha, in his history of the ideas of colonial identity-making, analysing colonial writings, theories, ethnography and imperial laws, identified the constitution of the colonised subject not only as hierarchically inferior but as essentially deferred in the dimensions of time (it was backward, behind), space (tropical heat and distance from Europe causes savagery), ethics (primitive) and their very biology (basic instincts). This in practice meant that, even as in liberal progressive European circles their humanity and its theoretical endowment with rights was generally acknowledged, its validity was deferred to a future when the colonial subject will have caught up with Europeans. This is the best-case scenario, of course, where liberals acknowledged a shared humanity; for conservatives like d'Argenlieu and de Gaulle, the world was structured around a global racial hierarchy where each civilisation stood as demonstration of its racial potential and might.[58]

Bhabha's conceptualisation of the deferred humanity of colonial subjects helps us understand the second wave of colonial ideology that was becoming widespread by the 1930s, especially among progressives, and which dominated Second World War and post-war colonial discourse.[59] The language of the Brazzaville Conference Declaration, and the conceptual structure underlying it, bears the influence of this 1920s 'progressive colonialism', also known as 'liberal imperialism'. It acknowledged, for example, that colonial subjects should have rights – but permanently deferred these to an unspecified future when they would be ready to wield such rights.[60]

Drawing on Bhabha's framework, this chapter now explores the conceptualisation of the 'deferred sovereignty' identified in this chapter established in the French Empire by the 1940s colonial reforms. This is an addition to the history of ideas of sovereignty – a far bleaker one than the sovereignty and self-determination explored elsewhere in this volume – historical understanding of the evolution of theories of the state, and ultimately of the ways identity participates in constituting global politics.[61] This is a concept of sovereignty that draws on the theories of identity that shaped politics at the time, of course, but, vitally, the question emerges of how it informed and thus helped constitute institutions like the staggeringly independent post-Second World War Indochinese regime. This is also relevant to understand the post-1910 Union of South Africa and other colonial administrative constructs like Algeria or Rhodesia, which went as far as breaking from or betraying their metropoles to protect racial orders. Further, the question also emerges as to how the concept, and its institutions, informed the practices of their agents and their doxa or logic of practice. This is particularly important since the post-war French empire called on its governors and military commanders to defend the 'principles of French colonialism' as they saw fit.[62]

By 1945, the sovereignty of a colony was acknowledged to belong to indigenous peoples by right. We can see this in de Gaulle's own reforms, the 1945 UN Charter, and it was also present in older arrangements like the League of Nations mandates. This acknowledgement was, additionally, a feature of the UN Trusteeship system, as well as US discourses on colonialism in the Philippines, which differed by having explicit end dates and thus not permanently deferring sovereignty. The core mechanism of this concept draws on the deferral of humanity common in ethnic theories of the time to defer their access, relation to and right over sovereign, administrative and representational power. In other words, it is acknowledged that natives, as humans within the liberal French Republic, should have an active share in sovereignty just as French citizens do. This share, however, is to be held in trust by more advanced peoples until racial readiness is reached.

This is how the Brazzaville Conference managed to acknowledge these principles whilst indefinitely rejecting autonomy, self-rule or independence. Deferred sovereignty, whilst creating sovereign rights for colonial subjects, permanently deferred them. They are deferred in time, awaiting progress; in race, as natives cannot become French, and thus citizens; and in ethics too, awaiting a time when they can be trusted. This had huge effects in practice, deferring removal of the colossal legal differences between French and native subjects, deferring too the time when they could no longer be subject to hierarchically established disciplining such as citizen punishment, collective punishment, torture and expropriation, and would acquire the right to vote, which is thus postponed and endowed onto European settlers alone.

Deferred sovereignty is therefore an identity-based concept of sovereignty justified as a temporal delay. Like other modern conceptualisations of sovereignty, it organises practices of sovereignty and how individuals, institutions and agents access and avail themselves of it. Furthermore, like other ideas of sovereignty, deferred sovereignty too shapes 'the conditions for knowing the state as such'.[63] I propose that, where this idea meets its practical applications and reifications, we might look at it as a *dispositif*: a conceptual mechanism that governs knowledge structures, agency and institutions and their administrative practices of power.[64] This specific dispositif draws on ethnonationalist theories of the state and humanity common in France in the nineteenth century – still common in the French Far Right today[65] – and ideas and practices of racialised governmentality common in French colonialism,[66] as well as the Christian-colonial ideology of the *mission civilisatrice* (civilising mission). This is worth noting because their structures inform this idea of sovereignty granted to but wielded on behalf of racially inferior peoples.

Deferred sovereignty is a theoretical and political dispositif that conceptually distributes who might wield sovereignty on the basis of race, birth and gender, and when. This is how Indochina established 'democratic' governance where elections were held on behalf of the territory, but in which only white French citizens could vote, or how d'Argenlieu could, on his own authority, separate Cochinchina from the rest of Vietnam on behalf of its people. By providing them with an ontological ideology and structural logic – indeed a veritable theory of the state – the dispositif of deferred sovereignty produced institutions such as the colonial government, puppet states and even still-colonial post-colonial states such as the Union of South Africa and Rhodesia. These institutions in turn produced agents that wielded power on their behalf, and they too were informed in their logic of practice – their doxa – by the same governing concept, for example, policing subjects differently on the basis of race in Indochina.

It is a powerful instrument for a state to wield, but because its core rests on identity theories, the latter are its true focus and paramount to its practice, not the metropole that issued it. This became evident as European states began to betray their colonist dependants and engage in decolonisation. At this juncture, deferred sovereignty allowed colonialists to prioritise ethnic domination as principle and as racially structured practice over defending France, quickly replacing the metropole and its wishes as the core focus of all colonial practice. The dominant idea of the instrument, its raison d'être, turned into a ghost that even tried to possess the French state when it stopped supporting colonial efforts. Even though this means venturing outside the period studied in this volume, it is worth exploring briefly to provide a view of the longer-term impact of these instruments on France itself.

As the French Republic hesitated to continue its bloody war against Algerian anti-colonial rebels in 1958, peace talks loomed on the horizon. Against the prospect of an independent Algeria, colonialist politicians, colonists and especially military leaders used the instrument of deferred sovereignty to defend French colonialism from France itself. A group of key colonial administrators like Maurice Challe, politicians like former premier Bidault and colonial generals like Raoul Salan (whom we met in Indochina) launched a coup from Algiers called the Algiers Putsch; claimed sovereignty over all of France; and launched an invasion of the metropole, landing paratroopers in Corsica, in order to 'correct' its course and reverse the policy on Algeria that might, as was being negotiated, allow non-whites to vote in an independence referendum. They demanded that de Gaulle's government resign so that the generals could resume the war to keep Algeria French. They failed, and France continued negotiating. When the 1962 Evian accords granted independence to Algeria, key members of the colonial military including Salan and politicians like Bidault formed the illegal *Organisation de l'Armée Secrète* (Secret Army Organisation, OAS) to once again force France to keep fighting in Algeria, staging a series of terrorist attacks and attempting to assassinate de Gaulle.

The instrument, its institutions, its agents, ultimately tried to remake the metropole in its own image.

A recent public intervention by key French military leaders on immigration and the role of Islam and former colonial subjects migrating to France suggests that key military institutions remain imbibed with the deferred sovereignty once promoted by de Gaulle, Salan and Bidault, which remains common in the military. In the letter, signed by numerous contemporary generals, it is possible to identify the self-same logic that France might once more need 'the intervention of our comrades on active duty in a perilous mission of protection of our civilisational values' against the rest of France. This time, I fear, the sovereignty being deferred is that of French citizens, in order to – seventy years after its inception – once again promote an ethnic hierarchical order.[67]

Conclusion

What can we learn from exploring the concept and practice of deferred sovereignty? This instrument, created on behalf of the interests of the French state but conceptualised around the perceived interests of the French race, ended up supporting the emergence of quasi-states with agents that wielded sovereign privileges. When the French state stopped supporting its colonial order at all cost, it came home to reform the state that created it. The state that created it had rejected the extremes (if not the core substance) of the colonial ideology that had given rise to the instrument in the first place, but the instrument tried to reform the metropole so that it would continue pursuing its colonial mission.

Focus on the instruments of international relations, rather than just sovereign states, is vital to enable this type of analysis and its insights. This approach allows analysis to recognise and account for when their practices vary and, as occurred in this chapter, do the unexpected, which in practice means that it is vital to include imperial polities and the ideas that sustained their practices in analyses of international order. Further, paying attention to the instruments themselves, rather than just the assumed holders of those instruments, has enabled this chapter to retrieve the decidedly difficult relations between France, her colonial ideology and the institutions and agents that were created to promote it, as well as the impact of this ideological–legal–practice nexus on the metropole to this day. It would, I suggest, be of interest to take this approach to analysis of other colonial ideologies and the institutions they gave rise to.[68]

In this chapter, therefore, international instruments are shown to be vital in shaping the institutional, national and international relations of our time. Crucially, paying attention to international instruments allows for two important but challenging historical and international lines of enquiry to be launched. Firstly, it becomes possible, and indeed necessary, to retrieve the role of ideology and complex conceptualisations like deferred sovereignty in giving rise to real-world actors and institutions, be they completely non-state or quasi-state like colonial Indochina, and relations among them. This makes it possible to, for example, recover and analyse important dynamics that would have escaped analysis focusing solely on the state or an institution, such as the fractious relationship between the French state and its colonial administrations. Such an approach also adds to post-colonial and decolonial approaches a detailed understanding of the specific practices involved, their fractious and often contradictory institutional drivers, and the ideas that informed them. The empirical approach additionally makes it possible to retrieve their present-day impact on extant cases of deferred sovereignty such as Western Sahara and the Chagos Islands, and thus ultimately on the making of contemporary world politics.

Focussing analysis on instruments, secondly, helps reveal how they inform and indeed often give rise to institutions, agents and practices. Studying these practices in light of an understanding of the instrument that informs them helps make sense of practices, for example, how and why the French Indochinese and later the French Algerian governments carried out their own diplomacy with other states, often dragging an unwilling France behind them. This had a vast impact on the Franco-Vietnamese War, in which the colonial administration and its diplomats played a vital role in persuading American diplomats that the Vietnamese rebels were dangerous Stalinist stooges, leading to the more famous American war in Vietnam. Finally, a focus on how French colonial institutions and agents turned the international instrument that created them against a metropole that would not support more war reveals the vast power of colonial instruments. In particular, it helps analyse the extent to which French colonialism – and the ethnonationalist ideas that sustained it – were reinforced in metropolitan France by those that had wielded the international instrument of deferred sovereignty on her behalf.

France's post-colonial story becomes far more interesting and revealing: from stubborn centralised Portugal-like resistance to decolonisation to a more nuanced, detailed and enlightening account of how internal French political battles on colonialism were won by colonialists, and indeed how those same colonialists came to shape contemporary France. The significant resilience of colonial ideology evident in the French military in the 1940s, 1950s and today suggests that ideological currents within it remain marked by its role as the key executor of deferred sovereignty and its government, colonialism more broadly, and thus ultimately of an extant ideology of ethnic order. International instruments, it turns out, can even remake their wielder.

Notes

1 Aileen Moreton-Robinson, *The White Possessive: Property, Power, and Indigenous Sovereignty*, Indigenous Americas (Minneapolis, MN: University of Minnesota Press, 2015).
2 David Marr, *Vietnam: State, War, and Revolution* (Berkeley, CA: University of California Press, 2013).
3 See Alfred Georges, *Charles de Gaulle et la guerre d'Indochine* (Paris: Nouvelles Editions Latines, 1974); Frédéric Turpin, *De Gaulle, Les Gaullistes et l'Indochine: 1940–1956* (Paris: Les Indes savantes, 2005); Institut Charles de Gaulle, *Le général De Gaulle et l'Indochine 1940–1946* (Paris: Plon, 1982);

Stein Tønnesson, *The Vietnamese Revolution of 1945: Roosevelt, Ho Chi Minh and de Gaulle in World at War* (London: PRIO Sage, 1991).

4 Douglas Little, 'Cold War and Colonialism in Africa: The United States, France, and the Madagascar Revolt of 1947', *Pacific Historical Review* 59:4 (1990), 527–52; James I. Lewis, 'The French Colonial Service and the Issues of Reform, 1944–8', *Contemporary European History* 4:2 (July 1995), 153–88; Laura M. Calkins, 'The Changing Strategies of Struggle, 1947–49', in *China and the First Vietnam War, 1947–54* (London: Routledge, 2013); Marilyn Young, *Vietnam Wars 1945–1990*, Harper Perennial edition (New York: Harper Perennial, 2020), p. 20.

5 Mark Mazower, *No Enchanted Palace: The End of Empire and the Ideological Origins of the United Nations* (Princeton, NJ: Princeton University Press, 2009).

6 See for example Tony Smith, 'A Comparative Study of French and British Decolonization', *Comparative Studies in Society and History* 20:1 (1978), 72.

7 Tony Smith, 'The French Colonial Consensus and People's War, 1946–58', *Journal of Contemporary History* 9:4 (1974), 217–47; Martin Shipway, 'Creating an Emergency: Metropolitan Constraints on French Colonial Policy and Its Breakdown in Indo-China, 1945–47', *The Journal of Imperial and Commonwealth History* 21:3 (1 September 1993), 1–16; Martin Shipway, *The Road to War: France and Vietnam 1944–1947* (New York: Berghahn Books, 2003); Martin Shipway, 'The Wind of Change and the Tides of History: De Gaulle, Macmillan and the Beginnings of the French Decolonizing Endgame', in L. J. Butler and Sarah Stockwell (eds), *The Wind of Change: Harold Macmillan and British Decolonization*, Cambridge Imperial and Post-Colonial Studies Series (London: Palgrave Macmillan UK, 2013), pp. 180–94.

8 Pablo de Orellana, *The Road to Vietnam* (London: I.B.Tauris, 2020), pp. 73, 79.

9 See, for example, edited by André Malraux and other leading 1930s French intellectuals, the volume Andrée Françoise Caroline d' Ardenne de Tizac, Andrée Viollis and André Malraux (eds), *Indochine S.O.S.* (Paris: Gallimard, 1935).

10 This was a big innovation of the 1940s and an expansion of the practice begun by Leopold II with the creation of the Congo Free State, and built on by the League of Nations Mandates, the British in India (1921), Egypt (1922) and Iraq (1932), as well as the Americans in the Philippines (1935) and FDR's proposals for UN Mandates. See Andrew Fitzmaurice, *King Leopold's Ghostwriter: The Creation of Persons and States in the Nineteenth Century* (Princeton, NJ: Princeton University Press, 2021).

11 Stephen Chan, *Exporting Apartheid* (London: Macmillan Education, 1990).

12 J Chalcraft (ed.), *Counterhegemony in the Colony and Postcolony* (London: Palgrave Macmillan, 2007); Vivienne Jabri, *The Postcolonial Subject: Claiming Politics/Governing Others in Late Modernity* (Abingdon: Routledge, 2012); For a good example of a similar expansion of these studies of colonial ideas into practices on the ground, administration, power, institutions and agents, see Moreton-Robinson, *The White Possessive*.

13 To help readers follow the sources and if needed find them, they are cited according to the institution of origin and its respective original archival reference as per each archive, including dating method of each reference system. AN refers to Archives Nationales de France, MAE to Ministère Affaires Étrangères, OM to the French Archives d'Autre-Mer, NA to the UK National Archives, NARA to the US National Archives, and Sainteny to the Jean Sainteny personal archive held at Sciences Po Paris.
14 For the figure of the older 'man on the spot' in colonial expansionism, see J. Gallagher and R. Robinson, 'The Imperialism of Free Trade', *The Economic History Review* 6:1 (1953), 1–15; Philip D. Curtin, *The World and the West: The European Challenge and the Overseas Response in the Age of Empire* (Cambridge: Cambridge University Press, 2002).
15 John J. Sbrega, 'The Anticolonial Policies of Franklin D. Roosevelt: A Reappraisal', *Political Science Quarterly* (1986), 65–84; Walter LaFeber, 'Roosevelt, Churchill, and Indochina: 1942–45', *The American Historical Review* 80:5 (1975), 1277–95; Tønnesson, *The Vietnamese Revolution of 1945*; Gary R. Hess, 'The First American Commitment in Indochina: The Acceptance of the "Bao Dai Solution", 1950', *Diplomatic History* 2:4 (1978), 331–50; Gary R. Hess, 'Franklin Roosevelt and Indochina', *The Journal of American History* 59:2 (September 1972), 353–68; Lewis, 'The French Colonial Service and the Issues of Reform, 1944–8'; David B. Woolner, Warren F. Kimball and David Reynolds, *FDR's World* (New York: Palgrave Macmillan, 2008).
16 See Frederick Cooper, *Citizenship between Empire and Nation* (Princeton, NJ, Princeton University Press, 2016).
17 Michael Collins, 'Decolonisation and the "Federal Moment"', *Diplomacy & Statecraft* 24:1 (1 March 2013), 21–40.
18 It is worth noting that only the oldest colonies from the 1600s, like Martinique, did allow some native 'qualified' representatives to join the Assemblée Nationale; Martin Deming Lewis, 'One Hundred Million Frenchmen: The "Assimilation" Theory in French Colonial Policy', *Comparative Studies in Society and History* 4:2 (January 1962), 129–53.
19 Charles de Gaulle, *Lettres, notes et carnets. 1943–1945* (Paris: Plon, 1983); Charles de Gaulle, *Lettres, notes et carnets: Tome 2, 1942 – mai 1958* (Paris: R. Laffont, 2010); Charles de Gaulle, *Le salut 1944–1946* (Paris: Pocket, 2010).
20 Gilbert Doho, *Le Code de l'indigénat, Ou Le Fondement Des États Autocratiques En Afrique Francophone* (Paris: L'Harmattan, 2017), pp. 1–297; Jennifer Anne Boittin, Christina Firpo and Emily Musil Church, 'Hierarchies of Race and Gender in the French Colonial Empire, 1914–1946', *Historical Reflections/Réflexions Historiques* 37:1 (1 March 2011), 60–90.
21 See Cooper, *Citizenship between Empire and Nation*, chapter 4.
22 Unlike the British Viceroy, High Commissioners of Indochina could, for example, make their own appointments to key colonial positions like lieutenant-governors, military positions and others, and, since the opium and liquor compulsory purchases produced substantial liquidity for the colonial government, also finance, budgets and currency.

23 'Note sur la politique qu'entend suivre le Gouvernement Francais en Indochine apres sa liberation', 8/45, AP127, 457, AN; see also de Orellana, *The Road to Vietnam*, p. 44 for a diagram of reporting pathways and analysis of how the Indochinese government ran its own diplomatic communications.
24 At the National Archives they remain to this day vaguely labelled 'New Indochina Files'.
25 Allocution 27/8/1945 in de Gaulle, de Gaulle, *Le salut 1944–1946*. For an introduction to this dignity-restoring exercise in colonialism, see Pierre Grosser, 'Indochine: combat pour une puissance perdue', *L'Histoire* (2022), https://www.lhistoire.fr/indochine-combat-pour-une-puissance-perdue.
26 De Gaulle to Sainteny following up on previously cited 'Note sur la politique en Indochine', August–December 1945, AS5.
27 S. Tønnesson, *Vietnam 1946: How the War Began* (Berkeley, CA: University of California Press, 2010), p. 65.
28 Martin Thomas, 'The Colonial Policies of the Mouvement Républicain Populaire, 1944–1954: From Reform to Reaction', *The English Historical Review* 118:476 (1 April 2003), 380–411.
29 For a good example of this perspective, see Martin Thomas, *Fight or Flight: Britain, France, and the Roads from Empire* (Oxford: Oxford University Press, 2014); Martin Thomas, 'Free France, the British Government and the Future of French Indo-China, 1940–45', *Journal of Southeast Asian Studies* 28:1 (1997), 137–60.
30 Allocution 27/8/1945 in de Gaulle, de Gaulle, *Le salut 1944–1946*. See also Turpin, *De Gaulle, Les Gaullistes et l'Indochine*.
31 de Orellana, *The Road to Vietnam*, p. 71.
32 HAUSSAIRE to COMINDO and Prime Minister, Memorandum 'Tournant politique en Indochine', both 26/4/46, AP 127, 457, AN; 26 Circulaire Février 1947, AP 127, 457, AN.
33 HAUSSAIRE to COMINDO, 26/7/45, AP 127, 457.
34 'Terrorisme excercé par le Viet-Minh sur les populations du territoire', in 'Secret circular' HAUSSAIRE to COMINDO, 8/3/1946, 174QO.46, Fond EA, MAE; 1946 'Terrorisme' file for COMINDO, in 174QO.46, Fond EA, MAE.
35 Underlined in the original, 'note pour M. Georges Bidault', 10/7/46, AP127, 457, AN. See for instance Note Verbale, 7/7/46, AP 127, 457, AN.
36 Indochine française. Haut-commissariat. *Le problème de la fédération indochinoise*, 02/05/46, HCI, ANOM.
37 See the many references to 'traitors' in Thierry d'Argenlieu, *Chronique d'Indochine: 1945–1947* (Paris: A. Michel, 1985).
38 Shipway, *The Road to War*; Rachel Chin, 'The Levant Mandates and Charles de Gaulle's Provisional Government: Power, Culture and Messages of Imperial Reform', *European Review of History: Revue Européenne d'histoire* 25:2 (4 March 2018), 312–29.
39 'Note sur la politique qu'entend suivre le Gouvernement Francais en Indochine apres sa liberation', 8/45, AP127, 457, AN.

40 Général de Gaulle: Présentation du Gouvernement d'unité nationale (23 novembre 1945), Assemblée Nationale.
41 Bernard B. Fall, 'Tribulations of a Party Line: The French Communists and Indo-China', *Foreign Affairs* 33:3 (1955), 499–510.
42 For a detailed narrative account, see chapter 5, p. 146, Tønnesson, *Vietnam 1946*.
43 Rapport 28/11/46, AP 127, 457, AN.
44 See, for examples of core contributions to researching the diplomacy of the conflict, Young, *Vietnam Wars 1945–1990*; Mark Philip Bradley, *Imagining Vietnam and America: The Making of Postcolonial Vietnam, 1919–1950* (Chapel Hill, NC: University of North Carolina Press, 2000); Mark Philip Bradley and Marilyn B. Young, *Making Sense of the Vietnam Wars: Local, National, and Transnational Perspectives* (Oxford: Oxford University Press, 2008); Philippe Devillers (ed.), *Paris-Saigon-Hanoi: les archives de la guerre, 1944–1947* (Paris: Gallimard, 1988); M. A. Lawrence, *Assuming the Burden: Europe and the American Commitment to War in Vietnam* (Berkeley, CA: University of California Press, 2005); Mark Atwood Lawrence, 'Transnational Coalition-Building and the Making of the Cold War in Indochina, 1947–1949', *Diplomatic History* 26:3 (2002), 453–80; Mark Atwood Lawrence, *The Vietnam War: A Concise International History*, Illustrated edition (Oxford: Oxford University Press, 2010).
45 This history of descriptions is the core focus of the book in de Orellana, *The Road to Vietnam*, chapters 13, 14 and 15.
46 Policy Statement, 27/9/1948, 711.51G, RG59, NARA.
47 See Tizac, Viollis and Malraux, *Indochine S.O.S.*
48 This is the policy that Graham Greene mocks as 'the Third Force' in his novel *The Quiet American* (London: Heineman, 1955).
49 Paris to State, 1/10/1947, 851G.00/1 0–147, RG59, NARA. Hanoi to State, 2/12/1947, 851G.00/1 2–247, RG59, NARA. 'Communism in Indochina', Saigon to State, 7/3/1947, 851G.00B/3–747, RG59, NARA. Saigon to State, 7/3/1947, 851G.00B/3–747, RG59, NARA.
50 'Les Philippines et l'expansionisme americain', 1/1946, Dossier Philippines-6–1946, INDO/HCI/CD/ 2–4, ANOM.
51 Dossier Philippines-6–1946, INDO/HCI/CD/ 2–4, ANOM.
52 'Rapport politique Octobre–Décembre 1948', CP 93/ HCI/INDO, ANOM.
53 For more on Pignon himself, see Daniel Varga, 'Léon Pignon, l'homme-clé de la solution Bao Dai et de l'implication des États-Unis dans la Guerre d'Indochine', *Outre-Mers. Revue d'histoire* 96:364 (2009), 277–313.
54 de Orellana, *The Road to Vietnam*, pp. 147–50.
55 'Rapport politique Fevrier-Mars 1949', CP 93/ HCI/INDO, ANOM.
56 Report to the National Security Council by the Department of State, S/S–NSC files, lot 63 D 351, NARA.
57 Homi Bhabha, 'Of Mimicry and Man: The Ambivalence of Colonial Discourse', *October* 28 (1 April 1984), 125–33; Homi K. Bhabha, *The Location of Culture* (London: Psychology Press, 1994).

58 Thomas Vaisset, *L'Amiral d'Argenlieu. Le moine soldat du gaullisme* (Paris: Humensis, 2017). Hilariously, his only major concerns about Nazism were its '*paganisme*' and its conquest of France.
59 For an in-depth understanding of the growing post-war globalism against the existing world of empires, which is relevant because in many ways deferred sovereignty could be said to have been a riposte to its expectations, see Or Rosenboim, *The Emergence of Globalism* (Princeton, NJ: Princeton University Press, 2017), chapters 4 and 6.
60 Institut Charles de Gaulle, *Le général De Gaulle et lIndochine 1940–1946*, part I.
61 See for example J. Bartelson, *A Genealogy of Sovereignty* (Cambridge: Cambridge University Press, 1995).
62 'Speech Made by General de Gaulle at the Opening of the Brazzaville Conference on January 30th 1944'. Charles-de-Gaulle.Org, 15 November 2014, https://web.archive.org/web/20141115095220/http://www.charles-de-gaulle.org/pages/stock-html/en/the-man/home/speeches/speech-made-by-general-de-gaulle-at-the-opening-of-the-brazzaville-conference-on-january-30th-1944.php.
63 This, I argue, fits as a colonial specification of the modern sovereignty explored by Bartelson, *A Genealogy of Sovereignty*, p. 189.
64 *Dispositif* means device or apparatus; the term is distinct from a concept of power in that it has explicit relations with practices, institutions and the doxa of the agents of said institutions. Michel Foucault, 'The confessions of the flesh' (interview) in M. Foucault and P. Rabinow, *Ethics: Subjectivity and Truth: The Essential Works of Michel Foucault 1954–1984* (London: Penguin, 1997). The concept is also explored in extreme detail of practice (governing sex and the body in this case) in the posthumous Michel Foucault, *Histoire de la sexualite IV: Les aveux de la chair* (Paris: Gallimard, 2018); see p. 79, for example, on the intellectual mechanisms, discourses, institutions and agents of sexual penitence.
65 See Pablo de Orellana and Nicholas Michelsen, 'Reactionary Internationalism: The Philosophy of the New Right', *Review of International Studies* 45:5 (December 2019), 748–67.
66 See Gilbert Doho, *Le Code de l'indigénat, ou Le fondement des États autocratiques en Afrique francophone*, Études africaines. Politique (Paris: L'Harmattan, 2017).
67 'La nouvelle tribune des militaires', *Valeurs actuelles*, 11 May 2021, https://www.valeursactuelles.com/societe/exclusif-signez-la-nouvelle-tribune-des-militaires.
68 An evident example that comes to mind is the government of the Dutch East Indies after the colonial reforms of 1922.

Index

Adatci, Mineichiro 180
Advisory Committee on the Traffic in Opium 137, 139–41, 143
advisory jurisdiction 178–88
Albania 62–71
Algerian War 206, 219
Allied Powers (First World War) 38–9, 63–4, 67, 70, 73–4, 85–6, 179
Allied Powers (Second World War) 204
Altamira, Rafael 180, 184
American opium policy 139–41
American Relief Administration 44, 46
Amery, Leo 24
ammunition 108, 110, 120
Anatolia 26
Angell, Norman 2
Anglo-Chinese Agreement (1907) 129
Anslinger, Harry J. 143, 145
anti-colonial politics 25, 106–8, 198–9, 213
apartheid 201, 204
arms control 104–20
arms trade 105–6, 108
Arms Trade Convention (1919) 111–19
asphyxiating gasses *see* chemical weapons
Asquith, Herbert Henry 133
Atlantic Charter (1941) 198
Australia 45–6, 132
Austria-Hungary 9, 21, 23–4, 26, 29, 45, 131
Austria 41
Austro-Marxists 21

Balkans 62, 69
Balkan Wars 17, 27
Bangkok Convention (1931) 127, 144–6
Bank of International Settlements 41

Battle of Annual (1921) 82
Beer, Max 161, 165–6
Belgium 60, 109–10, 112
Bidault, Georges 206, 209–11, 219
Bollaert, Émile 205
border delimitation *see* delimitation
Bourgeois, Léon 179–80
Brailsford, Henry 22–3
Branting, Hjalmar 116, 119
Brazzaville Conference (1944) 200–1, 203–8, 217–18
Brent, Charles 127–8, 130–4, 140–1
Briand, Aristide 61, 73
Britain *see* United Kingdom
British Commonwealth 19, 208
British Dominions 24, 39, 48, 60, 208
British Empire 60, 104–7, 147
British North Borneo 135–7, 141, 143
Brussels Declaration (1874) 83

Caldwell, John 142–4
Cecil, Lord Robert 115–19, 158, 179
Challe, Maurice 219
Chamberlain, Austen 185
Chatham House *see* Royal Institute of International Affairs
chemical weapons 81–99
Chirol, Valentine 26
'civilising mission' 84, 116, 205, 218
chlorine *see* chemical weapons
Churchill, Winston 104
Clarac, Achille 214
Cochinchina 209–10
Colombia 40
colonialism 4, 25, 28, 72–3, 84, 88, 90–2, 97–8, 104–9, 113–14, 127–30, 135–6, 145–6, 198–221
Commonwealth *see* British Commonwealth

Conference of Ambassadors 57, 62–73, 186–7
Congo Free State 49, 60, 222
Convention for Limiting the Manufacture and Regulating the Distribution of Narcotics (1931) 144
Coombe Tennant, Winifred 152, 167–72
Corfu incident (1923) 74
Crowdy, Rachel 43, 167, 169–70

Da Lat Conference (1946) 203–4, 208, 210–12, 215
Dalberg-Acton, John 22, 24
d'Argenlieu, Thierry 206, 208–12, 214–16
Darlan, François 204
Davies, David 3
Davis, John W. 136–7
decolonisation 20, 198–201, 204, 216, 218–19, 221
Decoux, Jean 204
de Gaulle, Charles 198–200, 203–9, 211, 216–19
Delevingne, Malcolm 137, 142–3
delimitation 58, 64–74, 185–7
Delimitation Commission 64–6, 185–7
demarcation 62–4
Deschamps, Edouard 179
diplomacy
  'new diplomacy' 6, 8, 113, 118–20
  'open diplomacy' 18, 155–9, 165–73
  'secret diplomacy' 155, 171
disarmament 37, 42, 104–6, 114–19, 158
Disarmament Committee (League of Nations) 115–17
Dorpat, Peace Treaty *see* Tartu, Peace Treaty (1920)
drug control 127–46
Drummond, Eric 64, 167
Du Bois, W. E. B. 96–7
Dutch East Indies *see* Netherlands, the, Netherlands East Indies (Indonesia)

Eastern Carelia (Karelia) 183–5, 189–90
Egypt 106–8
Entente Cordiale (1904) 2

Entente Powers *see* Allied Powers (First World War)
Ethiopia 81–99
ethnonationalism *see* nationalism
European Court of Human Rights (ECHR) 190

Far East French Expeditionary Corps 206
Fernandes, Raul 180
First Indochina War (1946–54) 211–13
First World War 20–2, 26–7, 84–6, 107, 179
Fisher, H. A. L. 116–18
Fontainebleau Conference (1946) 203–4, 208–11
Forbes, W. Cameron 136
Formosa (Taiwan) 128
France 40, 86–7, 92, 109, 112, 114, 130–2, 134, 166–7, 169–71, 177, 198–221
French Union 202–5, 208–9
Fried, Alfred H. 2

gas warfare *see* chemical weapons
Geneva 9, 114, 152–4, 157–61, 165–6
Geneva Opium Convention (1925) 141–4, 189
Geneva Protocol (1925) 10, 82–3, 87–90, 93, 96–8
Ghadar movement 106
Gilmore, Grant 190
Great Britain *see* United Kingdom
Greco-Turkish population exchange 27–9
Greece 26–8, 58, 62–3, 67–8, 185
Greenwood, Arthur 2, 22
Grey, Edward 130, 133
gun control 104–20

Habsburg monarchy *see* Austria-Hungary
Hagerup, Francis 180
Hague, The 180–1
Hague Conferences
  First Hague Conference (1899) 59–60, 83, 85–6
  Second Hague Conference (1907) 83, 85–6
Hague Convention (1912) *see* International Opium Convention (1912)
Haile Selassie 10, 91, 93–5, 99

Index

'Hai Phong Incident' 203–4, 211–12, 215
Harding, Warren 111, 137
Harrison, Francis 135–7
Hatay, State of 201
Health Organisation *see* League of Nations, Health Organisation
Hoare-Laval Pact (1935) 98
Hobson, J. A. 22
Howard-Ellis, Charles 165
Hudson, Manley O. 177–8, 188–91
humanitarianism viii, 27, 33–4, 35, 37, 84, 167–8
　humanitarian aid ix, 4, 43–8, 169
　humanitarian law 86, 94
　human rights 20, 43–5
Hurst, Cecil 116
Hymans Report (1920) 40

'idealism' in International Relations 5, 152, 173
imperialism 9–10, 17–24, 41, 60–2, 72–3, 104–120, 164, 200–2, 217
India 60, 104–9, 130–3, 198, 201
Indochina 198–221
inquiry commission 55–74, 143–4
Interministerial Committee for Indochina (COMINDO) 206, 209–11
International Anti-Opium Association 137
International Committee of the Red Cross 46, 85, 90
International Court of Justice (ICJ) 189–90
International Federation of League of Nation Societies 162
international jurisdiction 179–91
International Labour Organisation (ILO) 43–5, 181
international law 7–8, 38–9, 44–7, 86–9, 111, 119, 179–91
International Opium Commission of Shanghai (1909) 131–2
International Opium Convention (1912) 127, 131, 133–5, 138, 141, 146
international order 3, 116
International Relations (academic discipline of) viii, 2, 6–8, 15, 20, 22, 25, 79, 92, 102
International Relief Union 46

International Tribunal of the Law of the Sea (ITLOS) 190
internationalism, historiography of 3–6, 22–5, 105, 113–16, 156
IR *see* International Relations (academic discipline of)
Ireland 18, 24

Japan 92–3, 96, 103, 109, 112, 128, 130–1, 134, 204, 206, 208
Joint Commission of 'the Opium Trade and the Opium Habit in the Far East' 130

Kellogg-Briand Pact 1
Kelsen, Hans 36
Kitchener, Herbert 107
Kosovo 40

LaMotte, Ellen N. 138–9
Lange, Christian 115–16
Lapradelle, Albert de 180–2
Larnaude, Fernand 179
League of Nations 5, 9
　Assembly 10, 55, 57–8, 60–1 63–4, 86, 89, 94–5, 114, 117–20, 119–20, 152–77, 179–81, 183, 186, 189–90
　Council 10, 38–40, 55, 57–8, 60–71, 73, 75–6, 78, 82, 97–8, 114, 117–18, 153–4, 162–3, 177, 179–90
　Covenant 37–9, 40, 42–8, 58, 60, 94–5, 156, 168, 177, 179–81, 186, 189–91
　Health Organisation 43, 47, 92
　Information Section 157, 164
　Inquiry *see* inquiry commission
　Secretariat 39, 46–7, 56, 58, 61, 64–73, 76, 78–9, 118–19, 153
League of Nations Union 2, 161
Leclerc, Philippe 211
Lenin, Vladimir 21
liberal internationalism 5, 105, 113–15, 117
liminality 92–3, 98
Loder, Bernard 180
London Peace Conference *see* Conference of Ambassadors
Low, David 81–2
Lux, Štefan 163
Lytton Commission 57

Index

Macedonia 28–9
Madariaga, Salvador de 61, 73
Maisky, Ivan 2
Manchurian crisis 57–8, 61
mandate system 25, 39–40, 88, 153, 199–202
Mandatory Palestine 18, 28
March, Peyton C. 88
Maritza question 185–6, 189
Masaryk, Thomas 23
Meinich, Jens Christian 65
Mello Franco, Afranio de 186
Memel dispute 40
Mill, John Stewart 24
Miller, David Hunter 179
Milner, Alfred 112
minoritisation 27–9
minority protection 27–8, 43–5
Mirdita 63, 66, 68
Moltke, Frederick 65, 67
Moore, John Bassett 181
'moral disarmament' 42, 115, 158
Moutet, Marius 208, 212
Muir, Ramsay 23
multilateralism 4, 7, 10, 91–2, 127–30, 136, 145–6, 152–3
Murray, Gilbert 17–19

Nansen passport 45
narcotics 60–1, 127–46
nationalism 1, 9, 17, 19, 22, 24–7, 31, 35, 45, 51, 85, 106, 140, 153, 198, 208–9, 214, 218, 221
Nehru, Jawaharlal 198, 201
Netherlands, the 130–2, 134, 142, 185
  Netherlands East Indies (Indonesia) 133, 226
'new diplomacy' *see* diplomacy
New Europe 23–4
non-governmental organisations (NGOs) 35, 46
Nordic Inter-Parliamentary Union 115
North Borneo *see* British North Borneo
noxious gases *see* chemical weapons

obscene publications 166–72
'old diplomacy' *see* diplomacy
opium trade 10, 56–8, 127–46, 167, 205, 223
Organisation de l'Armée secrète 219
Orientalism 26, 91
Orlando, Vittorio E. 179

Ottoman empire 9, 18, 26, 29, 39, 41, 49, 62, 107

Palais des Nations 160–2
Palestine *see* Mandatory Palestine
Paris Peace Conference (1919–20) 17, 24, 62, 105, 109, 153, 179
'Paris system' 26–7
'Parliament of the World' *see* League of Nations, Assembly
Pashtuns 104, 113
Pelletier, Thomas 138
Permanent Armaments Commission (PAC) 114–15, 118
Permanent Central Opium Board 145
Permanent Court of Arbitration (PCA) 59–60, 178–80
Permanent Court of International Justice (PCIJ) 92, 177–91
Persian Gulf 105, 107–13
Philippine Opium Committee 127–8
Philippines 127–46, 199, 214–17
Phillimore, Walter 179–80
phosgene *see* chemical weapons
Pignon, Léon 212–15
Politis, Nikolaos 36, 188
Ponsonby, Arthur 2
population transfers 27–8
Pourtalès, M. H. de 65, 68
'practices' in International Relations 7–8, 20, 27–9, 36, 57–9, 71–4, 152, 155–6, 165–6, 171–3, 200–3, 217–21
Prentiss, Augustin 89–90
'preventive adjudication' 177–91
public opinion 66, 87, 93, 114, 138–40, 155–8, 168–73

quasi-state structures 199–200, 209, 214, 220

racism 9–11, 21, 43, 69–70, 92, 99, 105–6, 111, 116–17, 164, 198–205, 216–19
Radio Nations 157
'realism' in International Relations 5, 173
Red Cross *see* International Committee of the Red Cross
Reynaud, Paul 168–70
Ricci-Busatti, Arturo 180
Rif War (1921–26) 82, 88–90, 93, 96

Index

Rockefeller Foundation 44
Roosevelt, Theodore 131
Root, Elihu 180
Royal Institute of International Affairs 2–3, 17–18
Russia 183–4

Sainteny, Jean 208
Salan, Raoul 215, 219
Salandra, Antonio 184
Salle de la Réformation 158–61
sanctions 5, 38–9, 82, 87–8, 91–3, 97–8
Satow, Ernest 7
Save the Children International Union 46
Schaefer, Charles 65
Schmitt, Carl 36
Sederholm, Jakob Johannes 65, 67–71
self-determination 3–5, 9, 17–29, 38–9, 198–200
self-government 22, 24, 26, 40, 91, 96
Seton-Watson, Robert 23
Single Convention on Narcotic Drugs (1961) 146
Sino-Japanese War (1937–45) 82, 92
small-arms control *see* gun control
Smuts, Jan 115
social contract theory 19
sovereignty 5, 8–11, 18–22, 25, 35–49, 91–9, 198–203, 208–9, 211–12, 215–21, 226
statehood 9, 19, 25, 36–9, 43, 83, 153, 164, 202, 204
statelessness 20, 44–5
Statute on Freedom of Transit (1921) 189
Statute on the International Régime of Railways (1923) 189
submarines 86, 89
sulfur mustard *see* chemical weapons
Survey of International Affairs 27
suzerainty 40
Sykes, Mark 107–8, 116

Taezaz, Lorenzo 93
Taft, William Howard 60
Tartu, Peace Treaty (1920) 183–4
tear gas *see* chemical weapons
Temporary Mixed Commission on Armaments (TMC) 42, 118

Tenney, Charles 131
territorial disputes 2, 9, 17, 28–9, 39–40, 56, 58, 62, 68–74
territoriality (of political organisations) 17–18, 24–5, 39–41, 43–5, 91, 129, 202
The Hague *see* Hague, The
Thesleff, Rolf 65
Thomas, Albert 181
Tirana 65
Toynbee, Arnold J. 18–19
Treadway, Walter Lewis 145
Treaty of Lausanne (1923) 26–7, 185
Treaty of Versailles (1919) 40, 45, 86, 114, 138
Treaty relating to the Use of Submarines and Noxious Gases in Warfare (1922) 86–7
Turkey 17, 26–7, 185–6, 201

Ukraine x, 5
Union of Democratic Control 22
United Kingdom 10, 17, 24, 46, 92, 99, 105–15, 129–37, 142–3, 162, 166–7, 169–70, 177, 201
United Nations (UN) 4–5
  Charter 198–9, 217
  Security Council (UNSC) 190
United States of America 87–8, 97, 112, 127–46, 162–3, 182, 188, 198, 203–4, 214–15

Valluy, Jean 212, 215
Vietnam 198–221
Visscher, Charles de 183, 188
Viviani, René 114–16, 118

Wal-Wal incident (1934) 81
Washburn Wright, Elizabeth 136
Washington Naval Conference (1921–22) 42
Weber, Max 36
Westphalian system 36, 45
Wettum, W. G. van 142
Wilson, Woodrow 21, 25, 37–8, 60, 111, 136, 156, 179
'Wilsonianism' 21, 25
  Wilsonian liberalism 38
  'Wilsonian sovereignty' 37
Women's International League for Peace and Freedom (WILPF) 2
Woolf, Leonard 22

World Court *see* Permanent Court of
    International Justice (PCIJ)
World Disarmament Conference (1932)
    158
'world-making' 20, 24
Wright, Hamilton 131–2, 136

Young, Sanborn 144
Young Men's Christian Association 46
Yugoslavia 56, 62–3, 66, 171
Yugoslav Wars (1991–2001) 19

Zamoyski, Maurice 187

Milton Keynes UK
Ingram Content Group UK Ltd.
UKHW021437021224
3319UKWH00008B/193